AF815529

Competition Policy International (CPI) provides comprehensive resources and continuing education for the global antitrust and competition policy community. Created and managed by leaders in the competition policy community, CPI delivers timely commentary and analysis on antitrust and global competition policy matters through a variety of media and applications.

www.competitionpolicyinternational.com

CONTENTS

LETTER FROM THE EDITOR

Competition policy is increasingly taking on a more prominent role worldwide. Since the *CPI Journal* started in 2005, the number of authorities that oversee competition matters has grown noticeably. In 2005, for example, the International Competition Network's (ICN) membership was made up of 95 authorities from 84 jurisdictions; by 2012 it is close to 120 agencies and tribunals, with new working groups such as the unilateral conduct group being added. This growth underscores the necessity of finding a common ground in the economic analysis undertaken by the authorities and of providing legal certainty to businesses that have a global footprint.

Competition policy is now more relevant both as a result of the greater importance of up and coming market economies–China, India, and Brazil, for example–as well as the international reach of local antitrust decisions in a world marketplace. With antitrust's greater significance comes the realization of a need to speak a common technical language, to push for and implement best international practices, and to promote transparency in legal decisions. CPI's work has focused on these themes since its inception. We are a reference for competition professionals in more than 185 countries who have searched, commented, and contributed to our repository of knowledge since our creation.

The *CPI Journal* has set a reputation for a high level of exposition and discussion of complex analyses in competition policy–it is a trigger for the thoughtful exchange of ideas among practitioners and experts. For me, in my new role as President, it is a pleasure to join this group of talented professionals who will remain deeply involved with CPI.

The Spring 2012 issue of *Competition Policy International* takes a look back at articles that have challenged and advanced antitrust scholarship. We then take a step forward by asking the authors to provide updates on their works and explain how changes—or lack thereof—in competition law and policy have affected their views since the articles were published.

Alex Nourry, the Head of Clifford Chance's London Antitrust Practice, and Nelson Jung of the U.K. Office of Fair Trading revisit their concerns of an emerging wave of interventionism by EU Member States.

The next set of articles discuss antitrust sanctions: Judge Douglas Ginsburg & Joshua Wright, professor at George Mason University School of Law, argue that their 2010 proposal of optimal sanctions is still pertinent today. Sheppard Mullin Partner Donald Klawiter explains how the Ginsburg-Wright model would operate on the ground and describes enforcement trends in jurisdictions around the world.

Collusion theories in merger analysis are re-explored by Malcolm B. Coate of the U.S. Federal Trade Commission. Ken Heyer, also at the FTC, takes a second—but different—look at merger analysis by considering the use of welfare standards in the review process.

Rosa Abrantes-Metz, principal at Global Economics Group, provides a timely update on her article on the use of screens by discussing the ongoing LIBOR investigations.

We complete our retrospective with two of the best Classics in antitrust literature. Thomas McCraw's incisive study of Schumpeter's writings show why his text continues to resonate more than 50 years later. The second classic, Aaron Director & Edward Levi's seminal *Law and the Future: Trade Regulation*, set the ground for the Chicago School of antitrust. Their article is prefaced by Keith Hylton's introduction that observes its enduring legacy.

CPI would like to thank its contributors and global community of readers that make the exchange of ideas both fruitful and fascinating.

Elisa V. Mariscal, Editor-in-Chief
Competition Policy International, Boston, MA, U.S.A.
Centro de Investigación y Docencia Económicas (CIDE), and Instituto Tecnológico Autónomo de México (ITAM), Mexico.

PROTECTIONISM IN THE AGE OF AUSTERITY – A FURTHER UNLEVELLING OF THE PLAYING FIELD?

*Alex Nourry and Nelson Jung**

I. INTRODUCTION – ARE THE CONCERNS RAISED IN 2006 STILL VALID?

In our 2006 article,[1] we highlighted an emerging wave of interventionism by EU Member States that manifested itself in a variety of protectionist measures designed to prevent foreign takeovers and promote national champions. The European Commission had initiated infringement proceedings against several Member States that had invoked industry-specific national regulations in an attempt to prevent takeovers of national companies by foreign competitors, when those transactions had already been cleared unconditionally by the Commission under its exclusive jurisdiction under the EU Merger Regulation ("EUMR").[2]

In a number of further cases, the Commission had been powerless to prevent the (attempted) creation of national champions, as it was unable to assert its jurisdiction over mergers between largely domestic players that were subject to the EUMR's "two-thirds rule."[3] Member States were criticized for applying public interest considerations that were unrelated to competition policy to clear a merger creating a national champion.[4]

---

* Alex Nourry is a partner and Head of the London Antitrust Practice at Clifford Chance LLP. Nelson Jung is an Assistant Director at the Office of Fair Trading. The views expressed in this article are personal and should not be taken as representing those of either Clifford Chance LLP or the Office of Fair Trading.

[1] Alex Nourry & Nelson Jung, *EU State Measures against Foreign Takeovers: "Economic Patriotism" in All But Name,* 2(2) Comp. Pol'y Int'l 99 (2006).

[2] *See, e.g.,* Case COMP/M.4110, E.ON/Endesa, 2006 O.J. (C 114), Case COMP/M.4249, Abertis/Autostrade, 2006 O.J. (C 205), and Case COMP/M.3894, Unicredito/HVB, 2005 O.J. (C 235).

[3] Where each of the parties to the concentration achieves more than two-thirds of its aggregate Community turnover within one and the same Member State, it is for that Member State's national competition authority to assess the merger, even when such mergers have cross-border effects. *See* Article 1(2) of Regulation 139/2004 (EUMR).

[4] *See, e.g.,* Case COMP/M.3986, Gas Natural/Endesa, C (2005) 4468); Lettre du 28 janvier 2003 du ministre de l'économie, des finances et de l'industrie au conseil de la société Crédit Agricole relative à une concentration dans le secteur bancaire, BOCCRF, N° 5, 4 mai 2004 p. 364; the Bundeskartellamt decision to block the *E.ON/ Ruhrgas* merger (*Bundeskartellamt WuW/E DE-V 511-525 – E.ON/Ruhrgas*), and; the ministerial authorization overruling the Bundeskartellamt on the grounds of public interest (*WuW/E DE-V 573-598 – E.ON Ruhrgas* and *WuW/E DE-V 643-653 – E.ON/ Ruhrgas*).

The Commission's recent decisional practice demonstrates its continued resolve to block the creation of national—or even European—champions where it considers that such mergers would significantly impede effective competition.

Against this background, we examined the compatibility of a range of protectionist State measures with the Internal Market and queried whether the overriding interests of the Internal Market would justify the abolition of the two-thirds rule.[5]

Nearly six years later, in the wake of a global financial crisis that gives rise to protectionist temptations once again, the rule is still in place despite mounting criticism.[6] The economic crisis and the often painful adjustments arising from the ensuing debt consolidation process provide a seemingly compelling justification for some governments to resort to interventionist industrial policies based on the belief that governments can "pick winners" by creating or protecting national champions.

However, the Commission's recent decisional practice demonstrates its continued resolve to block the creation of national—or even European—champions where it considers that such mergers would significantly impede effective competition.

Last year, the Commission blocked the proposed merger between Olympic Air and Aegean Airlines, stating that it would have resulted in a quasi-monopoly of the Greek air transport market.[7] Despite the fact that the merging parties operate primarily in (and out of) Greece, the Commission was able to establish jurisdiction over this transaction without the two-thirds rule coming into play. Had this transaction occurred in a different sector where the bulk of each

---

[5] Alternately, we considered that the two-thirds rule could be included as an additional ground for the referral of mergers back to Member States under Article 9(2)(a) EUMR. We argued that this would allow the Commission to assess the cross-border impact of any merger, even when it concerns essentially domestic players, in exercising its discretion to accede to a Member State request for referral back. *See* Nourry & Jung, *supra* note 2, at 127.

[6] The two-thirds rule has not been abolished despite the Commission's finding in its 2009 report on the functioning of the EUMR that "public interest considerations other than competition policy have been applied in a number of cases falling under this threshold to authorise mergers which could have given rise to competition concerns" and that, therefore, "the present form of the two-thirds rule merits further consideration." *See Communication from the Commission to the Council: Report on the functioning of Regulation 139/2004*, COM (2009) 281 final (June 18, 2009). In 2010, Mario Monti called for improved cooperation between national competition authorities to ensure procedural and substantive convergence between regulators at both the national and the EU level. Monti also proposed abolishing the two-thirds rule. *See* Mario Monti, *A New Strategy for the Single Market*, Report to the President of the European Commission (May 9, 2010).

[7] Case COMP/M.5830, Olympic/Aegean Airlines, 2010 O.J. (C 174) 8. This was the Commission's second prohibition decision in an airline case. The first, in 2007, was a prohibition of the proposed acquisition of Aer Lingus by Ryanair (COMP/M.4439, Ryanair/Aer Lingus, 2006 O.J. (C 274) 10), which also amounted to a merger of two airlines based at the same "home" airport in the national capital.

party's turnover was allocated to their home jurisdiction, the two-thirds rule may have resulted in a different jurisdictional, and possibly substantive, outcome.[8]

More recently, the Commission blocked the merger between NYSE Euronext and Deutsche Börse.[9] Commissioner Joaquín Almunia argued that the merger would have created a near-monopoly in crucial markets to the detriment of thousands of EU companies and harmed innovation in financial services.[10] However, it has been reported that the decision to block the merger was signed off by the Commission after an unusually fierce debate among the 27 Commissioners, where a minority supposedly challenged the verdict because it hindered the emergence of European champions in a global market.[11]

The Commission's quest for an open and contestable Internal Market in the face of resurfacing protectionist tendencies is, of course, not confined to the exercise of its powers under the EUMR. Its agenda to create and maintain a level playing field by tackling protectionist measures is also illustrated by its infringement proceedings against Portugal's "golden shares" and other special rights in GALP Energia, Energias de Portugal ("EDP") and Portugal Telecom.[12]

Overall, the Commission continues to act as a guardian of the functioning of the Internal Market by seeking to ensure that unduly interventionist national industrial policies do not override competition policy objectives.

---

[8] It is not clear from publicly available information whether a different method of geographical allocation of turnover in Olympic/Aegean Airlines may have established the Greek competition authority's jurisdiction over this transaction on the basis of the two-thirds rule. In general, it is not inconceivable that different approaches to the geographic allocation of turnover in this specific sector may alter the jurisdictional analysis such that the two-thirds rule could establish jurisdiction of a national competition authority. In previous cases, the Commission has considered various different approaches to turnover allocation in airline mergers, including the country of destination method (allocating the turnover to the country of final destination); the 50/50 method (splitting the turnover between the country of origin and the country of final destination); the point of sale method (allocating the turnover to the country where the ticket sale occurred) and the place of departure method (allocating the revenue from a flight to the Member State where the place of departure of the flight is located – for round trips, this could be done by either splitting the two one-way flights of round trip tickets bought at the same time or allocating the entire turnover to the place of departure where the original outbound flight is located). For a more detailed assessment of each of these methods, see Case COMP/M.4439, Ryanair/Aer Lingus, ¶ 18 et seq.

[9] Case COMP/M.6166, Deutsche Börse/NYSE Euronext, 2012 O.J. (C 440).

[10] Joaquín Almunia, Vice President of the European Commission responsible for Competition Policy, Speech at the Concurrences Conference: Industrial Policy and Competition Policy: Quo Vadis Europa?, New Frontiers of Antitrust 2012 (Feb. 10, 2012), *available at* http://europa.eu/rapid/pressReleasesAction.do?reference=SPEECH/12/83&format=HTML&aged=0&language=EN&guiLanguage=en.

[11] *See* Alex Barker, Jeremy Grant & James Wilson, *Deutsche Börse-NYSE merger blocked*, FIN. TIMES, Feb. 1, 2012.

[12] *See* Cases C-212/09, Commission v Portuguese Republic, 2012 O.J. (C 25) 4; C-543/08, Commission v Portuguese Republic, 2011 O.J. (C 13) 5, and; C-171/08, Commission v Portuguese Republic, 2010 O.J. (C 234) 5.

II. STATE-OWNED ENTERPRISES: THE RISE OF STATE CAPITALISM IN RESPONSE TO THE FINANCIAL CRISIS

In reality, SOEs often enjoy certain privileges and immunities that are not necessarily available to their privately-owned competitors.

Beyond the European Union, industrial policies fostering national champions are becoming increasingly popular in the aftermath of the financial crisis, primarily in the guise of State-Owned Enterprises ("SOEs") in emerging economies.[13]

According to recent reports, state-backed companies account for 80 percent of the value of China's stock market and 62 percent of Russia's.[14] Overall, they accounted for a third of the emerging world's foreign direct investment between 2003 and 2010.[15]

One may therefore query what impact the rise of SOEs and state-directed capitalism will have on the competitive landscape globally, irrespective of the extent to which EU policies continue to embrace the concept of a level playing field. The concept of competitive neutrality requires that SOEs should not enjoy net competitive advantages over their private sector competitors simply by virtue of public sector ownership. Although, in principle, the Organisation for Economic Co-operation and Development ("OECD") Principles of Corporate Governance recommend a level playing field,[16] in reality, SOEs often enjoy certain privileges and immunities that are not necessarily available to their privately-owned competitors.[17]

The trend towards an increasingly visible hand gives rise to a number of challenges from an antitrust perspective, not least in respect of merger control where SOEs are taking over foreign

---

13 China, for instance, has promoted its strategic industries through a variety of measures, including subsidies, fiscal incentives, export restrictions, trading rights authorizations, local content rules, low wages and labor standards. The Chinese model of capitalism, dubbed the "Beijing consensus," is seen as more successful and more stable by other emerging economies who appear to be gradually abandoning (neo)liberal theories in favor of industrial policy. *See* Damien Geradin & Ianis Girgenson, *Industrial Policy and European Merger Control – A Reassessment* 17 (TILEC Discussion Paper No. 2011-053). *See also* Joe Leahy, *Brazil looks to China for Industrial Policy*, Fin. Times, Apr. 11, 2011. The Brazilian government, which embraced privatization in the 1990s, is now interfering with companies like Vale and Petrobras, and compelling smaller companies to merge to form national champions.

14 *See The rise of state capitalism*, The Economist, Jan. 21, 2012, *available at* http://www.economist.com/node/21543160.

15 *Id.*

16 *See* OECD, OECD Guidelines on Corporate Governance of State-Owned Enterprises (2005), *available at* http://www.oecd.org/dataoecd/46/51/34803211.pdf.

17 For a more detailed assessment of basic competitive advantages of SOEs, see Antonio Capobianco & Hans Christiansen, *Competitive Neutrality and State-Owned Enterprises: Challenges and Policy Options* (OECD Corporate Governance Working Papers No. 1, 2011), *available at* http://www.oecd.org/dataoecd/29/43/46452890.pdf.

companies.[18] In recent decisions where the Commission scrutinized takeovers by SOEs, the Commission assessed whether the SOE involved was an independent economic entity or whether it belonged to a wider economic group, including other enterprises over which the State (in these cases, the Republic of China) enjoyed decisive influence.[19] In its analysis, the Commission pointed out that this type of assessment was required regardless of whether the ultimate parent entity was state-owned or privately owned, thereby reinforcing the concept of competitive neutrality.

Encouragingly, there are recent signs that emerging economies are also taking competitive neutrality considerations seriously in applying their respective competition laws. Developments in China, for instance, indicate that domestic SOEs are not immune from antitrust scrutiny under the Anti-Monopoly Law.[20]

III. FOREIGN INVESTMENT RULES REMAIN PROBLEMATIC

Although there may be greater convergence in the application of national competition laws—insofar as national governments increasingly follow recommendations made by the OECD and the International Competition Network—the risk of foreign investment rules providing a framework to pursue a more protectionist agenda remains and appears to be growing in importance. In March 2012, French President Nicolas Sarkozy stepped up his campaign for a "Buy European Act" for public contracts, insisting that there was a need to protect industry from "savage" trade competition, and threatening to act unilaterally if the European Union failed to take action.[21] In the same week, Brazil's finance minister Guido Mantega insisted that Brazil "cannot keep [its] borders completely free while others are using non-competitive

[18] Other challenges relate to certain pricing practices by SOEs with market power, including predatory pricing or cross-subsidisation.

[19] *See* Cases COMP/M.6082, China National Bluestar/Elkem, 2011 O.J. (C 274) 3 and COMP/M.6113, DSM/Sinochem/JV, 2011 O.J. (C 177) 2.

[20] In China's first antitrust investigation of its own SOEs, the National Development and Reform Commission is currently assessing how to proceed against two telecom companies. China Telecom and China Unicom are reportedly accused of employing anti-competitive practices to maintain their dominant position in the broadband market. The applicability of China's Anti-Monopoly Law to its own SOEs is further evidenced by the Ministry of Commerce's recent decision to impose conditions on a transaction involving a joint venture between General Electric and the state-owned Shenhua Group.

[21] *See* Hugh Carnegy, *Sarkozy appeals to his populist base,* FIN. TIMES, Mar. 16, 2012, *available at* http://www.ft.com/intl/cms/s/0/f1455ffa-6f76-11e1-9c57-00144feab49a.html.

mechanisms" and warned that the country will be taking "defensive measures."[22] Other countries, including Germany and Austria, have recently introduced foreign investment rules that create new barriers to foreign investors seeking to acquire stakes in domestic companies operating in a variety of sectors.[23]

Foreign investment legislation allows governments to block transactions that do not have an adverse impact on competition. Such legislation often lacks a clear definition or guidelines against which a "national interest" criterion could be measured, making it more difficult to predict whether or not a proposed transaction might be blocked.[24] This resulting uncertainty may in and of itself dissuade pro-competitive transactions giving rise to consumer welfare-enhancing effects. In Russia, for example, it has become difficult for foreign investors to determine the scope of application of the law relating to foreign investment in companies operating in strategic sectors. This is partly because a transaction may be subject to clearance even if the relevant entity's principal operations do not concern the strategic sectors, since ancillary involvement is sufficient to trigger the operation of that law.[25] While very few transactions have been blocked by the clearing committee,[26] the burdensome approval process and the significant delays caused by it are a major concern for investors.

A high-profile example of what critics have called "resource nationalism"[27] involved BHP Billiton's unsolicited bid for Canada's Potash Corporation of Saskatchewan Inc. Canada eventually blocked the $39 billion deal under its foreign investment laws on the grounds

---

22 *See* Leahy, *supra* note 13.

23 Under the Austrian Foreign Trade Act 2011 (a law analogous to the one establishing the German regime in 2009), companies operating in areas of internal and external security (defense equipment industry, security services) or general public services, including social security (particularly hospitals, rescue services, fire brigades, energy or water supply, telecommunication services, traffic or education) shall be protected against foreign takeovers by an approval to be issued by the Federal Minister for Economy, Family and Youth.

24 *See, e.g.*, Russia's *Federal Law № 57-FZ, On the procedure of foreign investment in companies having strategic significance for the preservation of national defence and state security*, passed on May 5, 2008 and published in the Rossiiskaya Gazeta on May 7, 2008. The text of the law (in Russian) is available at http://www.rg.ru/2008/05/07/investicii-fz-dok.html.

25 *See A Legal Overview to Foreign Investments in Russia's Strategic Sectors*, Clifford Chance Client Briefing, Mar. 2011, *available at* http://www.cliffordchance.com/publicationviews/publications/2011/03/a_legal_overviewtoforeigninvestmentsi.html.

26 In 2010, for example, the clearing committee considered 57 merger applications from foreign investors, clearing 44 of these outright, permitting a further 4 mergers after the imposition of certain conditions and blocking just 3 applications. *See* OECD, 2010 Annual Report on Competition Policy Developments in the Russian Federation, June 15, 2011, *available at* http://www.oecd.org/officialdocuments/publicdisplaydocumentpdf/?cote=DAF/COMP/AR(2011)21&docLanguage=En.

27 *See Canada must avoid prairie populism*, Fin. Times, Oct. 25, 2010, *available at* http://www.ft.com/intl/cms/s/0/6bc935dc-e06a-11df-99a3-00144feabdc0.html.

that it would not provide a "net benefit" to Canada.[28] Similarly, in April 2011, Singapore Exchange's A$8.4 billion bid for the Australian Securities Exchange was rejected, with Australian officials commenting that the deal was "not in Australia's national interest" and that the acquisition would only be justifiable "if there were very substantial benefits" such as "greatly enhanced opportunities for Australian businesses and investors to access capital markets."[29]

In March 2012, the Indonesian government issued a decree that will prevent foreign companies from owning more than 49 percent of certain mines; Indonesia is the world's largest tin producer, and a leading exporter of coal, precious metals and other minerals.[30] Similar protectionist measures are being adopted by many African states with substantial mining industries. In Zimbabwe, the government's "indigenization" policy has gone one step further by forcing foreign companies to give a 51 percent share to Zimbabwean nationals, without compensation.[31] The most recent example of "resource nationalism" is Argentina's expropriation of 51 percent of YPF shares owned by the Spanish company Repsol, which is highlighted by the European Commission in its latest Report on Potentially Trade Restrictive Measures as part of a rising trend of trade-related restrictive measures covering foreign direct investment amongst the EU's main trading partners, including the G20 countries.[32]

IV. JUST HOW LEVEL WILL THE PLAYING FIELD BE?

Mario Monti noted in his report on a new strategy for the Single Market that "Europe needs an industrial policy that does not conflict, rather builds on its competition rules."[33] He added that competition rules did not stand in the way of the European companies'

---

[28] *See* Bernard Simon, Helen Thomas & William MacNamara, *Canada rejects BHP bid for Potash*, FIN. TIMES, Nov. 4, 2010, *available at* http://www.ft.com/cms/s/0/7ec4f380-e798-11df-8ade-00144feab49a.html#axzz1r58MtV1t.

[29] *See* Peter Smith, *Australia confirms rejection of SGX-ASX deal*, FIN. TIMES, Apr. 8, 2011, *available at* http://www.ft.com/intl/cms/s/0/f2809c78-6184-11e0-a315-00144feab49a.html.

[30] *See* Sarah Mishkin & Helen Thomas, *Indonesia limits foreign ownership of mines*, FIN. TIMES, Mar. 7, 2012, *available at* http://www.ft.com/intl/cms/s/0/e9d9e570-684f-11e1-a6cc-00144feabdc0.html.

[31] *See Wish you were mine*, THE ECONOMIST, Feb. 11, 2012, *available at* http://www.economist.com/node/21547285.

[32] EUROPEAN COMMISSION DIRECTORATE-GENERAL FOR TRADE, NINTH REPORT ON POTENTIALLY TRADE RESTRICTIVE MEASURES IDENTIFIED IN THE CONTEXT OF THE FINANCIAL AND ECONOMIC CRISIS, SEPTEMBER 2011 – 1 MAY 2012, June 6, 2012.

[33] *See* Mario Monti, *A New Strategy for the Single Market: At the Service of Europe's Economy and Society*, Report to the President of the European Commission, May 9, 2010, *available at* http://ec.europa.eu/bepa/pdf/monti_report_final_10_05_2010_en.pdf.

search for the best scale and size to compete globally, citing the European Aeronautic Defence and Space Company ("EADS") as an example.

Rather than resorting to protectionist industrial policies in a political knee-jerk reaction to an economic crisis, in the long run, creating an environment that stimulates competition on the merits and removes barriers to expansion and growth is indeed more likely to benefit consumer welfare. By contrast, shielding domestic companies from competition is more likely to leave them underprepared for global competition than to truly assist them, let alone the economy overall.

Rather than resorting to protectionist industrial policies in a political knee-jerk reaction to an economic crisis, in the long run, creating an environment that stimulates competition on the merits and removes barriers to expansion and growth is indeed more likely to benefit consumer welfare.

The Commission's recently-announced proposal to allow local authorities to dismiss tenders from countries that discriminate against EU-based companies[34] are, however, difficult to reconcile with Monti's recommendations. The Commission qualified the proposal by specifying that foreign bidders could not be excluded from the tender process without the Commission's prior approval[35] and that it is intended to encourage others to open their markets,[36] emphasizing that "Europe is and will remain open for business."

Nevertheless, criticisms have been levied against the proposal on several levels: (i) a "protectionist signal" of this kind would undermine the EU's credibility as it seeks to eliminate protectionist measures elsewhere; (ii) the measure could trigger retaliatory action from foreign governments, which could potentially cause further harm to EU businesses, and; (iii) the principal aim of public procurement in obtaining "value for money" for the taxpayer would be undermined if certain bidders were eliminated by reason of the nationality of their incorporation.[37]

---

[34] *Commission Proposal for a Regulation of the European Parliament and of the Council on the access of third-country goods and services to the Union's internal market in public procurement and procedures supporting negotiations on access of Union goods and services to the public procurement markets of third countries,* COM (2012) 124 final (Mar. 21, 2012), *available at* http://ec.europa.eu/internal_market/publicprocurement/docs/international_access/COM2012_124_en.pdf.

[35] The Commission also specified that contracts under €5 million would remain open to all bidders.

[36] Michael Barnier, the single market commissioner, has argued that European companies lose roughly €12 billion a year in export sales due to foreign markets not being open to EU businesses.

[37] *See* Alex Barker, Joshua Chaffin & Stanley Pignal, *Germany warns on keeping EU market open*, Fin. Times, Mar. 22, 2012, *available at* http://www.ft.com/cms/s/0/69821548-7374-11e1-94ba-00144feab49a.html.

V. CONCLUSION

It remains to be seen whether the Commission will advance its recent proposals in relation to public procurement contracts, or if an amended form of the measures announced on March 22, 2012 will be taken forward. Aside from these proposals, the Commission's efforts to ensure competition policy in the European Union is not sterilized by interventionist industrial policies is laudable. However, the global playing field is at risk of becoming even less level than before the financial crisis if SOEs are favored over their private sector competitors without an objective justification, and if national foreign investment rules are used to protect national champions or state resources where merger control rules no longer would.

EU STATE MEASURES AGAINST FOREIGN TAKEOVERS: "ECONOMIC PATRIOTISM" IN ALL BUT NAME

*Alex Nourry & Nelson Jung**

ABSTRACT:
Protectionist tendencies of EU Member States have always been evident in sectors of industry that previously were dominated largely by state-owned companies, namely, the banking, defense, energy, postal, telecommunications, transport, and water sectors where, following privatization, Member States have sought to preserve or create so-called "national champions." However, a new wave of protectionism or economic patriotism by Member States has broken out recently, as exemplified by the long-running saga of the takeover of Endesa, the Spanish electricity group. This article examines the compatibility of special rights and other state measures with the EC's single market objectives within the framework of the EC Treaty and their impact on foreign takeovers and investments. It also examines the initiatives taken by the Commission in order to eliminate such measures and analyzes the potential remedies available to foreign investors when confronted with such measures. Such remedies include the application of the Commission's powers under Article 21 of the EC Merger Regulation that arguably could be used to even greater effect with the abolition or curtailment of the two-thirds rule.

I. INTRODUCTION

Protectionist tendencies of EU Member States have always been a concern to the European Commission in the context of the EU's single-market objectives. Such tendencies have been especially evident in sectors of industry that previously were dominated largely by state-owned companies, namely, the banking, defense, energy, postal, telecommunications, transport, and water sectors where, following privatization, Member States have sought to preserve or create so-called "national champions."

---

* Alex Nourry is a partner and U.K. Head of the European Competition and Regulation group at Clifford Chance LLP. Nelson Jung is an associate at Clifford Chance LLP in the same group. The authors would like to thank their colleagues Dimos Dakanalis, Christos Nifadopoulos, and Trupti Reddy for their valuable contributions to this article.

This protectionism has manifested itself either through very direct and blatant means such as the grant of State aid as in the case of the French government's rescue of Alsthom, or through the exercise of other state measures, including special rights in privatized companies or the application of legislative or regulatory powers. These state measures, although now less prevalent as a result of Commission intervention, have tended to deter and, in some cases, have prevented foreign takeovers.

A new wave of protectionism or economic patriotism by Member States has broken out recently, as exemplified by the long-running saga of the takeover of Endesa, the Spanish electricity group. Endesa, having been, originally, the target of a proposed takeover by its Spanish rival, Gas Natural, in a clear attempt by the Spanish government to create a national champion in the energy sector, is also the subject of a proposed takeover by the German energy group, E.ON. While E.ON's proposed acquisition of Endesa received unconditional clearance from the Commission under the EC Merger Regulation (ECMR)[1] on the basis that the two groups do not have competing activities, the Spanish National Energy Commission (CNE) approved the merger on condition that E.ON sell up to 30 percent of Endesa's generation capacity on security grounds, thereby severely undermining the viability of the merger. The Commission reacted very swiftly and strongly to the CNE ruling, requesting that the Spanish government refrain from its protectionist obstruction of E.ON's takeover of Endesa.[2] Meanwhile, Iberdrola, another Spanish utility, also joined the fray by appealing against the Commission's clearance of the E.ON-Endesa deal, motivated by its agreement with Gas Natural to buy up to EUR 9 billion of excess assets following a merger with Endesa.[3]

The takeover battle for Endesa also highlights the inherent limitations of the Commission's exclusive jurisdiction under the ECMR to examine mergers between largely domestic players, even when such mergers may have a substantial impact on the single market. The

[1] Council Regulation 139/2004 of 20 January 2004 on the control of concentrations between undertakings, 2004 O.J. (L 24) 1.

[2] On the same day of its challenge to the Spanish government's obstruction of E.ON's takeover of Endesa, the Commission also called on the Italian government to explain its move to block the planned merger between Italian highway operator, Autostrade and Spain's Abertis. The Italian government had argued that the merger would be in breach of an Italian law that prohibits construction companies from holding shares in a concessionary. However, the Commission cleared the merger between Albertis and Autostrade on 22 September, 2006, and Italy's Infrastructure Minister Antonio di Pietro has, in the meantime, acknowledged that the Commission's clearance decision overrules the Italian law. *See* EUROPEAN COMMISSION, PRESS RELEASE NO. 1244 (2006).

[3] This issue of *Competition Policy International* went to print on October 2, 2006. The authors, therefore, were not able to discuss new developments after that date.

Commission was unable to assert its jurisdiction over Gas Natural's proposed takeover of Endesa because of the ECMR's so-called "two-thirds rule," as both parties derived over two-thirds of their respective turnover from activities within Spain. As a result, it fell to the Spanish authorities to review the proposed merger, which they ultimately approved subject to certain conditions.

At the time, in a paper to her fellow Commissioners, European Commissioner Neelie Kroes was reported to have called for wide-ranging reform of the EC's merger regime and, in particular, the abolition of the two-thirds rule on the grounds that it no longer reflected "an optimal allocation of competence between the national and the Community level, and even constitutes in some instances, an obstacle to a consistent treatment of cases."[4] The paper also pointed to the merger of E.ON and Ruhrgas, the German energy group, as another merger that the Commission, rather than the national competition authority, should have examined. Although that merger was blocked by the Bundeskartellamt, the German competition authority's decision was overruled by the German government.

The Commissioner's paper also raised the issue of other sectors, in particular, the financial services sector, where some of the largest mergers also fell outside the Commission's competence due to the application of the two-thirds rule, citing the takeover of Credit Lyonnais by Credit Agricole and of Paribas by BNP as examples in the French banking sector.

This article examines the compatibility of special rights and other state measures (other than State aid) with the EC's single market objectives within the framework of the EC Treaty and their impact on foreign takeovers and investments. It also examines the initiatives taken by the Commission in order to eliminate such measures and analyzes the potential remedies available to foreign investors when confronted with such measures. Such remedies include the application of the Commission's powers under Article 21 of the ECMR that arguably could be used to even greater effect with the abolition or curtailment of the two-thirds rule.

II. THE EU LEGAL FRAMEWORK

A. Fundamental Principles of Eu Law

The single or internal market freedoms of free movement of goods (Article 28 of the EC Treaty), services (Article 49 EC), capital (Article 56 EC), and right of establishment (Article 43 EC) enshrined in the Treaty constitute fundamental principles of EU law. Over the past

[4] Tobias Buck, *Kroes calls for more powers over mergers*, Fin. Times, Nov. 16, 2005.

decade, the principles governing the application of the Treaty freedoms have converged to a considerable extent. Essentially, any measure by a Member State that is liable to hinder or make less attractive the exercise of any of the freedoms is likely to be in breach of the Treaty unless it can be justified. The range of grounds on which Member States can validly rely to justify such a measure depends on whether the measure constituting a hindrance to the single market discriminates on the grounds of nationality (either directly or indirectly) or if it is indistinctly applicable. Discriminatory measures can be justified only by the limited and narrowly construed grounds set down explicitly in the Treaty, such as public policy, public security, or public health.[5] Non-discriminatory measures, however, are justifiable by overriding requirements in the general interest (a non-exhaustive list of such requirements having been developed by the EC Courts) provided that they comply with the principle of proportionality. Restrictions on the Treaty freedoms can never be justified by purely financial or economic reasons.

State measures restricting foreign takeovers generally come within the ambit of the free movement of capital as they are liable to deter or dissuade cross-border capital transactions. Article 56 EC gives effect to the free movement of capital between Member States, and between Member States and third countries. To that end, it provides that all restrictions on the movement of capital between Member States as well as between Member States and third countries are prohibited as a matter of principle. According to settled case law,[6] Directive 88/361, together with the nomenclature annexed to it, may be used for the purposes of defining a capital movement.[7] By way of example, direct investment in the form of participation in an undertaking by means of shareholding or the acquisition of securities on the capital market constitute capital movements within the meaning of Article 56 EC.[8]

Restrictions on acquisitions of controlling stakes in a domestic company by EU investors are also caught by the freedom of establishment as guaranteed in Article 43 EC. In fact, restrictions on the free movement of capital in the context of state measures preventing takeovers by EU investors are usually inextricably linked to the right of establishment.[9]

---

[5] In this respect, see, e.g., Articles 30, 46, 55, and 58(1)(b) of the EC Treaty.

[6] Case C-222/97, Trummer and Mayer, 1999 E.C.R. I-1661, at paragraphs 20 & 21.

[7] 1988 O.J. (L 178) 5; *see also* Communication of the Commission on certain legal aspects concerning intra-EU investment, 1997 O.J. (C 220) 15.

[8] The explanatory notes in Council Directive 88/361 of 24 June 1988 for the implementation of Article 67 of the Treaty, Annex I, 1988 O.J. (L 178) 5, state that direct investment is characterized by the possibility of participating effectively in the management of a company or in its control.

[9] Special Rights in Privatised Companies in the Enlarged Union - A Decade Full of Developments, Annex 1 (Commission Staff Working Document, Jul. 22, 2005).

It should be noted that Article 295 EC, which lays down the Treaty's neutrality between public and private ownership, does not have the effect of exempting the Member States' system of property ownership from the ambit of the Treaty freedoms. Thus, while Member States are not obliged to privatize state-owned companies, once a company is privatized, there is only limited scope for intervention. Member states can also not easily escape the application of the freedoms by invoking security concerns. Article 296 EC sets out the conditions under which Member States may legitimately invoke the protection of their essential security interests, in which case the freedoms do not apply.

B. The Commission's Exclusive Jurisdiction Over Mergers with A Community Dimension

Whether a transaction falls within the ambit of the ECMR and, as a consequence, is subject to the exclusive jurisdiction of the Commission, will play a crucial role in determining the powers that the Commission will have at its disposal and the effectiveness of any remedies available to a bidder when faced with state measures which restrict or seek to prevent a foreign takeover. Article 21(3) ECMR provides that no Member State shall apply its national legislation on competition to any concentration that has a Community dimension (i.e., mergers that meet the turnover thresholds set out in the ECMR).

Where the concentration significantly affects competition in a distinct market within a Member State, however, that Member State can request a referral back to its competent authorities under Article 9 ECMR. The notifying parties can also ask for a concentration with a Community dimension to be reviewed at national level by making a submission to the Commission under Article 4(4) ECMR prior to notifying.[10]

Apart from these mechanisms, whereby the whole or part of a concentration may be referred to the national competition authorities on request, Member States cannot intervene in a merger that is subject to the Commission's jurisdiction, unless they can successfully invoke the protection of their "legitimate interests" under Article 21(4) ECMR. Examples of legitimate interests include public security, plurality of the media, and prudential rules. Legitimate interests grounds are interpreted narrowly given that they constitute exceptions

[10] Article 4(4) of Council Regulation 139/2004 of 20 January 2004 on the control of concentrations between undertakings (hereinafter ECMR), 2004 O.J. (L 24) 1, requires the notifying parties to make a reasoned submission to the effect that the concentration may significantly affect competition in a market within a Member State which presents all the characteristics of a distinct market and should therefore be examined, in whole or in part, by that Member State.

to the Commission's exclusive jurisdiction to vet mergers with a Community dimension. However, there is a limitation to the Commission's exclusive jurisdiction where each of the parties to a merger achieves more than two-thirds of its turnover in the same Member State. Therefore, where the two-thirds rule is met, mergers are not subject to the Commission's scrutiny, but are reviewed instead by national competition authorities, irrespective of what impact they might have on the single market.

However, there is a limitation to the Commission's exclusive jurisdiction where each of the parties to a merger achieves more than two-thirds of its turnover in the same Member State. Therefore, where the two-thirds rule is met, mergers are not subject to the Commission's scrutiny, but are reviewed instead by national competition authorities, irrespective of what impact they might have on the single market

III. THE LEGAL AND ECONOMIC IMPACT OF SPECIAL RIGHTS

A. What Are Special Rights and How Are They Perceived by the Commission?

Special rights, often referred to as "golden shares," are measures used by Member States to retain control over privatized companies, usually to prevent them from being taken over or to prevent the companies' management from taking actions which are contrary to national government policy for the sector in which they operate. While the former constitutes a direct restriction on investment, the latter will only indirectly affect investment decisions by making the investment potentially less attractive.

Golden shares are one of the most commonly used types of special rights, enabling the government to veto specific events or changes in the company's structure. They are usually enshrined in the articles of association of the company and cannot be changed without the government's consent. Special rights may also be conferred on governments by legislation, either under a general framework law covering several economic sectors or specific legislation aimed at an economic sector or a company. Governments may also seek to assert special rights over companies that are awarded concession contracts to provide services of general interest (e.g., in the gambling and broadcasting sectors).

Typically, Member States justify special rights on the grounds that they are necessary to achieve certain policy objectives, usually of a public-interest nature. However, by restricting (directly or indirectly) cross-border mergers or investments, special rights are liable to infringe the principles of free movement of capital (Article 56 EC) and right of establishment (Article 43 EC) and as such can only be compatible with EU law if they meet the strict criteria that have been laid down by the European Court of Justice (ECJ).

In the 2003 paper, *Capital Movements in the Legal Framework of the Community*,[11] the Commission was critical of the margin of appreciation that Member States had at their disposal on the basis of the Treaty, and was concerned over restrictive practices by the Member States against non-EU bidders targeting companies in the European Union. The paper described the situation as amounting to the creation of a "fortress Europe," hostile to outside investment.

The Commission therefore focused its capital movements paper on international trade and the obligations of the Member States towards the Organization for Economic Co-operation and Development and other international organizations.

The Commission is responsible for monitoring the proper and timely application of Treaty rules governing the freedom of capital movements as well as other internal market freedoms. Its objective is to secure the removal of all remaining restrictions to the free movement of capital in the internal market through ongoing cooperation and dialogue with Member States. Where Member States fail to comply with their obligations under the Treaty, this responsibility will require the Commission to initiate infringement procedures against the Member States concerned.

In its staff working document, Special rights in privatized companies in the enlarged Union—a decade full of developments,[12] the Commission outlined three principal concerns about special rights, being that they can:

- hinder privatized companies from achieving the full benefits of privatization;
- distort market driven cross-border activity in terms of both direct and portfolio investment in privatized companies; and,
- prove one of the obstacles to achieving a level playing field in the EU market for corporate control.

The Commission also raised concerns about the strong economic implications that special rights can have for the functioning of the single market since the companies in which Member States retain special rights often play a significant role in the economy. It identified 141 companies operating in sectors ranging from telecommunications, energy, and postal services to banking and insurance in which Member States retained special rights. Of these

[11] *Capital Movements in the Legal Framework of the Community, in* The EU Economy 2003 Review 320, 320-28 (Directorate General for Economic and Financial Affairs, 2003).

[12] Special Rights in Privatised Companies in the Enlarged Union - A Decade Full of Developments, Annex 1 (Commission Staff Working Document, Jul. 22, 2005).

141 companies,[13] 14 percent were accounted for by the fifteen old Member States (EU 15) and 86 percent by the ten new Member States (EU 10).

While special rights are still widely present in the EU 10 and affect a broader range of industries, including alcoholic beverages, food processing, textiles, and pharmaceuticals, in the Commission's view, this is largely due to the timing and scale of the privatization process in these countries and, in most cases, the Member States concerned have put in place a process to deal with the issue. In other cases, the Commission believes the special rights can be justified by exceptions provided in the Treaty or are structured in a way that is compatible with EU law. Overall, the Commission's assessment is that special rights in privatized companies are being phased out and that this can be attributed to two key factors:

- the proactive approach the Commission has taken in engaging in a dialogue with Member States, and
- the impact of the rulings of the ECJ in a series of landmark cases.

The Commission also identified the development of a more robust regulatory environment in specific sectors (e.g., telecommunications and energy) as another relevant factor both at the EU and national level, which has allowed Member States to protect the services of general interest in a relatively less restrictive manner. However, where special rights still persist, whether in the EU 15 or EU 10, that are not compatible with EU law, the Commission will not hesitate to proceed with infringement proceedings against the Member States concerned.

The latest report published by the Commission in November 2005,[14] assesses the microeconomic impact of special rights in privatized EU companies on company performance, investment in the companies, and share values. The report, however, does not address the broader impacts of special rights on economic performance in the industry sectors concerned, or on consumers, or on the European Union as a whole.

In its conclusions, the report found that:

- special rights held by public authorities tend to have a negative impact on the longer-term economic performance of EU privatized companies;

---

[13] This number includes a number of regional companies, including 29 regional waterworks in the Czech Republic and 21 energy companies in Hungary.

[14] Oxera, Special Rights of Public Authorities in Privatised EU Companies: The Microeconomic Impact (2005) (report prepared for the European Commission).

- both existing and new empirical research provide strong evidence that special rights can constitute important barriers to direct investment;
- special rights have an adverse impact not only on the market for corporate control, by restricting takeover activity and distorting the level playing field in the market, but also on portfolio investors, who would otherwise benefit from increases in the value of their shares during a takeover;
- to the extent that special rights restrict the free movement of capital across EU borders, they impede further financial market integration; and
- regulation may be seen as a potentially less restrictive and more transparent means of achieving public policy objectives, especially if carried out by an arm's-length regulatory authority.

On the basis of this report, it is likely that the Commission will continue and possibly intensify its efforts against special rights and may try to steer national governments more proactively towards entrusting independent regulatory bodies with the protection of public interest concerns rather than resort to special rights or other similar state measures.

B. Conditions for Compatibility of Special Rights with EU Law

In its July 2005 document, the Commission regarded the rulings delivered by the ECJ in a series of seven infringement cases initiated by the Commission pursuant to Article 226 EC, as the most significant development in the field of special rights. In these cases, the Court set down very strict criteria for the use of special rights and their compatibility with EU law.

The ECJ's rulings[15] essentially confirm that special rights can be compatible with EU law even when they may be at odds with the principles of free movement of capital (Article 56 EC) and right of establishment (Article 43 EC) provided they are:

- justifiable, based on the exceptions explicitly listed in the Treaty or by reference to requirements in the general interest (where this constitutes a genuine and serious threat);

[15] Case C-58/99, Commission v. Italy, 2000 E.C.R. I-3811; Case C-367/98, Commission v. Portugal, 2002 E.C.R. I-4731; Case C-483/99, Commission v. France, 2002 E.C.R. I-4781; Case C-503/99, Commission v. Belgium, 2002 E.C.R. I-4809; Case C-98/01, Commission v. United Kingdom, 2003 E.C.R. I-04641; Case C-463/00, Commission v. Spain, 2003 E.C.R. I-4581; Case C-174/04, Commission v. Italy, 2005 E.C.R. I-4933.

- necessary to protect the interests concerned and this protection cannot be obtained by less restrictive measures (i.e., proportionate);
- objective, non-discriminatory, and transparent; and
- subject to a legal remedy.

The ECJ also confirmed that the Treaty provisions on the free movement of capital do not draw a distinction between private undertakings and public undertakings.[16]

The cases concerned proceedings against Belgium, France, Portugal, Spain, the United Kingdom, and two cases against Italy. They all essentially concerned veto rights in favor of the state relating to the ownership of shares or capital of privatized companies. In all of the cases, with the exception of the case against Belgium, the ECJ ruled in favor of the Commission. While the Commission considers the ECJ's decisions in all seven cases as landmark rulings, those in the cases against Belgium, France, and Portugal delivered in 2002 stand out in particular. However, the cases against Italy, Spain, and the United Kingdom are also briefly examined, as well as the current status of pending cases and ongoing Commission intervention.

1. Portugal

The case against Portugal[17] concerned a general framework law relating to the privatization of undertakings in the banking, insurance, energy, and transport sectors that specified maximum levels of foreign participation (ranging between 5 and 40 percent) in the privatized companies. The ECJ found the law to constitute a restriction on the free movement of capital within the meaning of Article 56 EC. The Portuguese government sought to justify the law on the grounds that it was necessary for the pursuit of national economic policy objectives, for choosing a strategic partner, for strengthening the competitive structure of the market concerned, or modernizing and increasing the efficiency of means of production. However, none of these objectives were found by the ECJ to constitute a valid justification for restrictions on the fundamental Treaty freedoms.

[16] Case C-174/04, Commission v. Italy, 2005 E.C.R. I-4933.

[17] Case C-367/98, Commission v. Portugal, 2002 E.C.R. I-4731.

2. France

The case against France[18] concerned legislation that vested in the state a golden share in Société Nationale Elf-Aquitaine, and gave the Minister of Economic Affairs the right to:

- approve any direct or indirect shareholding by a natural or legal person, acting alone or in conjunction with others, in excess of one-fifth, one-tenth or one-third of the capital of, or voting rights in, the company, and
- oppose any decision to transfer or use as security the majority of the capital of four subsidiaries of that company.

In addition, the law provided for the appointment of two state representatives on the board of directors of the company, without entitlement to vote.

The ECJ ruled that the French law was incompatible with the free movement of capital, despite the fact that it applied without distinction to French nationals and to nationals of other Member States. It held that:

> "even though the rules in issue may not give rise to unequal treatment, they are liable to impede the acquisition of shares in the undertakings concerned and to dissuade investors in other Member States from investing in the capital of those undertakings. They are therefore liable, as a result, to render the free movement of capital illusory."[19]

The French government's justification for adopting the law was the safeguarding of supplies of petroleum products in the event of a crisis. The ECJ accepted that, in principle, this objective could be a valid public interest justification for the French law. However, the provisions of the law were too wide and "investors concerned were given no indication whatsoever as to the specific, objective circumstances in which prior authorization would be granted or refused."[20] Therefore, the legislation went beyond what was necessary in order to attain the objective indicated and constituted an unjustifiable restriction of the free movement of capital.

---

[18] Case C-483/99, Commission v. France, 2002 E.C.R. I-4781.

[19] *Id.* at paragraph 41.

[20] *Id.* at paragraph 50.

3. Belgium

The Belgium case[21] also involved legislation whose objective was to secure energy supplies at a time of crisis. Belgium had passed laws vesting in the state a golden share in, *inter alia*, Distrigaz. The law provided that:

- advance notice of any transfer, use as security or change in the intended destination of the company's system of lines and conduits that are used, or are capable of being used, as major infrastructures for the domestic conveyance of energy products must be given to the Minister responsible, who can oppose such operations if he considers that they adversely affect the national interest in the energy sector, and
- the Minister may appoint two state representatives to the board of directors of the company who can propose to the Minister the annulment of any decision of the board of directors which they regard as contrary to the guidelines for the country's energy policy, including the government's objectives concerning the country's energy supply.

The ECJ found that the measures were restrictive but allowed them on the basis that they were justified, as being necessary to attain the stated objective (to maintain minimum supplies of gas in the event of a real and serious threat) and because there were no less restrictive measures to attain the general interest objective. In particular, the ECJ found that the measures were acceptable because:

- the law established a system of opposition not prior approval (see the France case discussed above) and the public authorities were obliged to adhere to strict time limits when exercising the right to oppose an acquisition;
- the right was limited to certain decisions in relation to certain strategic assets of Distrigaz (lines and conduits); and,
- any intervention by the Minister had to be supported by a formal statement of reasons and was subject to judicial review by the courts.

Cumulatively, these three factors meant that the law did not grant a wide discretion to the state to intervene and established objective criteria on which the state could do so.

---

[21] Case C-503/99, Commission v. Belgium, 2002 E.C.R. I-4809.

4. Italy

The first decision against Italy, in 2000, concerned investment restrictions contained in a 1992 general framework law on privatization that, although amended by the Italian government in 2001, the Commission still considered to unduly restrict the freedoms of capital movements and establishment, and therefore referred it to the ECJ.

The second decision against Italy, in 2005, concerned a law of 2001 aimed at avoiding anticompetitive attacks on Italian companies operating in the electricity and gas sectors by public entities operating in the same sectors in other Member States, and enjoying a dominant position in their domestic markets. The law was also designed to safeguard energy supplies. In rejecting the Italian government's justifications for the law, the ECJ said that Italy had failed to show how energy supplies would be threatened by the acquisition of an Italian energy company specifically by a buyer dominant in another Member State as opposed to any other type of buyer. The ECJ also ruled that "an interest in generally strengthening the competitive structure of the market in question cannot constitute valid justification for restrictions on the free movement of capital"[22] and, in any case, that objective could be served by the ECMR. Following the judgment, the Commission called on Italy to comply with the ECJ's ruling as it was not convinced that the amendments subsequently made to the law fully implemented the ruling of the Court.[23]

5. Spain

The decision against Spain in 2003 concerned a law of 1995 relating to the privatizations of Repsol SA, Telefónica de España SA, Telefónica Servicios Móviles SA, Argentaria, Tabacalera SA, and Endesa SA., that gave the Spanish government a right of prior approval of certain management decisions.[24] In rejecting the measures, the ECJ ruled that the fact that the legislation concerned introduced regimes that would last only ten years did not make the measures proportionate since an "infringement of Treaty obligations does not cease to be an infringement merely because it is limited in time."[25] Following the ECJ's ruling in 2003, it was not

---

[22] Case C-174/04, Commission v. Italy, 2005 E.C.R. I-4933, at paragraph 37.

[23] European Commission, Press Release No. 439, Free Movement of Capital: Commission Calls on Italy to Apply Court of Justice Ruling on the Law on Investment in Energy Companies (2006); Eur. Commission, Press Release No. 1270, Free Movement of Capital: Commission Calls on Italy to Modify Law on Privatised Companies and to Apply Court Ruling on Investment in Energy Companies (2005).

[24] Case C-463/00, Commission v. Spain, 2003 E.C.R. I-4581.

[25] *Id.* at paragraph 81.

until May 2006 that the Spanish government fully eliminated the restrictions concerned, after the Commission had called on Spain to comply with the ECJ's judgment, and had sent Spain a reasoned opinion as part of infringement proceedings under Article 228 EC.

6. United Kingdom

The decision against the United Kingdom, concerned a golden share held by the U.K. government in British Airports Authority plc (BAA), that limited all interests in the company to 15 percent of voting shares and provided the U.K. government with a veto right over the disposal of shares. Following the ECJ's ruling in 2003, the U.K. government relinquished its golden share, that otherwise might have prevented the recent takeover of BAA by Spain's Ferrovial.[26]

7. Pending Cases

Infringement cases concerning golden shares are also pending before the ECJ against Germany and the Netherlands. The case against Germany concerns the 1960 law privatizing Volkswagen (VW) that to date still prevents any shareholder from acquiring more than 20 percent of voting rights, and confers a special blocking minority right on any shareholder who has 20 percent of voting rights. Traditionally, both the German government and the Land of Lower Saxony (the Land) held 20 percent voting rights in VW, although the Land is now the only shareholder with 20 percent voting rights and two mandatory members of the board. The Commission brought the case before the ECJ in 2004[27] claiming that these provisions of the VW Act make it substantially less attractive for other EU investors to acquire the company's shares with a view to participating effectively in management decisions or controlling it, and so are contrary to the Treaty provisions on free movement of capital and the right of establishment.

The two cases against the Netherlands, initiated by the Commission pursuant to Article 226 EC, concern golden shares held by the Dutch government in Koninklijke KPN N.V. (KPN) and TNT Post Groep N.V. (TPG). Conferring a major influence over KPN's and TPG's financial decision-making and the management of the two companies, the Commission took the view that the golden shares may deter EU investors from investing in the capital of the two companies and, consequently, were contrary to the Treaty rules on free movement of

[26] Case COMP/M.4164, Ferrovial/Quebec/GIC/BAA, 2006 O.J. (C 182) 11.

[27] European Commission, Press Release No. 1209, Free Movement of Capital: Commission Takes Germany to the Court of Justice on Volkswagen Law (2004).

capital and the right of establishment.[28] On April 6, 2006, Advocate General Poiares Maduro came to the conclusion that the Netherlands has indeed failed to fulfill its obligations under Article 56 EC by retaining its golden shares in KPN and TPG and this view was endorsed by the ECJ in its judgment of September 28, 2006.[29]

The Commission continues to monitor compliance with the Treaty provisions governing free movement of capital; and in this context is actively considering infringement procedures against a number of Member States (some of which have already been mentioned), including Denmark (possible obstacles to investment from other Member States in Copenhagen Airports); France (authorization procedure for foreign investments in certain sectors and ban on stock market listing for football clubs);[30] Hungary (privatization framework law); Luxembourg (veto rights over shareholdings in the satellite companies SES Astra and SES Global); and Spain (law amending functions of Spanish energy regulator).

IV. THE NEW WAVE OF INTERVENTIONISM

A. "Economic Patriotism" in All but Name

Based on the Commission's own assessment special rights, or golden shares, are being phased out by Member States, including among the EU 10. This probably also coincides with the fact that privatization programs in a number of Member States have now largely run their course.

The Commission appears disposed to encouraging Member States to entrust independent regulatory bodies with the protection of public interest concerns rather than resort to special rights or other interventionist measures. While Member States may be receptive to such an approach, possibly with the exception of certain sectors, such as defense,[31] this does not necessarily guarantee that Member States will refrain from interventionism in the pursuit of national interests.

---

[28] EUROPEAN COMMISSION, PRESS RELEASE NO. 1753, FREE MOVEMENT OF CAPITAL: COMMISSION TAKES THE NETHERLANDS TO COURT OF JUSTICE ON SPECIAL POWERS IN KPN AND TNT (2003).

[29] Cases C-282/04 & C-283/04, Commission v. Netherlands (not yet reported).

[30] France recently lifted its ban on the listing of sports clubs. *See* Adam Jones, *Olympique Lyonnais Leads Listing Field*, FIN. TIMES, Sept. 25, 2006.

[31] For example, it is unlikely that the U.K. government would relinquish its golden shares in BAE Systems and Rolls-Royce or France its golden shares in Thales and EADS.

Indeed, recently, a new wave of interventionism by Member States has emerged. This has manifested itself in the adoption or exercise of legislative and regulatory measures, or the blatant promotion of national champions in preference to a foreign takeover. Such interventionism is well illustrated, for example, by the Spanish government's actions in relation to the contested takeover of Endesa or by the French government's defense of Danone following rumors that PepsiCo was preparing a takeover bid in a sector that few would credit as being strategic or in the general interest, but nevertheless Danone was deemed by the government "a French icon and off-limits to foreign ownership."[32]

Recently, a new wave of interventionism by Member States has emerged. This has manifested itself in the adoption or exercise of legislative and regulatory measures, or the blatant promotion of national champions in preference to a foreign takeover

While such government interventions may be perceived to be in the national interest, in the long run they are unlikely to be in the best interests of domestic consumers since they are prone to result in higher prices and lower innovation. They are also undesirable from an internal market perspective as they create an unlevel playing field for business and ultimately are more likely to undermine rather than enhance the competitiveness of EU industry.

B. Legislative and Regulatory Measures

Controversially, in December 2005, France adopted a law[33] creating an authorization procedure for foreign investments in certain sectors that could affect public policy, public security, or national defense. The protected sectors include gambling (e.g., casinos); private security services; research, development, or production of chemical or biological antidotes; activities concerning equipment for intercepting communications or eavesdropping; services for evaluation of security of computer systems; dual-use (civil and military) technologies; cryptology; activities of firms that are repositories of defense secrets; research, production, or trade in arms, munitions, explosives, or other military equipment; or any other industry supplying the defense ministry any of the aforementioned goods or services.[34]

On April 4, 2006, the Commission sent a formal request to France, after informal dialogue that led the Commission to believe that the French law could potentially lead to restrictions in the freedom of movement of capital (Article 56 EC) and the right of

[32] Arturo Bris, *Global Growing Pains*, Fin. Times, Apr. 6, 2006.

[33] Decree 2005-1739 of 30 December 2005, O.J., December 31, 2005, No. 45.

[34] *See id.*

establishment (Article 43 EC).[35] Although the French law appeared to make wider use of an independent regulator for the purposes of protecting the public interest (along the lines of the proposals contained in the Commission's report of November 2005),[36] the Commission was concerned that the ambit of the powers conferred on the French regulator was considerably wider than appeared necessary for achieving the stated objectives of public policy, public security, and national defense and consequently not proportionate.

The Commission also challenged the inclusion of casinos in the category of companies for which there is public policy concern, especially as the transposition of the Money Laundering Directive could provide adequate public protection. The Commission is therefore likely to require France to amend its legislation, failing which it will be forced to pursue infringement proceedings against France under Article 226 EC.

In February 2006, Spain adopted new legislation extending the powers of the CNE, Spain's National Energy Commission, requiring the authorization of the CNE for the acquisition of over 10 percent of the share capital, or any other percentage resulting in significant influence, in companies engaged directly or indirectly in regulated activities in the energy sector. In exercising such powers, the CNE is able to take into consideration a variety of factors, including any risks in relation to the regulated activities, the inability to perform such activities, and the protection of the general interest and reasons of public security. In the Commission's view, these factors are vague and indeterminate and as a result give the CNE wide discretionary powers. In May 2006, the Commission announced that it had opened infringement proceedings under Article 226 EC by requesting in a formal letter that Spain provide more information concerning the new legislation, having already warned the Spanish government that the law was likely to violate EU law, insofar as it hindered or rendered less attractive the free movement of capital and the right of establishment.[37]

The Spanish legislation is particularly sensitive given that it was adopted in the context of competing takeover bids for the Spanish electricity operator, Endesa. On February 21, 2006, the German energy company E.ON announced its intention to launch a public bid for Endesa, countering the bid that Spain's Gas Natural had made for the company

---

[35] European Commission, Press Release No. 438, Free Movement of Capital: Commission Scrutinises French Law Establishing Authorisation Procedure for Foreign Investments in Certain Sectors (2006).

[36] *See* Oxera, *supra* note 14.

[37] European Commission, Press Release No. 569, Free Movement of Capital: Commission Opens Infringement Proceedings Against Spain Regarding Law Amending Functions of Spanish Electricity and Gas Regulator (2006).

in September 2005. Just three days after E.ON's announcement (on February 24, 2006), Spain adopted the law[38] extending the CNE's powers to allow it to block foreign takeovers. This move was widely criticized as a blatant attempt by the Spanish government to deter E.ON from pursuing its bid. Nevertheless, E.ON notified its proposed takeover of Endesa to the Commission on March 16, 2006, and this was cleared unconditionally on April 25, 2006. The CNE subsequently also approved E.ON's proposed takeover of Endesa, on July 28, 2006, but subject to substantial conditions, including, most significantly, the sale of 30 percent of Endesa's domestic generation capacity. In light of the CNE's decision, the Commission announced that it would take the appropriate measures to ensure that its clearance decision in *E.ON/Endesa*[39] was respected and, accordingly, on August 3, 2006, sent the Spanish government a letter based on Article 21 ECMR, requesting "clarifications" regarding the CNE's decision.[40] In its reply of August 10, 2006, the Spanish government accused the Commission of exceeding its authority and countered that the conditions imposed on E.ON do not prevent it from acquiring Endesa. According to the Commission's preliminary conclusions, however, most of these conditions raise serious doubts as to their compatibility with EC law. Competition Commissioner Neelie Kroes vowed to remain vigilant in this case and to continue to take a firm stance in similar cases.[41] Not surprisingly, therefore, on September 26, 2006, the Commission announced that it had adopted a decision finding that Spain has breached Article 21 ECMR by virtue of the conditions imposed by the CNE on E.ON's bid for Endesa.[42] The Commission also announced that it had sent Spain a reasoned opinion alleging that the legislation that extended the power of the CNE to authorize mergers in the energy sector infringes Articles 43 and 56 EC. In addition, both E.ON and Endesa have appealed the CNE's decision.[43]

---

[38] Act of 24 February by which the Functions of the National Commission of Energy are Modified (B.O.E., 2006, 3436).

[39] Case COMP/M.4110, E.ON/Endesa, 2006 O.J. (C 68) 09.

[40] EUROPEAN COMMISSION, PRESS RELEASE NO. 1096, STATEMENT BY COMMISSION SPOKESPERSON: RECEIPT OF LETTER FROM SPANISH AUTHORITIES ON EON/ENDESA MERGER (2006).

[41] *See* Competition Commissioner Neelie Kroes' speech on "Cross-border mergers and energy markets" given at the Villa d'Este Forum in Cernobbia, Italy, on 2 September 2006, Speech/06/480.

[42] EUROPEAN COMMISSION, PRESS RELEASE NO. 1265, MERGERS: COMMISSION RULES AGAINST SPANISH ENERGY REGULATOR'S MEASURES CONCERNING E.ON'S BID FOR ENDESA (2006).

[43] EUROPEAN COMMISSION, PRESS RELEASE NO. 1264, FREE MOVEMENT OF CAPITAL: COMMISSION CALLS ON SPAIN TO MODIFY THE LAW AMENDING THE FUNCTIONS OF THE SPANISH ELECTRICITY AND GAS REGULATOR (2006).

C. Promoting Mergers to Create National Champions

Member States are not averse to resorting to even more blatant industrial engineering when they cannot rely on legislative or regulatory measures in order to create national champions.

When Italy's Enel expressed interest in the French energy company Suez, the French government orchestrated a defensive merger between Suez and Gaz de France in February 2006. President Jacques Chirac summarized his opposition to Enel's bid for Suez by declaring: "France doesn't want to surrender to a purely financial operation."[44] Although France was cleared in May 2006 of breaching EU internal market rules by promoting the defensive merger, it was criticized by the Commission for considering maintaining a golden share in the merged entity.[45] The Commission decided on June 19, 2006, that it would investigate the merger on the basis of competition concerns raised in the Belgian gas and electricity supply market.[46] It outlined its main concerns in a Statement of Objections issued on August 19, 2006,[47] and is expected to adopt a decision on the compatibility of the merger between Suez and Gaz de France with the common market on November 17, 2006.[48]

A national champion was created in the German *E.ON/Ruhrgas* case. The German Federal Cartel Office prohibited the acquisition of a majority stake in Ruhrgas by E.ON in 2002 on the basis of competition concerns.[49] However, in spite of the merger being blocked by the Bundeskartellamt, the Federal Minister of Economics ultimately granted a special ministerial authorization and cleared the merger. This special authorization could, of course, not have been granted had the transaction triggered the Commission's exclusive jurisdiction under the ECMR. However, the Commission had reached the decision that it was not competent to review the case given that E.ON and Ruhrgas achieved more than two-thirds of their EU-wide turnover within Germany. The U.K.'s energy regulator, Ofgem, argued at the time that the merger should have been reviewed at EU level, claiming that E.ON's subsequent acquisition of U.K. energy company Powergen took it above the two-thirds limit. In Ofgem's view, E.ON

---

44 Bris, *supra* note 32.

45 *France to keep control over GdF/Suez assets*, Reuters, May 23, 2006.

46 European Commission, Press Release No. 802, Mergers: Commission Opens In-Depth Investigation Into Merger Between Gaz De France and Suez Group (2006).

47 European Commission, Press Release No. 1109, Mergers: The European Commission Adopts a "Statement of Objections" Regarding the Merger Project Between Suez and Gaz de France (2006).

48 In view of remedies proposed by Suez and Gaz de France on September 20, 2006, the deadline for the Commission's decision was extended by 15 working days; MEMO/06/340.

49 *See* the Bundeskartellamt's press release relating to its decision to prohibit the acquisition *available at* http://www.bundeskartellamt.de/wEnglisch/News/Archiv/ArchivNews2002/2002_02_28.shtml.

had effectively side-stepped the Commission's exclusive jurisdiction over the merger. At the time, the E.ON/Ruhrgas merger attracted widespread criticism that it was incompatible with the spirit of competition and undermined the liberalization of the EU energy market.

D. State Intervention in the Context of Article 21 ECMR

The ability of Member States to successfully resort to interventionist measures is far more limited when it comes to takeovers with a Community dimension falling within the exclusive jurisdiction of the Commission under the ECMR. Member States do not have the power to intervene in mergers that have a Community dimension unless they can justifiably invoke legitimate interests (e.g., public security, media plurality, or prudential rules) within the meaning of Article 21(4) ECMR. To the extent that this provision constitutes an exception to the Commission's exclusive competence to vet mergers falling within the ECMR, the provision is to be narrowly construed, so that any measures invoked by Member States pursuant to Article 21(4) ECMR must be proportionate and compatible with EU law.

1. The Champalimaud *Case*

In *BSCH/Champalimaud*,[50] the acquisition by Banco Santander Central Hispanico (BSCH), a Spanish bank, of the Champalimaud group of Portuguese banks and insurance companies fell within the ECMR and was therefore notified to the Commission. However, the Portuguese Minister of Finance adopted a decision freezing Champalimaud's shares on the basis that the transaction failed to comply with Portuguese financial rules. While the Portuguese authorities claimed that their decision was based on prudential grounds, the Commission doubted that this was in fact the case and suspected the decision to be driven by protectionist considerations. Moreover, the Portuguese authorities had not communicated the interests they wanted to protect to the Commission in accordance with Article 21(4) ECMR. As a consequence, the Commission initiated infringement proceedings and adopted an interim measures decision suspending the application of the Portuguese authorities' decision pending further investigation.

The Commission was not only concerned with an apparent attempt to undermine its exclusive jurisdiction under the ECMR, but also raised the issue whether the Portuguese decision violated the principles of free movement of capital and freedom of establishment. However, the Portuguese authorities refused to suspend their decision and instead suspended certain voting rights in the Champalimaud group. The Commission cleared the concen-

[50] Case IV/M.1616, BSCH/A.Champalimaud, 1999 O.J. (C 197) 5.

tration in August 1999 and initiated further infringement proceedings against Portugal in September 1999 for not complying with the interim measures decision. On October 20, 1999, the Commission adopted a final decision declaring that Portugal had infringed Article 21 ECMR. Following the withdrawal of the Portuguese measures, BSCH went on to acquire control of Banco Totta & Açores, SA. and Banco de Crédito Prédial Português, both subsidiaries of the Champalimaud group.

2. *The* Cimpor *Case*

This case involved a proposed bid for the Portuguese cement company Cimpor, in which the Portuguese state held golden shares. In 2000, Holderbel, a Belgian subsidiary of Holderbank of Switzerland and Portuguese cement company, Secil, launched a public bid to acquire Cimpor. Given that the transaction had a Community dimension it was notified to the Commission under the ECMR. However, the Portuguese Minister of Finance prohibited the transaction. The Commission issued a decision finding that Portugal did not protect any legitimate interests under Article 21 ECMR, and that Portugal was acting in breach of the Commission's exclusive jurisdiction to review the concentration.[51] The Commission decided that Portugal should withdraw its prohibition measures in order to comply with Community law.

Portugal challenged the Commission's decision claiming that the Commission had no legal basis for it. Portugal had not made a request for the protection of legitimate interests under Article 21 ECMR and argued that non-compliance with the procedure in Article 21 was not sufficient for the Commission to reach its infringement decision. Furthermore, Portugal claimed that, if anything, the Commission should have opened an infringement procedure against Portugal under Article 226 EC rather than relying on Article 21 ECMR to reach its decision. However, in its ruling of June 22, 2004, the ECJ dismissed Portugal's appeal on the basis that the Commission acted legitimately in making a decision under Article 21 ECMR.[52]

3. *The Polish Banking Case*

In March 2006, the Commission began infringement proceedings against Poland under Article 21 ECMR. The Commission considered that Poland had breached the Commission's exclusive jurisdiction to review mergers with a Community dimension by requiring the bank UniCredit to divest its shares in the Polish bank BPH, the acquisition of which had already been approved

---

51 Case COMP/M.2054, Secil/Holderbank/Cimpor, 2000 O.J. (C 198) 5. The parties subsequently withdrew their notification.

52 Case C-42/01, Portugal v. Commission, 2004 E.C.R. I-6079; for an analysis of the implications of the decision in terms of remedies, see infra, Section V.

by the Commission as part of UniCredit's takeover of German bank HVB.[53] The Polish Treasury instructed UniCredit to sell its shares in BPH on the basis that UniCredit was bound by a non-compete clause in a privatization agreement it had entered into when it acquired the Polish bank Pekao in 1999 from the Polish state. Poland insisted that this non-compete clause continued to prevent UniCredit, for a period of ten years, from opening subsidiaries and/or branches in Poland, acquiring control of banks active in Poland, or making any capital investment in any company active in the Polish banking sector. The Commission reminded Poland that Member States can neither apply their national competition law to concentrations with a Community dimension, nor can they adopt measures which could prohibit or prejudice (de jure or de facto) such concentrations unless they can rely on legitimate interests under Article 21(4) ECMR, and the specific measure is proportionate and compatible with EU law.

The Commission considered the Polish government's decision to invoke the non-compete clause to constitute a measure that can de facto prevent, or seriously prejudice, the *UniCredit/HVB* concentration. In addition, the Commission noted that Poland had not communicated to it any other hypothetical legitimate interests under Article 21(4) ECMR, and that, in any event, the non-compete clause itself appeared to be incompatible with the free movement of capital and the freedom of establishment.[54] The Commission emphasized that it could adopt a decision under Article 21 ECMR requiring the Polish government to refrain from invoking the non-compete clause. Moreover, the Commission stressed that such a decision would be directly applicable, meaning that it could be invoked directly before a national court or public authority in Poland by aggrieved third parties.

In April 2006, Poland entered into an agreement with UniCredit according to which UniCredit agreed to sell 200 of the 483 branches of Poland's BPH bank. The Commission, however, announced that this agreement did not necessarily mean an end to proceedings against Poland for violating Article 21 ECMR.

4. The Italian Banking Cases

The Italian central bank's handling of foreign takeover bids has also given rise to concerns recently. In one case the Commission cleared the public takeover bid by the Dutch banking group ABN Amro for Italian bank Antonveneta. However, the governor of Italy's central bank,

[53] Case COMP/M.3894, Unicredito/HVB, 2005 O.J. (C 235) 4.

[54] Note that the Commission started infringement proceedings under Article 226 EC with regard to a possible violation of Articles 43 and 56 EC. *See* Eur. Commission, Press Release No. 276, Free Movement of Capital: Commission Opens Infringement Procedure Against Poland in Context of UniCredit/HBV Merger (2006).

who holds a personal veto over banking mergers, appeared to have favored a rival bid from the Italian bank BPI, and reportedly overruled a number of senior Italian regulators who expressed concerns about the viability of BPI's bid. After a long takeover battle, ABN Amro ultimately succeeded, becoming the first foreign bank to acquire an Italian financial institution, and the governor of the Italian central bank, Antonio Fazio, was forced to step down amid a criminal investigation into allegations of insider trading and abuse of office.

The Italian banking cases have sparked a wider drive by the Commission to combat protectionism in Europe's fragmented financial services sector. The Commission appears particularly keen to clarify the role of central banks and other financial regulators, that are tasked, among other things, with ensuring that cross-border mergers do not undermine the stability of domestic financial markets. The Commission argued that the present regime gives national institutions too much scope to obstruct foreign takeovers. To this end, on March 16, 2006, the Commission announced that it may look to overhaul rules for the policing of mergers in the banking, insurance, and securities sectors with the aim of reducing protectionism and harmonizing supervisory practices.[55] More recently, the Commission said it was going to table a proposal to change the banking directive to the effect that national supervisors will only be able to oppose a merger in this sector if one of the objective and non-discriminatory criteria set out in the directive is met.[56]

V. REMEDIES AGAINST STATE MEASURES AVAILABLE TO FOREIGN INVESTORS

A. Overriding Political and Commercial Considerations

State measures that restrict foreign takeovers or investments and do not meet the conditions for compatibility with EU law laid down by the ECJ will render Member States in violation of their obligations to comply with the Treaty rules on the free movement of capital (Article 56 EC) and the right of establishment (Article 43 EC).

---

[55] Charlie McCreevy, EU Commissioner for Internal Market and Services, has commented that "the tendency by national regulators to encourage national champions" is one reason for the currently limited cross-border banking consolidation. Charlie McCreevy, *European Banking - challenges and changes ahead*, Address to Institut International de'Etudes Bancaires (May 20, 2005).

[56] According to Fin. Times, Sept. 6, 2006, the criteria set out in the draft proposal are (i) the reputation of the acquirer and its ability to meet the standards set out in the banking directive, (i) the reputation and experience of the people charged with steering the merged group, (iii) the financial soundness of the acquirer, (iv) its ability to meet all the criteria and obligations laid out in the directive and other sectoral rules, and (v) suspected links to money laundering and terrorist financing.

Violations of the Treaty will in principle give rise to a range of potential remedies for a foreign bidder or investor at both the EU and national levels. The challenge, however, is whether any of these remedies can provide effective and meaningful redress within the context of a contested cross-border merger. Even to the extent that remedies are available that would afford such redress within an acceptable timeframe, aggrieved parties will inevitably have to face up to the political and commercial realities of having to challenge the government of a Member State with which it aspires to do business not only in the immediate future but possibly also over the longer term. These overriding considerations may, in practice, prove to be the greatest obstacle to foreign investors pursuing remedies against Member States, whether at the EU or national level.

B. Remedies at the EU Level

An aggrieved investor's principal remedy at the EU level will be to lodge a complaint with the Commission against the Member State concerned, with a view to the Commission initiating one or more of the enforcement procedures available to it under either Article 86 or 226 EC. Where the transaction falls within the ambit of the ECMR, the Commission also has the additional option of taking enforcement action under Article 21 ECMR.

1. Article 86 EC

An aggrieved investor could challenge a state measure that it feels confers special rights on a company by complaining to the Commission. Article 86(3) EC imposes a duty on the Commission to ensure that Member States do not keep in place measures that are contrary to Article 86(1) EC,[57] and gives the Commission power to adopt decisions or directives that are legally binding. Failure to comply with such a decision or directive can be the basis for an action before the ECJ. However, while decisions and directives of the Commission are subject to challenge by the Member State or the company that is the subject of the state measure, a failure by the Commission to issue a decision or directive following an investigation cannot be challenged by a complainant because it is does not constitute a legally binding act.[58]

[57] In essence, Article 86(1) EC is designed to prevent Member States from evading the competition (and other) rules of the Treaty by maintaining public ownership of undertakings or by granting undertakings special or exclusive rights.

[58] *See* Case C141/02, Commission v. Max-mobil, 2005 E.C.R. I-1283.

It has been suggested that the Commission has the power to adopt interim measures under Article 86(3) EC, although it has never done so.[59] This is on the basis that the Commission's powers arising from Article 86(3) EC may be similar to its powers in relation Articles 81 and 82 EC, that allow it to adopt interim measures in urgent cases and on the basis of a prima facie finding of infringement.

2. Article 226 EC

The Commission can (on its own initiative or following a complaint) investigate and issue a reasoned opinion under Article 226 EC in respect of a Treaty violation by a Member State. If the Member State concerned fails to comply within the time limits laid down in the reasoned opinion, the Commission may bring an action before the ECJ. Once the ECJ upholds the Commission's opinion, and if the Member State fails to comply with the finding of the ECJ, the Commission can, after giving the Member State an opportunity to submit its observations, issue a reasoned opinion specifying the points on which the Member State has not complied with the ECJ's judgment. If, following the second reasoned opinion, the Member State fails to take the necessary steps within the time limit laid down, the Commission may then bring a further action before the ECJ, requesting the imposition of a penalty payment against the Member State under Article 228 EC.

It will be readily apparent that the enforcement procedure under Article 226 EC is a long and complicated one, that is not well-suited to the commercial realities of a contested takeover, as is well illustrated by the still unresolved VW case and KPN and TPG cases. Moreover, a final decision under Article 228 EC will be of little practical use to the parties to a prospective merger since they are likely to have been driven to abandon the deal well before the ECJ has issued its decision.

3. Article 21 ECMR

Where a proposed merger falls within the ambit of the Commission's exclusive jurisdiction under the ECMR, Article 21 ECMR probably offers the most effective and timely remedy for an aggrieved investor above any other remedy available

For the first time in the *Champalimaud* case, and more recently in the *Cimpor* and *UniCredit* cases, the Commission initiated proceedings on the basis of Article 21 ECMR, requiring Member States to refrain from adopting measures (ostensibly on the grounds of legitimate national interest under Article 21(3) ECMR) that would amount to an infringement of the Commission's exclusive jurisdiction under the ECMR to vet mergers with a Community dimension.

---

[59] *See* John Temple Lang, European Union legal rules on State measures restricting competition, Paper Presented at the 2005 Summit at Como (Oct. 2005) (on file with the author)

In reaching an Article 21 ECMR infringement decision, the Commission initially forms a preliminary view as to the incompatibility of the Member State measures with Article 21 ECMR, and sends the Member State concerned a letter asking it to justify its actions. The Member State then has fifteen working days to reply to the Commission's initial findings. If, following this consultation period, the Commission still believes that Article 21 ECMR has been infringed, it can adopt a decision requiring the Member State to withdraw the infringing national measure. This decision is addressed to the Member State, is binding on it and, crucially, is directly applicable against the Member State to which it is addressed and, as such, is enforceable in the national courts by any party affected by the decision which, in this context, would include an aggrieved foreign investor. Moreover, the Commission may also adopt interim measures in the course of Article 21 ECMR proceedings (as it did in *Champalimaud* case, where it provisionally lifted Portugal's suspension of the merger).

In its 2004 ruling in *Portugal v. Commission*,[60] the ECJ crucially confirmed that Article 21 ECMR proceedings could be initiated by the Commission regardless of whether the Member State concerned had invoked legitimate national interests under Article 21(3) ECMR. In other words, the fact that a Member State had chosen not to follow the Article 21(3) ECMR procedure did not preclude the Commission from using Article 21 to secure the withdrawal of protectionist measures that are not justified or proportionate under EU law.

In its decision, the ECJ emphasized that:

> "if the Commission were reduced, in the absence of any communication by the Member State concerned [under Article 21 ECMR] to the sole option of bringing an action for failure to fulfill obligations under Article 226 EC, it would be impossible to obtain a Community decision within the short time-limits laid down by the Merger Regulation, with a consequent increase in the risk that such a decision may be taken only after the national measures have already irretrievably prejudiced the merger with a Community dimension."[61]

Apart from the political pressure that Article 21 ECMR proceedings bring to bear on the Member State concerned, that alone may result in the withdrawal of an offending national measure, an Article 21 ECMR infringement decision may also be a powerful weapon in the hands of an aggrieved investor before the national courts.

[60] *See supra* note 52.

[61] *See id.* at paragraph 55.

C. Remedies at A National Level

It is a well-established principle of EU law that national courts are under a general duty to disregard any national measure that is inconsistent with EU law.[62] Article 10 EC stipulates that Member States "shall abstain from any measure which could jeopardize the attainment of the objectives of the Treaty," and, as such, requires all Member States, including their courts and competition authorities, to take all necessary measures to guarantee the application and effectiveness of EU law.[63] Article 10 EC embodies the so-called "effet-utile" of EU law and the EC courts have held that it places numerous practical duties and obligations on Member States in the context of complying with both the letter and the spirit of the Treaty.

National courts are under a duty to enable companies to challenge state measures that are contrary to EU law, for example, through judicial review or a declaration that the national measures are contrary to EU law. While the procedures for mounting such a challenge are governed by national law, they must not make it impossible or excessively difficult to exercise the rights granted by EU law.[64]

In *Fiammiferi*,[65] the ECJ extended the duty to set aside national provisions conflicting with Community law to non-judicial bodies such as competition authorities. According to the ECJ, since a national competition authority is responsible for ensuring, inter alia, that Article 81 EC is observed, then Article 81, in conjunction with Article 10 EC, imposes a duty on Member States to refrain from introducing (or to withdraw) measures contrary to the EC competition rules, as otherwise those rules would be rendered less effective if the competition authority were not able to disregard a national measure that is contrary to the combined provisions of Articles 10 and 81 EC.[66]

Where the proposed merger does not fall within the Commission's exclusive competence (i.e., because the parties each achieve two-thirds of their turnover in one and the same Member State), an aggrieved investor will usually be left with a claim that the protectionist

---

[62] *See* Case 106/77, Amministrazione delle Finanze dello Stato v. Simmenthal SpA, 1978 E.C.R. 629; Cases C-46 & 48/93, Brasserie du pecheur / Bundesrepublik Deutschland and The Queen / Secretary of State for Transport, ex parte Factortame and others, 1996 E.C.R. I-1029; Case 66/86, Ahmed Saeed Flugreisen and others / Zentrale zur Bek_mpfung unlauteren Wettbewerbs, 1989 E.C.R. 803.

[63] *See, e.g.*, Case 68/88, Commission v. Greece, 1989 E.C.R. 2965, at paragraph 23.

[64] *See, e.g.*, Case C-312/93, Peterbroeck, Van Campenhout & Cie / Belgian State, 1995 E.C.R. I-4599.

[65] Case C-198/01, Consorzio Industrie Fiammiferi (CIF) v. Autorità Garante della Concorrenza e del Mercato, 2003 E.C.R. I-8055.

[66] *See id.* at paragraph 50.

measure infringes the rules on free movement of capital (Article 56 EC) and the right of establishment (Article 43 EC). In this scenario, the national court will have to determine whether the national measure at issue is in breach of the Treaty freedoms, and, if so, if it is justified under the criteria set down by the ECJ. If the matter is not clear-cut, it is likely to be referred by the national court to the ECJ for a preliminary ruling under Article 234 EC.[67] Even if there is no referral to the ECJ, inevitably, there will be a risk of several time-consuming appeals before the finding of an infringement of EU law becomes final. Such an action could be pursued in parallel with Article 226 EC infringement proceedings against the Member State concerned.

As already mentioned, where a proposed merger falls within the ambit of the ECMR, then Article 21 ECMR is likely to offer the most effective and timely remedy for an aggrieved investor. Ideally, an aggrieved investor bringing an action before a national court would be armed with both a Commission clearance decision under the ECMR in respect of the proposed merger, and a Commission Article 21 ECMR infringement decision condemning the infringing state measure, in which case the national court would have little choice but to set aside the state measure concerned. Furthermore, in such a scenario, it is unlikely that questions of EU law would arise that the national court would feel compelled to refer to the ECJ under Article 234 EC, and the scope for a Member State to appeal an adverse judgment of the national court is also likely to be considerably diminished. Overall, this should also result in a much speedier resolution of any claim.

On bringing an action before a national court, it would also be open to an aggrieved investor to apply for interim measures. In the *Factortame* case,[68] the ECJ held that national courts are obliged to provide interim relief against the state even if such a remedy was not available under national law. This means that a national court would have a duty to suspend the application of any state measures contrary to EU law. Insofar as a blocked bid may result in losses for a frustrated bidder, it would also be open to the bidder to bring an action for damages against the Member State concerned, as the national courts also have a duty to award compensation for breaches of EU law.[69]

---

[67] Under Article 234 EC, any court or tribunal of a Member State may (and in certain circumstances must) refer a case to the ECJ for a preliminary ruling concerning the interpretation of EU law. The ECJ rules on the issues referred to it and sends the case back to the national courts which then apply the EU law in question as interpreted by the ECJ to the case at hand.

[68] Case 213/89, R v. Secretary of State for Transport, *ex parte* Factortame, Ltd.,1990 E.C.R. I-2433.

[69] Cases C-6 & 9/90, Francovich and Bonifaci v. Italy, 1993 E.C.R. I-5357.

D. Do the Overriding Interests of the Internal Market Justify the Abolition of the Two-Thirds Rule?

Arguably, the two-thirds rule, which was introduced as part of the EC's first merger control regime in 1989, is outdated and inconsistent with its overriding internal market objectives.

The Commission has shown in its prohibition decision in *EDP/ENI/GDP*[70] that it will not hesitate to block the creation of a national champion where it considers that such a merger would significantly impede effective competition in the European Union. Moreover, the Commission appears equally determined to ensure that its clearance decisions and its exclusive jurisdiction under the ECMR are not obstructed by interventionist measures, from Member States, designed to prevent foreign takeovers. European Commissioner Neelie Kroes recently stated that "the EU's single market will descend into chaos" if Member States stand in the way of mergers falling within the Commission's exclusive competence.[71] The Commission's determination to tackle protectionist measures is well illustrated by the vigorous stance it has taken against Spain's attempts to obstruct E.ON's proposed takeover of Endesa as well as its infringement decisions under Article 21 ECMR against the Portuguese government in the *Champalimaud* and *Cimpor* cases.[72]

However, the Commission is effectively powerless to prevent the creation of national champions, regardless of what impact this might have on the internal market, when it comes to mergers which fall outside its exclusive jurisdiction under the ECMR because of the application of the two-thirds rule. Much to Commissioner Kroes' frustration, this was the case with Gas Natural's proposed takeover of Endesa, that led the Commissioner to call for the abolition of the two-thirds rule.[73]

Arguably, the two-thirds rule, which was introduced as part of the EC's first merger control regime in 1989, is outdated and inconsistent with its overriding internal market objectives. However, it is worth noting that, at the time of its review of the ECMR in 2003, the Commission was of the opinion that the two-thirds rule should be retained on the grounds that it applies to less than 10 percent of filings and is a reasonable expression of the principle of subsidiarity.

---

[70] Case COMP/M.3440, EDP/ENI/GDP, 2005 O.J. (C 288) 2.

[71] European Commission, Press Release No. 277, Mergers: Commission Launches Procedure Against Poland for Preventing UniCredit/HVB Merger (2006).

[72] *See supra* notes 50 & 51.

[73] *See supra* note 4.

Aside from the two-thirds rule, the ECMR provides for mechanisms whereby concentrations with a Community dimension, that affect competition in a distinct market within a Member State, can be reviewed at the national level. Under Article 9(2)(a) ECMR a Member State can request a referral back to its competent authorities where a concentration "threatens to affect significantly" competition in a distinct market within that Member State. Where the Commission considers that such a threat exists, it can either assert its exclusive jurisdiction and deal with the case itself, or refer the whole or part of the case to the Member State's competition authorities. In this scenario, the Commission has a wide margin of discretion in deciding whether or not to refer the case to the competent national authorities.

According to Article 9(2)(b) ECMR, a request for a referral back can also be made by a Member State where a concentration "affects competition in a distinct market which does not constitute a substantial part of the common market" (i.e., in a local or regional market within that Member State). If the Commission considers such a local or regional market to be affected by the concentration, it is obliged to refer the whole case or that part of the case which relates to this market, to the Member State's competition authorities.[74]

Given that amendments to the ECMR require unanimous approval in the Council,[75] all Member States would ultimately have to agree to abolish the two-thirds rule." This may, of course, be difficult to achieve given the protectionist tendencies of Member States. Even those Member States that may be willing to give more discretion to the Commission may not be keen to make further changes to the ECMR relatively soon after its recent overhaul.

However, rather than completely abolishing the two-thirds rule, a more palatable solution for Member States might be to include the two-thirds rule as an additional ground for the referral of mergers back to Member States under Article 9(2)(a) ECMR. This would allow the Commission to assess the cross-border impact of any merger, even when it concerns essentially domestic players, in exercising its discretion to accede to a Member State request for referral back. This would effectively eliminate the possibility of Member States frustrating foreign takeovers or the objectives of the internal market by the creation of national champions from mergers falling outside the Commission's exclusive jurisdiction under the ECMR.

---

[74] There is also a referral mechanism under Article 4(4) ECMR which can be initiated by the notifying parties. *See supra* note 10.

[75] As the legal basis for the ECMR itself is Article 83 EC in conjunction with Article 308 EC, which requires unanimity, any amendments to the ECMR can only be adopted unanimously on the same legal basis.

INTERVIEW:
UPDATE ON "ANTITRUST SANCTIONS"

As part of our Spring 2012 issue, CPI is presenting a retrospective of our best articles in the past and providing updates. One of our selections is "Antitrust Sanctions," originally appearing in the Fall 2010 issue of the Journal. Douglas Ginsburg and Josh Wright, the two co-authors, are here to discuss developments since the article was published. They will also be exploring some of the issues raised in depth. But first, some background information on the authors:

Scan our QR code with your mobile device to listen to the recorded interview. Note: you must have a scanner app or installed software to read the QR code.

Douglas H. Ginsburg is a Judge of the United States Court of Appeals for the District of Columbia Circuit, to which he was appointed by President Reagan in 1986 and which he served as Chief Judge from 2001 to 2008. He is also a Professor of Law at New York University, and Visiting Professor, University College London, Faculty of Laws. Judge Ginsburg was previously a Professor at Harvard Law School and Assistant Attorney General in charge of the Antitrust Division of the United States Department of Justice.

Josh Wright is a Professor of Law at George Mason University School of Law. His areas of expertise cover antitrust, law and economics, consumer protection, and intellectual property. Josh has published dozens of law review articles and co-edited three books: Pioneers of Law and Economics, Competition Policy and Patent Law Under Uncertainty, and the Research Handbook in The Law and Economics of The Family. He is the co-editor of the Supreme Court Economic Review, and also serves on the Editorial Advisory Board of our own Antitrust Chronicle.

Could you provide an update on what trends have continued or changed since you wrote "Antitrust Sanctions"? In particular, has the use of fines continued to rise in frequency as well as amount, and does incarceration continue to lag behind fines as an antitrust sanction?

DG: It is not so much a matter of frequency as it is the amount of the fine, and whether the fine is still the usual sanction in most jurisdictions, which it is. I have little doubt that the amounts have continued to increase—they certainly have not fallen off. In fact, not long ago, the Mexican competition authority imposed a fine of $1 billion USD.

JW: I would add that it is certainly the case that incarceration trends in the U.S. have remained relatively stable since the article, both in terms of average length of sentence and the rate of incarceration. For our purposes in the article, the most important trend has been that the mix of sanctions has remained relatively constant in the U.S. and the EU as between corporate fines, jail, and the absence of debarment.

DG: Since we wrote the article, though, Mexico has instituted a system of criminal sanctions and Japan has increased the penalties for criminal antitrust violations, but I don't think there's been a criminal case concluded in either of those jurisdictions.

You propose shifting high fines away from the corporation in favor of increasing fines on the individual wrongdoers at the firm as a more optimal sanction. Since you've written the article, anti-corporation sentiment has flared up. Given this more hostile climate, and also considering any type of political atmosphere, are there any adjustments you'd now make to account for public reception?

DG: If the analysis was right when we wrote it, then it is still right now. You are certainly correct that the political environment has changed a bit, but that might actually make it more likely that individuals would be sanctioned in jurisdictions where previously it was only the companies that were sanctioned. After all, individuals who were at the helm of some major companies have come in for a large share of criticism over the last several years, along with their companies.

JW: Another point is that our proposal is to adjust the mix of sanctions, holding constant the level of corporate fines and increase accountability or culpability for individuals within the firm. Professor Harrington, in his response to our article in CPI, incorrectly presumed our proposal would require a reduction in current levels of corporate fines. It may well be the case that such a reduction would

Our proposal begins with the modest observation that increases in corporate fines to date haven't been associated with any marginal gains in deterrence, and that holding corporate fines at current levels, the proposed shift in the mix of sanctions would improve deterrence

improve the efficiency of deterrence if coupled with an increase in individual accountability and debarment. Our proposal begins with the modest observation that increases in corporate fines to date haven't been associated with any marginal gains in deterrence, and that holding corporate fines at current levels, the proposed shift in the mix of sanctions would improve deterrence. Perhaps the fact that the corporate fines would remain constant might make the move more, rather than less, palatable in the current environment, as Judge Ginsburg just observed. I agree that if the analysis was right on the merits then, it remains so.

If it is the individual who is engaging in the criminal violations, then shaming seems to me quite appropriate

It's worth pointing out, as we do in the article, that a shift in debarment would be consistent with modern trends in the U.S., where we're already moving toward an increase in criminal sanctions and individual accountability. Recall that the evolution of debarment as a sanction at the SEC for white-collar crime arose out of the SEC's decision to start pursuing it, rather than any legislative action. That general trend toward greater individual sanctions hasn't been coupled with debarment before in the antitrust context, at least here in the U.S., but it has been adopted as an antitrust sanction in other countries. And we even have debarment here in the U.S. at other agencies, indeed even right down the road at the Federal Trade Commission, for different types of violations. It may only be a matter of time before the DOJ takes a closer look at adding debarment to the enforcement toolkit.

Is there a concern that with a sanction like debarment or a focus on the individual, that it might actually be counterproductive because it might be seen as a shaming penalty or scapegoating?

DG: If it is the individual who is engaging in the criminal violations, then shaming seems to me quite appropriate. Individuals are going to have limited resources available for fines, which punish their families as well as them individually. There is a good case for a modest amount of jail time, and the shame of jail is certainly much greater than it is for any other individual sanction. I think that has been an important source of deterrence for individuals ever since the Department of Justice started seeking real jail time—not just a very short sentence that was often suspended—but some real time in jail starting in the mid-1980s, and increasing since then.

JW: I'd like to add two additional related points about the economics of reputational sanctions and the efficacy of deterrence. The first, as we discussed in our article, is that the constant increase in corporate fines over the past twenty years doesn't appear to have generated much bang for your buck in the way of marginal deterrence. When analyzing whether to add another penalty to the mix such as debarment with its potential to increase reputational sanctions, the economist immediately turns to the "compared to what" question. Likewise, if there are potential fairness concerns with increasing individual penalties, even if they produce greater returns for consumers because of increased or more efficient deterrence, one must compare them to the fairness concerns with ever-increasing corporate fines. Recall that the corporate fines are borne in large part by passive shareholders and consumers, neither of whom seem like particularly fair targets for penalties. Measuring these things in the antitrust context, in terms of fairness, is a mixed bag. That is why, in antitrust at least, thinking about deterrence in terms of efficiency and the consumer welfare standard is a much more fruitful avenue of thought. It's certainly the avenue of thought that the DOJ has in mind, and it is responsible for starting this shift towards increasing individual accountability.

the constant increase in corporate fines over the past twenty years doesn't appear to have generated much bang for your buck in the way of marginal deterrence

The second important economic point is that one of the benefits of increasing reputational sanctions for price-fixing as an offense potentially cuts in the other direction—that is, in favor of a reduction in corporate fines. The greater the reputational sanction, the less—for any specific given level of deterrence—is required to achieve efficient or optimal deterrence. The economic logic is that we can rely to a lesser extent upon more inefficient methods of deterrence which tax passive shareholders and consumers. We can aim the deterrence more directly at the perpetrator, who is in the position to stop the offense—in this case, price-fixing. So there is an efficiency gain as well, and one way to think about that efficiency gain is the marginal gain from increasing the reputational sanction. Debarment is not in use as an antitrust sanction at all in the U.S. currently. There's much more to gain there in terms of increasing reputational sanctions from its current level of zero up the scale to one or two, than the potential gains from a further dollar increase in level of the corporate fines, which are already at very high levels.

If you're working at a corporation and there is some gray area in your line of work—an example that you use is non-collusive vertical restraints versus price-fixing—and let's say you yourself are not sure whether what you're doing is an antitrust violation, how do you take this into account when formulating an appropriate punishment model?

As soon as they are in a gray area, it is appropriate to bring a civil action, not a criminal action; only when it has been clarified that what may have been gray in the past is actually unlawful, then is it be appropriate to bring a criminal case

DG: The enforcement agencies that have criminal sanctions available—the U.S., of course, but also Canada, the UK, Australia, and several others—have been appropriately careful never to bring a criminal case where the conduct is in a gray area, where it is just anything other than naked price-fixing or market division, which any reasonable business person would know is against the law. As soon as they are in a gray area, it is appropriate to bring a civil action, not a criminal action; only when it has been clarified that what may have been gray in the past is actually unlawful, then is it be appropriate to bring a criminal case. A noteworthy example of how this has been practiced by the Antitrust Division is the much-publicized current filing involving Apple and some book publishers. This was brought as a civil case because it is not just a bunch of competitors getting together and fixing prices, it is a little bit different, and requires the Department to proceed cautiously.

JW: The Apple example is a good one. It's an example where, in addition to some agreement or alleged agreement among publishers in the DOJ's complaint, you've got other factors going on. Although the DOJ's complaint alleges a horizontal conspiracy, it is a complicated agreement. The agreement may not directly be on price, instead, it may be to move to something like the agency model, something more akin to an agreement between rivals to adopt resale price maintenance without further agreement on what the minimum prices will be. It's a more complicated arrangement—the technology is more complicated, the involvement is more complicated. So in these sorts of cases, the DOJ, even in the presence of horizontal agreement doesn't bring criminal cases.

The second example that comes to mind is the FTC's invitation to collude cases. Although the FTC does not have authority to pursue a criminal case, it certainly can refer those cases to the DOJ. But in its invitation to collude cases, rather than refer them to the DOJ for criminal investigation, largely what it's done is to pursue those cases under Section 5 of the FTC Act and treat them a little bit differently. When in that gray area somewhere short of what appears to be a plain vanilla hardcore cartel offense that would traditionally be the subject of criminal jurisdiction, I think the stance of the agencies, in the United States at least, is to exercise appropriate caution in making use of criminal sanctions.

DG: To follow up on what Josh was saying, soliciting a price-fixing agreement was first litigated in the American Airlines case in 1984. If you recall, the president of American Airlines called the president of Braniff and suggested they fix prices, but the president of Braniff instead taped the conversation and sent it to the New York Times, which put it on the front page. It was not entirely clear, however, until the Fifth Circuit made it clear, that this was a violation of the Sherman Act. Now the FTC has brought a number of civil cases, and I think the Department of Justice would be entirely justified if it had a clean-cut solicitation case to prosecute it as a crime. The public is on notice that it is a flat-out violation of the Sherman Act; it is not a gray area anymore, even if it was 25 years ago.

How has your proposal been received in the European Union?

DG: The problem is that the European Commission has a very limited toolkit. They don't have, at the European level, a criminal sanction; in fact, they cannot even fine an individual for price fixing. I do not think they have any specific authorization for debarment, but of course, if that seems to be the right thing to do, they could seek that authorization. So they're quite limited at present, but potentially interested in some new ideas. At least, I hope so.

Thank you for taking the time to provide an update on your article, "Antitrust Sanctions," and it's been great talking to the both of you.

ANTITRUST SANCTIONS

*Douglas H. Ginsburg & Joshua D. Wright**

ABSTRACT

In this article, we first discuss traditional deterrence theory as applied to optimal criminal antitrust penalties. Then we evaluate both the U.S. and EU experience with ever- increasing corporate fines and the available empirical evidence on the deterrent value of cartel sanctions. In the next part we turn to our claim that the conventional wisdom of ever-increasing corporate fines to solve the problem of under-deterrence is misguided. The determination of the optimal sanction for price-fixing should be guided by two principles: (1) the total sanction must be great enough, but no greater than necessary, to take the profit out of price-fixing; and (2) the individuals responsible for the price-fixing should be given a sufficient disincentive to discourage them from engaging in the activity. We propose altering the distribution of criminal sanctions for corporations and the individuals who fix prices on their behalf, and introducing sanctions for negligent officers and directors consistent with our two fundamental principles. Finally, we discuss the experience with debarment as a sanction in other contexts, and how it might operate in the context of U.S. antitrust enforcement.

I. INTRODUCTION

Antitrust authorities across the world are increasingly concerned with fighting cartels, especially international cartels.[1] Countries previously without cartel prohibitions, including many in Latin America, Asia, and Africa, have in recent years adopted antitrust laws and begun to

* Douglas H. Ginsburg is Professor at NYU School of Law and Senior Judge on the United States Court of Appeals for the District of Columbia Circuit. Joshua D. Wright is Associate Professor at George Mason University School of Law and Department of Economics. We gratefully acknowledge the research assistance of Eric M. Fraser, Jan Rybnicek, and Judd Stone and helpful comments from John Connor, David K. Kessler, Bruce Kobayashi, Abel Mateus, and participants at the American Law and Economics Association Annual Meeting.

[1] In the United States, it has been estimated that over 90 percent of recent fines for antitrust violations are attributable to international cartel activity and said that "the typical international cartel likely consists of a U.S. company and three or four of its competitors that are market leaders in Europe, Asia, and throughout the world." Scott Hammond, An Update of the Antitrust Division's Criminal Enforcement Program, Address Before the ABA Section of Antitrust Law Cartel Enforcement Roundtable 2005 Fall Forum 2 (Nov. 16, 2005), *available at* http://www.usdoj.gov/atr/public/speeches/213247.htm.

enforce them. Countries with longstanding cartel prohibitions have adopted corporate leniency policies and increased the resources they dedicate to antitrust enforcement, with the result that more cartels than ever are coming to light and being sanctioned. This development has also spurred closer cooperation among national enforcement agencies.[2] The widespread introduction of more aggressive efforts to detect and prosecute cartel activity has led to dramatically larger corporate fines and a slow but growing movement toward criminalization.[3]

Antitrust laws and enforcement agencies have largely followed the conventional wisdom that the primary cure for insufficient deterrence of hard-core cartel activity, such as price-fixing, is to increase corporate fines. For example, the United States and the European Union have in recent years pointed with pride and a sense of accomplishment to the large and increasing fines levied upon companies that participate in cartels.

In the United States, the statute governing fines for antitrust offenses was amended first in 1987 to provide the option of a fine set by doubling the greater of the defendant's gain or the victims' losses.[4]At that time, antitrust fines set without using this alternative option were capped at $100,000 for individuals and $1 million for corporations.[5]It was amended again in 1990 to increase the maximum personal fine to $350,000 and the maximum corporate fine to $10 million,[6]and yet again in 2004 to increase the maximum personal fine to $1 million, the maximum corporate fine to $100 million and the maximum jail sentence from three years (which it had been since 1974) to ten years.[7]The maximum fine that the European Commission may impose upon a company that violates the EU's competition laws is 10 percent of the company's global turnover but, under the 2006 EC Guidelines, in most cases hard-core cartel offenses warrant baseline fines up to 30 percent of relevant sales, which can be adjusted upward with virtually no limit.[8]

---

[2] OECD, Hard Core Cartels: Third Report on the Implementation of the 1998 Council Recommendation 30 (2005), http://www.oecd.org/dataoecd/58/1/35863307.pdf (stating that "OECD members and observers have found that international cooperation in discovering, investigating, and prosecuting international cartels has reached unprecedented levels").

[3] The growing list of nations with antitrust laws providing for criminal sanctions includes Australia, Brazil, Canada, Chile, Germany, Ireland, Israel, Japan, Korea, Poland, Russia, the United Kingdom, and other jurisdictions. *See* Appendix.

[4] 18 U.S.C. § 3571.

[5] 15 U.S.C. § 1 (1989) (amended 1990).

[6] Antitrust Amendments Act of 1990, Pub. L .No. 101-588, 104 Stat. 2879 (codified at 15 U.S.C. § 1 (2000)).

[7] *See* Antitrust Criminal Penalty Enhancement and Reform Act of 2004, Pub. L. No. 108- 237, § 215, 118 Stat. 665, 668 (2004) (codified as amended at 15 U.S.C. §§ 1-3).

[8] *See Guidelines on the Method of Setting Fines*, Official Journal C 210, Sept. 1, 2006, at ¶ 21–27, 32; UK Office of Fair Trading, An Assessment Of Discretionary Penalty Regimes (October 2009). Under the new guidelines, the base fine of a recidivist can be increased by up to 100 percent for each previous infringement. *See Guidelines on the Method of Setting Fines, supra*, at ¶ 28.

Despite the large and ever-increasing corporate fines, cartels—particularly international cartels—remain a substantial problem, and recidivism among price-fixers is not infrequent.

In both the United States and the EU, the average corporate fine has increased dramatically over the last 15 years. The EU has gone from collecting an average corporate fine of EUR 2 million in 1990-94, to EUR 46 million in 2005-09; U.S. average corporate fines have grown almost a hundredfold from $480,000 during 1990-94, to $44 million more recently.[9]

Despite the large and ever-increasing corporate fines, cartels—particularly international cartels—remain a substantial problem, and recidivism among price-fixers is not infrequent. The impossibility of observing how many cartels go undetected renders the empirical evidence that bears upon the issue subject to more than one interpretation, but the data are largely consistent with cartel formation rates that, despite the growth in fines and the introduction of corporate leniency programs, imply current antitrust sanctions are an insufficient deterrent.

Although the corporation is the current focus of deterrence, there are in fact two potential targets for antitrust sanctions: The corporation and the individual who fixes prices on its behalf. There also two sources of antitrust sanctions: Law enforcement, which may fine both types of offenders, incarcerate individuals, and, as we propose, debar them from serving as corporate officers or directors; and the market, which imposes reputational penalties upon both types of offenders. The challenge for antitrust law is to coordinate these various corporate and individual sanctions to achieve the optimal total sanction.

We believe determination of the optimal sanction for price-fixing (and other cartel activities) should be guided by two fundamental principles. First, the total sanction must be great enough, but no greater than necessary, to take the profit out of price-fixing. If the expected value of price-fixing net of legal sanctions is positive, that is, if price-fixing is profitable, then the market will produce it. This point illustrates the complex interactions between corporate and individual sanctions. Where the conduct is profitable to the firm, and therefore increases its share price, it is more likely that both firm and the individual perpetrator are rewarded rather than penalized by the market, thus increasing the total sanction necessary to provide optimal deterrence.

Whether the first principle is satisfied depends, in part, on the level of sanctions imposed upon the corporation. With an appropriately calibrated corporate sanction, reputational penalties imposed upon the corporation and its agents will reduce the individual fines and jail sen-

9 *See* Figures 2 and 4, *infra*.

tences necessary to achieve the desired level of deterrence.[10] On the other hand, if the corporate sanction exceeds this level, then it risks over-deterrence by providing an incentive for excessive corporate monitoring and compliance expenditures that are ultimately passed on to consumers in the form of higher prices and foregone products and, in any event, is likely inefficient. This point remains valid even if the optimal level of cartel activity is zero.

The available anecdotal and quantitative data suggest further increasing the fines imposed upon corporations is not likely to solve the problem

The second principle is that the individuals responsible for the cartel activity, whether they are engaged in, complicit with, or negligent in preventing the price-fixing scheme, should be given a sufficient disincentive to discourage them from engaging in that activity.[11] The U.S. Antitrust Division reasonably believes that "individual accountability through the imposition of jail sentences is the single greatest deterrent" to cartel activity.[12] A survey done for the U.K. Office of Fair Trading confirms that criminal penalties are the penalties of greatest concern to business people.[13] A penalty scheme that is faithful to the first principle implies that at least part of the disincentive for the responsible individual will be market-based; the career prospects for a convicted price-fixer should be diminished, and certainly not enhanced, by his record of price-fixing. Because reputational sanctions are likely to be highly imperfect, however, it is important that the sanction be targeted directly at the responsible individuals, and not at their employers. The sanctions should also be proportional to fault. That is, the individual perpetrator should face a more serious sanction than the director or officer who negligently supervised the perpetrator. Note that although the first principle focuses upon calibrating sanctions to the optimal level of deterrence, the second principle emphasizes the efficient allocation or mix of deterrent capital between the corporation and the individuals who act on its behalf.

While in principle there is certainly some fine or a combination of fine and jail time sufficiently high to deter individuals from price-fixing, the available anecdotal and quantitative data suggest further increasing the fines imposed upon corporations is not likely to solve the

---

10 Jonathan Karpoff, D. Scott Lee, & Gerald S. Martin, *The Consequences to Managers for Financial Misrepresentation*, 88 J. FIN. ECON. 193 (2008) (finding the likelihood of termination or ouster for individuals responsible for SEC and Department of Justice financial misrepresentation enforcement actions increases substantially with the cost of the misconduct to shareholders).

11 *Cf.* Donald I. Baker, *The Use of Criminal Law Remedies to Deter and Punish Cartels and Bid-Rigging*, 69 GEO. WASH. L. REV. 693, 713-14 (2001).

12 Scott D. Hammond, Ten Strategies for Winning the Fight Against Hardcore Cartels, Oct. 18, 2005 (Paris Working Party No. 3 Prosecutors Program).

13 UK Office of Fair Trading, The Deterrent Effect of Competition Enforcement by the OFT (November 2007).

problem. It is here that we offer an alternative solution: De-emphasize fines for publicly traded corporations and, instead, debar individuals responsible for price-fixing from further employment in a position from which they could again violate or negligently enable their subordinates to violate the antitrust laws. As we shall argue below, imposing ever-higher corporate fines is misguided; criminally sanctioning the persons directly engaged in or complicit with price-fixing and debarring negligent directors and officers whose conduct do not warrant a greater sanction would deter more price-fixing than would increasing the fines levied upon the corporation that employed them. Debarment has already been authorized as a sanction for price-fixing in some countries, including the United Kingdom, Australia, and Sweden, and has been proposed by the Competition Commission of South Africa.[14]

Our proposal to reform antitrust sanctions for price-fixing has two key components: the overall level of deterrence, which entails making debarment and jail time available to enforcement agencies that do not now have those options, and the mix, as opposed to the level, of criminal sanctions. Guided by the two fundamental principles set out above, we propose to shift sanctions away from the corporation and toward perpetrators and other responsible individuals.

In Part II we discuss traditional deterrence theory as applied to optimal criminal antitrust penalties. In Part III we evaluate both the U.S. and EU experience with ever-increasing corporate fines and the available empirical evidence on the deterrent value of cartel sanctions. In Part IV we turn to our claim that the conventional wisdom of ever-increasing corporate fines to solve the problem of under-deterrence is misguided. We propose altering the distribution of criminal sanctions for corporations and the individuals who fix prices on their behalf, and introducing sanctions for negligent officers and directors consistent with our two fundamental principles. In Part V we discuss the experience with debarment as a sanction in other contexts, and how it might operate in the context of U.S. antitrust enforcement. Part VI concludes.

II. TRADITIONAL DETERRENCE THEORY AND OPTIMAL ANTITRUST PENALTIES

The economic analysis of optimal legal sanctions and criminal punishments is built upon the foundational insight that penalties should be sufficient to induce offenders to internalize the full social cost of their crimes.[15] In a simple setting where detection of crimes and enforcement of

[14] Recently proposed legislation in South Africa would allow the Competition Commission to seek a court order debarring an offender from serving as a director of a firm.

[15] The seminal analysis is in Gary S. Becker, *Crime and Punishment: An Economic Approach*, 76 J. Pol. Econ. 169 (1968). *See also* William M. Landes, *Optimal Sanctions for Antitrust Violations*, 50 U. Chi. L. Rev. 652 (1983).

the law are both perfect (probability of punishment = 1) and costless, the optimal sanction will be equal to the total social harm of the crime. In the more realistic setting in which the probabilities both of detection and of punishment are less than perfect and enforcement costs are positive, optimal penalties must exceed the social cost of the crime so that the expected sanction facing each potential violator is equal to the harm his violation will cause. This economic insight of optimal penalty theory is captured in our first principle. Because the furtive nature of cartel activity reduces the probability of detection and successful prosecution, the optimal total sanction must consist of a fine equal to the perpetrator's expected gain from the violation multiplied by the inverse of the probability of detection (plus the variable enforcement costs of imposing the sanction, which we ignore henceforth). The key insight of the economic approach to optimal penalties generally, which applies with full force to antitrust sanctions, is that the penalty must be sufficient to render the expected value of the illegal behavior equal to zero.

The key insight of the economic approach to optimal penalties generally, which applies with full force to antitrust sanctions, is that the penalty must be sufficient to render the expected value of the illegal behavior equal to zero

Within this framework, therefore, the central determinants of the optimal antitrust sanction are the probabilities that price-fixing is detected and that an enforcement action is successful. In the simplest model of optimal antitrust penalties, the trebling of damages implies a detection rate of less than 33 percent. Although it is inherently difficult to determine the actual detection rate because some cartels go undetected, the best available estimate places the rate much lower, between 13 and 17 percent.[16] Although that estimate is somewhat dated, as it was based upon data from cartels indicted by the U.S. Antitrust Division between 1961 and 1988, more recent estimates based upon data for the EU suggest a detection rate consistent with the low end of that range.[17] On the other hand, there is some evidence the detection rate in the United States has increased by as much as 60 percent in recent years as a result of the corporate leniency program;[18] although there are no comparable data for the EU, the effect of its corporate leniency program should be similar. Therefore, assuming a prior detection rate of about 15 percent in both the EU and the United states, the current rate would be approximately 25 percent.

---

[16] Peter G. Bryant & E. Woodrow Eckard, Jr., *Price Fixing: The Probability of Getting Caught*, 73 REV. ECON. & STAT. 531 (1991).

[17] Emannuel Combe, Constance Monnier, & Renaud Legal, *Cartels: The Probability of Getting Caught in the European Union* 21 (Working paper, 2008), *available at* http://papers.ssrn.com/sol3/papers.cfm?abstract_id=1015061 (estimating a probability of detection between 12.9 and 13.2 percent).

[18] Nathan H. Miller, *Strategic Leniency and Cartel Enforcement*, 99 AM. ECON. REV. 750, 760 (2009).

The pertinent question is whether antitrust sanctions and the threat thereof impose costs greater than necessary to deter cartel activity

The relatively low probability of detection raises the probability of underdeterrence and hence the need for increased sanctions. At the same time, care must be taken lest excessive penalties deter efficient conduct and cause corporations to overinvest in compliance.[19] The pertinent question is whether antitrust sanctions and the threat thereof impose costs greater than necessary to deter cartel activity.[20] There are two important potential sources of over-deterrence in criminal antitrust sanctions. The first is the possibility that criminal penalties will be used to deter socially efficient conduct, such as non-collusive vertical restraints, which could be mistakenly attacked as price-fixing.[21] Although the antitrust statutes could be used that way, there is no modern support for extending criminal penalties to non-cartel activity, nor is there evidence that this potential for mischaracterization has led to a reduction in socially efficient business practices. Accordingly, we strongly favor the modern de facto limitation of criminal penalties to cartel activities, such as naked horizontal price-fixing, bid-rigging, and market division.[22]

A second potential source of over-deterrence involves agency costs. A firm incurs agency costs to the extent its incentives diverge from those facing its employees and agents. Because agency costs create an environment that facilitates criminal conduct by the firm's agents, corporate fines are meant to provide a counter-incentive for the corporation to monitor, detect, and prevent crimes committed by its agents.[23] If the fine is greater than the total social cost of the crime, however, it will induce the firm to make excessive, i.e., socially inefficient, investments in monitoring and prevention.[24] The social costs of the monitoring and compliance expenditures made in response to an increase in antitrust fines raise the firm's marginal costs and are passed on to consumers in the form of higher prices—a detriment that must be weighed

---

[19] *See* Becker, *supra* note 14, at 191–193 (describing model for optimal levels of sanctions).

[20] *See* Bruce H. Kobayashi, *Antitrust, Agency, and Amnesty: An Economic Analysis of the Criminal Enforcement of the Antitrust Laws Against Corporations*, 69 Geo. Wash. L. Rev. 715, 733-734 (2001).

[21] Mark A. Cohen & David T. Scheffman, *The Antitrust Sentencing Guideline: Is the Punishment Worth the Costs?*, 27 Am. Crim. L. Rev. 331,352-54 (1989).

[22] We make the simplifying assumption throughout our analysis that criminal penalties will be limited exclusively to naked cartel activity. This assumption should have no effect upon the practical scope of our analysis; we are aware of no criminal cases involving non-cartel activity since 1980, when the Antitrust Division of the U.S. Department of Justice brought such a case based upon resale price maintenance. *See* U.S. v. Cuisinarts, Inc., Crim. No. H-80-49 (D. Conn. Sept. 17, 1980).

[23] *See* Kobayashi, *supra* note 20, at 736-38.

[24] *Id.* The firm may also have an incentive to increase investments in avoiding detection and conviction. These investments, in turn, reduce the probability of cartel detection and increase the level of the optimal sanction. *See* Edward A. Snyder, *The Effect of Higher Criminal Penalties on Antitrust Enforcement*, 33 J. L. & Econ. 439, 440 (1990).

against any potential increase in the probability of detection when assessing the optimal level of deterrence.[25]

To our knowledge, however, there is no empirical evidence that suggests consumers anywhere are currently paying the cost of an overzealous cartel enforcement regime.[26]

To our knowledge, however, there is no empirical evidence that suggests consumers anywhere are currently paying the cost of an overzealous cartel enforcement regime

Attention to agency costs in determining the optimal antitrust penalty brings to light the key distinction between the level of penalties required for optimal deterrence and the efficient allocation of those penalties as between the corporation and its agents. The simple model of optimal antitrust penalties ignores that distinction as well as a number of other complications. For example, reputational sanctions in the employment market can reduce the requisite level of legal sanctions.[27] The risk preferences of individuals and the possibility of legal error also alter the optimal sanction. Finally, other penalties—particularly the costs incurred by defendant corporations in private suits for damages—are also relevant to identifying optimal antitrust penalties because they, too, influence firm behavior ex ante.[28]

The standard economic approach to optimal sanctions suggests that, because fines and damage awards are transfers that do not reduce social welfare, monetary sanctions should be used as often as possible; alternative sanctions are called for only to the extent fines provide insufficient deterrence. This approach, therefore, leads to an antitrust enforcement system with a low probability of detection, very high fines, and very few cartels. There are a number of reasons, however, to believe fines alone will not provide sufficient deterrence

---

[25] Kobayashi, supra note 20, at 736-38.

[26] There is some evidence of a related form of over-deterrence in other areas of law. While the impact of increased exposure to liability and compliance costs can be small when spread across industries, in particular settings it can be quite large. *See* Tomas J. Philipson & Eric Sun, *Is the Food and Drug Administration Safe and Effective?*, 22 J. Econ. Persp. 85, 94–95 (2008) (finding the deadweight losses due to price increases resulting from product liability litigation in the pharmaceutical industry are in the tens of billions of dollars); Paul Rubin & Joanna Shepherd, *Tort Reform and Accidental Deaths*, 50 J.L. & Econ. 221 (2007) (estimating product liability has increased accidental deaths by raising the prices of safety-enhancing goods and services); Richard L. Manning, *Changing Rules in Tort Law and the Market for Childhood Vaccines*, 37 J. L. & Econ. 247, 273 (1994) (concluding the price of vaccines went up twenty-fold after product liability was imposed).

[27] There is at present, however, little quantitative evidence that antitrust offenders suffer serious reputational losses when convicted. *See* Cindy R. Alexander, *On the Nature of the Reputational Penalty for Corporate Crime: Evidence*, 42 J. L. & Econ. 489 (1999); *see also* Jonathan M. Karpoff & John R. Lott, Jr., *The Reputational Penalty Firms Bear from Committing Criminal Fraud*, 36 J. L. & Econ. 757 (1993).

[28] We put these issues aside for the purpose of our analysis.

and alternative sanctions such as imprisonment, which is costly, and debarment, which is not costly, should also be used in antitrust enforcement.[29]

As both a theoretical and a practical matter, given the inherent uncertainty about the probability of detection and other key empirical inputs, it is likely impossible to pinpoint the optimal level of total antitrust sanctions, much less to identify precisely the mix of the potentially available sanctions that would lead to the uniquely efficient level of deterrence. Still, the economic framework is useful for thinking about the tradeoffs between various types of sanctions and their likely consequences.

III. ARE CARTELS BEING UNDERDETERRED? THE EXPERIENCE IN THE UNITED STATES AND THE EU

The bulk of scholarly opinion is consistent with the view that despite ever-increasing levels of corporate fines and longer jail sentences, cartel activity is currently under-deterred.[30] Whether current sanctions under-deter is ultimately an empirical question, however, and the rate of cartel formation over time is unobservable, which makes impossible any confident conclusion about whether current sanctions are over-deterring, under-deterring, or just right. Nonetheless, the experience in the United States and the EU with ever-increasing fines gives some reason to doubt the efficacy of further extending this approach or, indeed, of maintaining the status quo.

A. Increasing Fines in the United States and the EU

In the United States, corporate fines have increased dramatically since 1990. As Figure 1 illustrates, the enforcement agencies are clearly exercising their enhanced statutory authority, for total corporate fines collected by the Antitrust Division have increased from $142 million during the period 1990-94 to $3.35 billion during 2005-09. Annual average total fines collected increased from $28 million during the period 1990-94 to $670 million during 2005-2009, an increase of more than 2000 percent.

[29] *Cf.* Gregory J. Werden & Marylin J. Simon, *Why Price Fixers Should Go to Prison*, 32 Antitrust Bull. 917 (1987); A. Mitchell Polinsky & Steven Shavell, *Should Employees Be Subject to Fines and Imprisonment Given the Existence of Corporate Liability?*, 13 Int'l Rev. L. & Econ. 239 (1993).

[30] *See, e.g.*, Yoliya Bolotova & John M. Connor, *Cartel Sanctions: An Empirical Analysis* (Working Paper, Apr. 2008), *available at* http://papers.ssrn.com/sol3/papers.cfm?abstract_id=1116421; Gregory J. Werden, *Sanctioning Cartel Activity: Let the Punishment Fit the Crimes*, EUR. Competition J. 19 (2009); OECD, Cartel Sanctions Against Individuals (2003).

FIGURE 1 United States Antitrust Division Total Corporate Fines 1990–2009

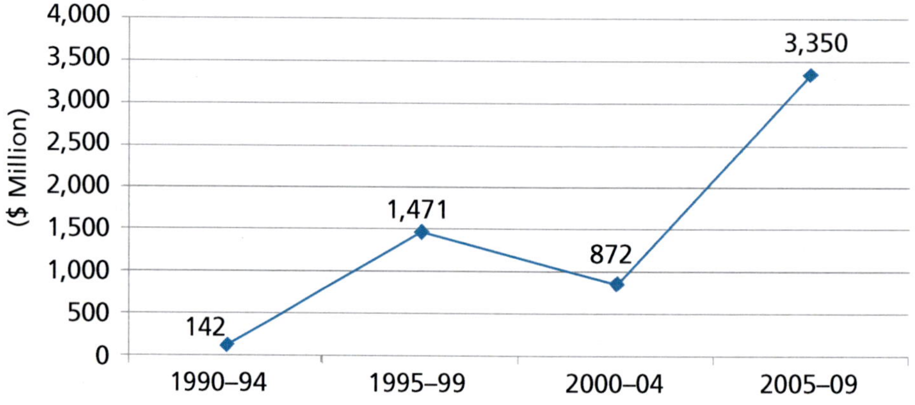

As Figure 2 illustrates, this upward trend in corporate fines over the last 20 years, and especially the last decade, is significant. Average corporate fines have increased almost 10,000 percent snot the product of a small number of extremely large fines, but rather includes 73 fines of more than $10 million during 1996-2009, 18 of which were more than $100 million.

FIGURE 2 United States Antitrust Division Average Corporate Fines 1990–2009

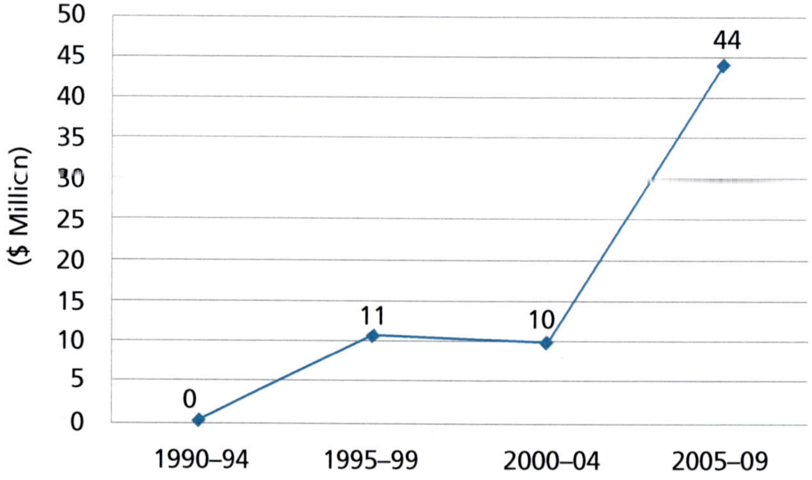

FIGURE 3 EU Total Corporate Fines 1990–2009

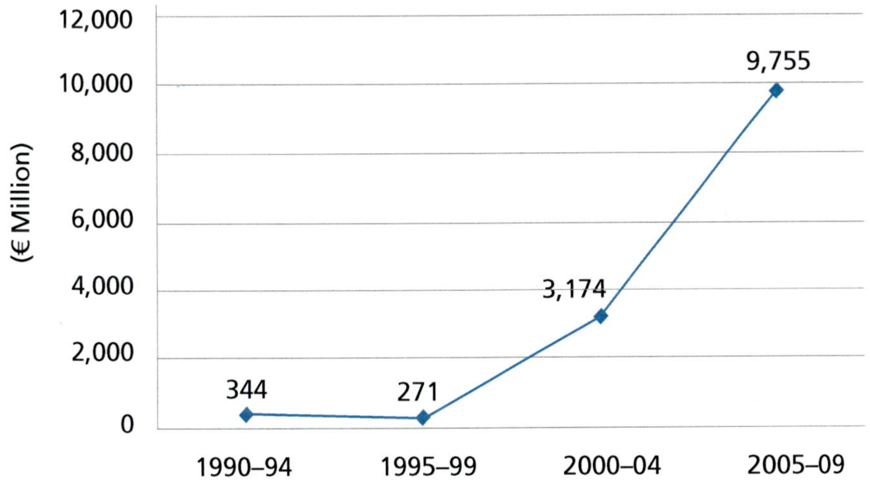

The EU now fines price-fixers even more aggressively than does the United States.[31] As shown in Figure 3, total EU corporate fines in the last quinquennium were almost EUR 10 billion, or 27 times what they had been in 1990–94, reflecting an even greater rate of growth than that of total U.S. corporate fines. The United States collected more in fines only during 1999, which may reflect simply that the United States fined Hoffman-La Roche for its participation in the vitamin cartel in 1999 whereas Europe did so in 2001.

Figure 4 shows that average corporate fines in the EU increased from less than EUR 2 million during the period 1990-94 to more than EUR 45 million during 2005-09. Over the same interval, total fines levied upon corporations each year went from EUR 19 million to EUR 450 million, representing an increase of almost 24 times.

A critical question for our purposes is whether the greatly increased level of fines since 1990 has resulted in increased deterrence. Professor Connor finds that while "[i]nternational cartel discovery rates have been increasing since 1990, from four to six per year in the early 1990s

[31] The United Kingdom has also levied large fines. The largest fines in a single case totaled £225 million. *See* Press Release, Office of Fair Trading, *OFT Imposes £225m Fine Against Certain Tobacco Manufacturers and Retailers Over Retail Pricing Practices, available at* http://www.oft.gov.uk/news/press/2010/39-10 (Apr. 16, 2010).

FIGURE 4 EU Average Corporate Fines 1990–2009

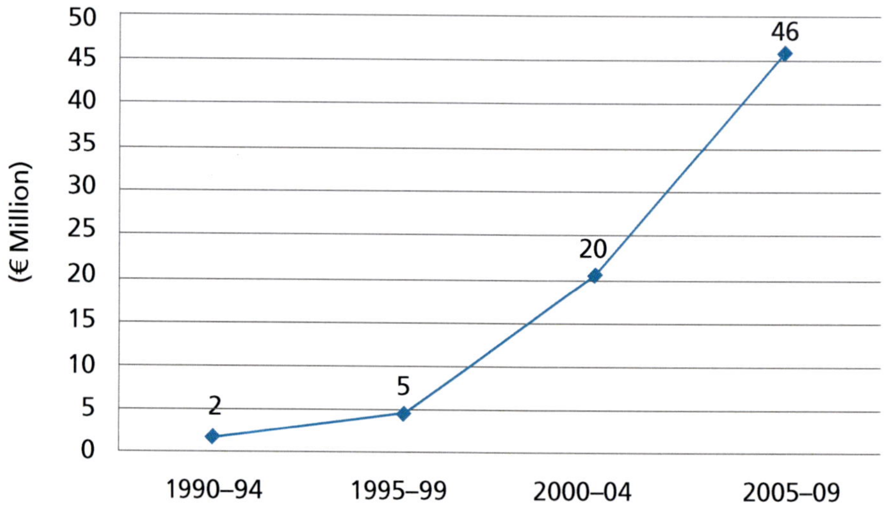

to about 35 per year in 2003-2005," detected instances of price-fixing remained relatively frequent from 1990 to 2005, extracting from consumers (in constant 2005 dollars) aggregate overcharges exceeding $200 billion, with an average overcharge of $2.1 billion per cartel.[32]

The significance of the increase in aggregate cartel fines is ambiguous. Perhaps enforcement agencies are becoming more successful in discovering and prosecuting price-fixers; or perhaps companies are even more frequently fixing prices despite the increase in the average fine. If the best way to deter price-fixing is to increase fines, then we should expect the number of cartel cases to decrease as fines increase. At this point, however, we do not have any evidence that a still higher corporate fine would deter price-fixing more effectively. It may simply be that corporate fines are misdirected, so that increasing the severity of sanctions along this margin is at best irrelevant and might counter-productively impose costs upon consumers in the form of higher prices as firms pass on increased monitoring and compliance expenditures.

---

[32] John M. Connor & C. Gustav Helmers, *Statistics on Modern Private International Cartels, 1990-2005* 37–38 (Working Paper, January 2007), *available at* http://papers.ssrn.com/sol3/papers.cfm?abstract_id= 1103610; Miller, *supra* note 18, provides evidence that the introduction of the corporate leniency program in the United States significantly enhanced detection rates and deterrence.

FIGURE 5 US Antitrust Division Total Incarceration Days 1990–2009

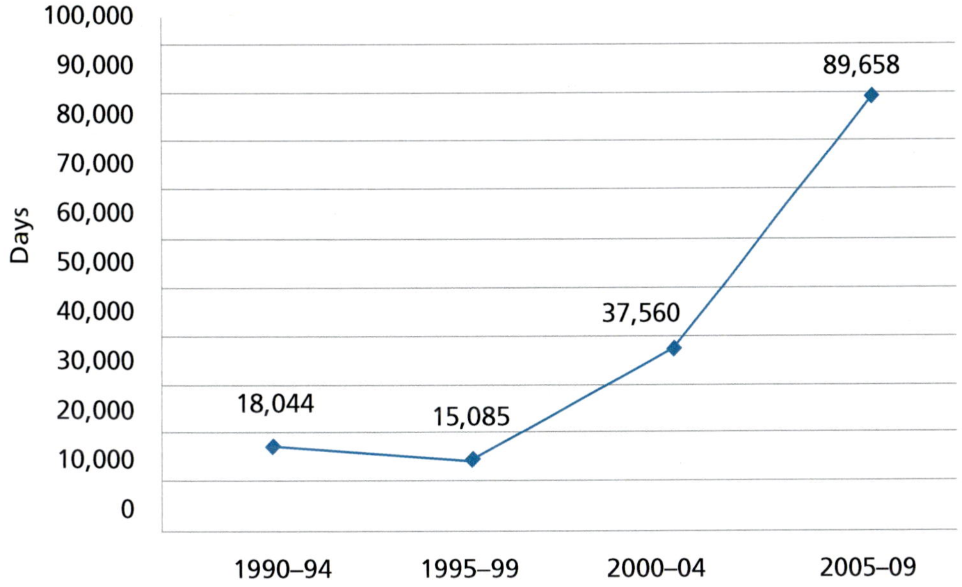

B. Increasing Jail Sentences in the United States

Corporate fines are not the only sanction imposed in the United States. As Figure 5 demonstrates, since 1990 the U.S. Antitrust Division has been sending more individuals to jail for longer periods of time, but the number of individuals sentenced has increased at a lesser rate than have fines.[33]

Perhaps more important, as Figure 6 shows, the average length of the sentence meted out also increased, especially after 2004, when the maximum lawful sentence was increased from three to ten years.[34]

---

[33] Total incarceration days in 2005–2009 were about four times what they had been during 1990–1994.

[34] The average sentence during 2005–2009 is almost twice the average sentence during the 1990–2004 period. The average duration of incarceration increased despite a simultaneous increase in the number of persons sentenced from 73 to 125. In 2009, eighty percent of criminal defendants were sentenced to jail. The average sentence was 24 months. See U.S. Antitrust Division Update 2010, Criminal Program, http://www.justice.gov/atr/public/update/2010/criminal-program.html (last visited Sept. 23, 2010).

FIGURE 6 US Antitrust Division Average Jail Sentence 1990–2009

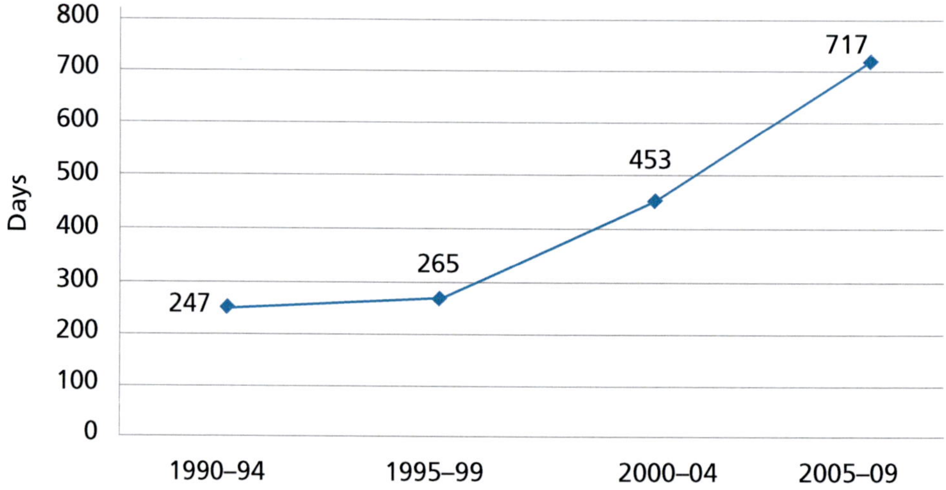

Comparable data are not available for the EU because there is no provision for imposing any sanction—fine or jail time—upon an individual. In some instances, however, individual sanctions may be sought by the competition agency of a member country.

C. The Proliferation of Criminal Antitrust Sanctions Around the World

Over the last decade a number of countries have increased the sanctions for cartel offenses. Penalties include not only corporate and individual fines but also jail sentences and debarment.

Fines imposed by national competition agencies can be quite significant. The U.K. Office of Fair Trading assessed an average corporate fine of £4.7 million during the period 2001–06.[35] During the same period, the German Bundeskartellamt collected a total of EUR 969.2 million in corporate and individual fines.[36] The French Competition Council imposed fines of EUR 2.0 billion from 2001to 2008 and EUR 631.3 million in 2008 alone.[37]

---

[35] UK Office of Fair Trading, An Assessment of Discretionary Penalty Regimes 148 (2009).

[36] Bundeskartellamt, Our Activities in 2005 and 2006 at 46 (2007).

[37] Natasha G Assadi-Tardif & Marc Lévy, *France: Cartels, in* European Antitrust Review 2010 (2009).

There is no indication that the dramatic increase in both corporate fines and the average length of jail sentences has resulted in a significant decline in cartel activity

National competition laws have also increasingly authorized incarceration for cartel offenses. For example, public prosecutors in Germany obtained a 34-month sentence for bid rigging in the Pipes Cartel case.[38] The Appendix summarizes the availability of antitrust sanctions in 39 countries. In 18 of those countries, competition laws authorize prison time for price-fixing. Criminal sanctions, however, are rarely imposed outside the United States and now Canada, where fines have been the usual penalty but imprisonment is now more frequently being sought. The overwhelming majority of these penalty regimes provide for both corporate and individual fines, while a few provide for debarment.

D. Are Conventional Penalties Deterring Cartels?

There is no indication that the dramatic increase in both corporate fines and the average length of jail sentences has resulted in a significant decline in cartel activity. Corporate fines are unlikely to efficiently deter conduct by an individual employee because he will internalize almost none of the fine imposed against his employer. The data are consistent with this understanding. While it is impossible to quantify what, if any, effect the increase in criminal antitrust sanctions has had upon the level of cartel activity, the available data on the duration of price-fixing conspiracies, on stock price movements in response to cartel related indictments, and on recidivism among companies all suggest current penalties under-deter.

The best available estimate of average cartel duration, from a study of 40 recent cases brought either by the U.S. Antitrust Division or the European Commission, is six years.[39] Although the sample of cartels leading to indictments is biased, there is no a priori reason

---

[38] Florian Wagner-von Papp, *Criminal Antitrust Law Enforcement in Germany: 'The Whole Point Is Lost If You Keep It a Secret! Why Didn't You Tell the World, Eh?'*, forthcoming in CRIMINALISING CARTELS: CRITICAL STUDIES OF AN INTERDISCIPLINARY REGULATORY MOVEMENT (C. Beaton-Wells & A. Ezrachi, eds., 2010).

[39] *See* Simon J. Evenett et al., *International Cartel Enforcement: Lessons from the 1990s*, 24 WORLD ECON. 1221, 1226 (2001); Margaret C. Levenstein & Valerie Y. Suslow, *What Determines Cartel Success?*, 44 J. ECON. LIT. 43, 49-50 (2006) (reporting an average cartel duration of five years across several studies, with a range of 3.7 to ten years). Levenstein & Suslow report no trend in average cartel duration over time. *Id.* at 51.

to believe the sample selection biases upward the estimate of average cartel duration.[40] That these cartels persisted undetected for so long suggests price-fixing may be more profitable than was previously thought,[41] which in turn suggests the need for greater sanctions if cartels are to be deterred.

Stock price movements following indictments for price-fixing also suggest inadequate deterrence. A well-documented empirical regularity, both across jurisdictions and over time, is that share values in indicted firms initially fall significantly. The most recent studies evaluating EU antitrust enforcement find a large loss of value upon the initiation of an enforcement action, only a small fraction of which can be attributed to fines and legal costs.[42] Similar results obtain in the United States. For example, the total loss of stock market capitalization for a sample of firms indicted from 1962 to 1980 is approximately $2.18 billion (in 1982 dollars), less than 13 percent of which can be attributed to fines, private treble damages, and other legal costs.[43] A similar loss of value following indictments of publicly traded firms was found in a

---

40 One possibility is indicted cartels are those that have been in operation the longest, increasing the probability of detection and suggesting the average cartel duration rate is less than prevailing estimates based upon indicted cartels. On the other hand, it is equally plausible indicted cartels are less skilled at keeping their illegal activities covert, which would suggest the average duration is greater than estimated.

41 *See* George Stigler, *A Theory of Oligopoly,* 72 J. Pol. Econ. 44, 46 (1964) ("It is a well-established proposition that if any member of the agreement can secretly violate it, he will gain larger profits than by conforming to it . . . . The literature of collusive agreements . . . is replete with instances of the collapse of conspiracies because of 'secret' price-cutting.") In addition to emphasizing the threat to cartel stability posed by the incentive to deviate from collusive agreements with secret price-cutting, economists also viewed skeptically the claim that firms could sustain a price-fixing agreement without government support. *See* Harold Demsetz, *Two Systems of Belief About Monopoly, in* Industrial Concentration: The New Learning 164 (Harvey J. Goldschmid et al. eds., 1974) ("The key to sustained monopoly power is the ability of an industry to restrict or retard the expansion and utilization of productive capacity. Government can offer to industry much greater powers of coercion to accomplish this end than can be supplied by the industry itself.")

42 See Andrea Gunster & Mathijs A. van Dijk, The Impact of European Antitrust Policy: Evidence from the Stock Market 2, 21–22 (Working Paper, Apr. 2010), available at http://papers.ssrn.com/sol3/papers.cfm? abstract_id=1598387 (finding a total market value loss of EUR 24 billion associated with enforcement events, of which roughly seventy-five percent cannot be explained by fines and legal costs); see also Gregor Langus, Massimo Motta, & Luca Aguzzoni, The Effect of EU Antitrust Investigations and Fines on a Firm's Valuation (Working Paper, Jul. 2009), available at http://www.barcelonagse.eu/tmp/pdf/motta_fines_july09.pdf.

43 Jean-Claude Bosch & E. Woodrow Eckard, Jr., *The Profitability of Price Fixing: Evidence from Stock Market Reaction to Federal Indictments,* 73 Rev. Econ. Stat. 309, 309 (1991).

study spanning 1981 to 2000.[44] One reasonable interpretation of these findings is that the residual loss in value is associated with the expectation that the price of the firm's products will drop to the competitive level, with a concomitant loss of monopoly profits.[45] The share price data also suggests a strong incentive for recidivism; even after accounting for fines and legal costs, price-fixing remains profitable.

Indeed, subsequent studies demonstrate that the stock prices of the overwhelming majority of indicted firms return to pre-indictment levels within one year.[46] Again, this result holds for indictments between 1962 and 1980 as well as between 1981 and 2000. Given the substantially greater corporate fines imposed in the latter time period, the consistency of the stock price recovery across both periods suggests increased fines did not significantly increase cartel deterrence.[47] Regardless of the interpretation assigned to the initial post-indictment decrease in the stock price,[48] the systematic recovery of pre-indictment stock prices within a year suggests current sanctions have no more than a transitory impact upon market outcomes and little, if any, deterrent value.

Recent recidivism data in Figure 7 are also consistent with the view that sanctions are not adequately deterring cartel activity.

---

44 John S. Thompson & David L. Kaserman, *After the Fall: Stock Price Movements and the Deterrent Effect of Antitrust Enforcement*, 19 Rev. Indus. Org. 329 (2001).

45 One alternative interpretation is that the announcement of an indictment creates market expectations of lower operational efficiency, perhaps because of the loss of key management personnel, or the risk of future illegal activity that could lead to further prosecution and fines.

46 *See* Thompson & Kaserman, supra note 44 (finding the share price of eighty-five percent of the firms in the sample involving indictments between 1962 and 1980 had regained one hundred percent of their pre-indictment levels within one year); Alla Golub, Joshua Detre & John M. Connor, *The Profitability of Price-Fixing: Have Stronger Antitrust Sanctions Deterred?* 11 (Working Paper, Apr. 2005), *available at* http://papers. ssrn.com/sol3/papers.cfm?abstract_id=1188515 (finding the share prices of eighty-seven percent of the firms in a sample involving indictments between 1981 and 2001 had regained one hundred percent of their pre-indictment levels within one year).

47 It is possible that the significant increase in sanctions in both the United States and abroad after 2000 has resulted in greater deterrence. We are not aware of any empirical studies that test whether the stock price recovery patterns discussed above continue after 2000.

48 One possible explanation of the stock price recovery pattern is the market overreacts to the initial announcement of the indictment before quickly reverting to pre-indictment share price levels. This overreaction hypothesis, however, is not inconsistent with under-deterrence. From an optimal deterrence perspective, the key fact is that equilibrium share prices revert to collusive levels. Further, the overreaction interpretation requires one to believe not only that the market dramatically overreacts to negative information, resulting in short-term share prices reflecting the dissipation of future cartel rents and legal costs despite that the former are transitory, but also that the market has not improved its ability to form accurate expectations over a 40-year period despite experience with hundreds of indictments involving publicly traded corporations.

FIGURE 7 The World's Leading Recidivists

Company	Number of Judgments Worldwide 1990–2009
BASF	26
Total S.A. (TotalFina, Elf, Atofina)	18
F. Hoffman-La Roche	17
Azko Nobel	14
Aventis	14
ENI	14
Shell	14
Degussa (Evonik)	13
Bayer	11
Mitsubishi	10
Mitsui	10

Source: Connor & Helmers, Statistics on Private Int'l Cartels, 1990-2005 (Working Paper, 2008)

Professor Connor has identified seven companies that averaged about one or more judgments annually over the 15-year period 1990-2005. In addition to these exceptionally persistent recidivists, he found 86 companies with three or more judgments worldwide in this period. For the same 15-year period the filings of the U.S. Antitrust Division alone include three cases against Bayer and two each against Hoffman-La Roche, Degussa (now Evonik) Chemical, and Archer Daniels Midland, which again tends to suggest there is a problem with recidivism.[49]

[49] Statistics on the Department of Justice Antitrust Division criminal enforcement filings are available at http://www.justice.gov/atr/public/workstats.pdf.

Evaluating these data, Connor concludes that although "[m]onetary sanctions imposed upon international cartelists since 1989 have been the highest in antitrust history ... extensive recidivism implies that present cartel sanctions are inadequate to deter cartel formation."[50] He calculates that "even under the most optimistic assumptions about discovery, lenience, and prosecution rates, the average conspirator can reasonably expect to make a profit on the typical global price-fixing scheme .... To ensure optimal deterrence of global cartels, total financial sanctions should be four times the expected global cartel profits (the overcharge)."[51] This conclusion is remarkably consistent with our earlier estimate that perhaps twenty-five percent of cartels are now detected.

If one accepts that cartels are being under-deterred, then Connor's prescription reflects the prevailing view of how to solve the problem: Increase corporate fines, *simpliciter*. In our view, however, the prevailing view is in need of re-examination and is almost certainly wrong. Instead of expecting ever-larger corporate fines to reduce cartel behavior, we believe an alternative approach that shifts deterrence efforts away from the corporation and toward the individuals responsible for the violation will provide greater deterrence than does the current approach. We expect the increase in deterrence to be particularly large where individuals are not held criminally or civilly liable for their role in price-fixing. As for the United Kingdom, we think it is on a better trajectory than either the United States or the EU for reasons that appear below.

IV. OUR PROPOSAL

The model of the firm reflected in the approach currently taken by the antitrust enforcement agencies implicitly views "the corporation" as an entity looming above and apart from its employees, which view envisions the corporation as monitoring, investigating, and reporting their misdeeds. Therefore, it is no surprise that the standard economic approach to penalties, as applied by the enforcement agencies, yields a policy that focuses upon the corporation.

Whatever the merits of the conventional view as applied to a closely held corporation, a more granular model of the publicly traded corporation brings into clearer focus the incentives

---

50 Connor & Helmers, *supra* note 32 at 38. These recidivism data are consistent with earlier studies of price-fixing indictments finding approximately fourteen percent of firms were repeat offenders. *See* Bosch & Eckard, *supra* note 43 at 309 n. 1 (evaluating price-fixing indictments from 1962-1980); Richard A. Posner, *A Statistical Study of Antitrust Enforcement*, 13 J. L. & Econ. 365, 394–395 (1970) (finding 46 of 320 corporations indicted for price-fixing violations between 1964 and 1968 had been convicted previously and ten had three or more prior convictions).

51 John M. Connor, Optimal Deterrence and Private International Cartels (working paper, May 2005).

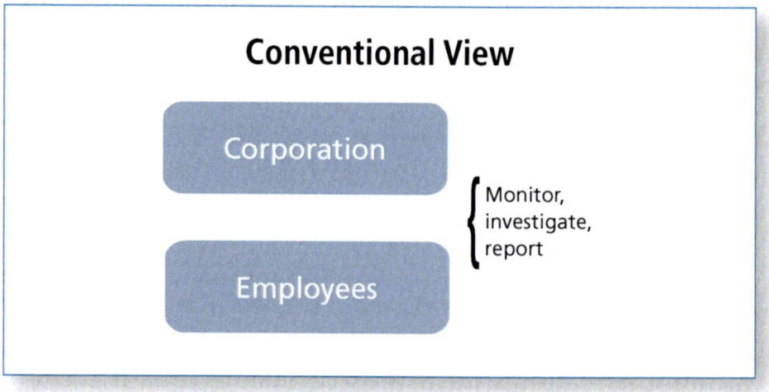

and abilities of the individuals who operate within and on behalf of the firm. In this model, the directors oversee the officers, who manage the employees. The shareholders are passive investors; they have no influence over the day-to-day operations of the firm. Public authorities (and, in the United States, plaintiffs' class action lawyers) monitor, investigate, and enforce the antitrust laws but, because they are firm outsiders, they have less information and exert less direct influence over employee behavior than do the senior managers and the directors.

The granular model makes it easier to see why a shift from further increasing penalties for corporations in favor of increasing the sanctions imposed upon the individual employ-

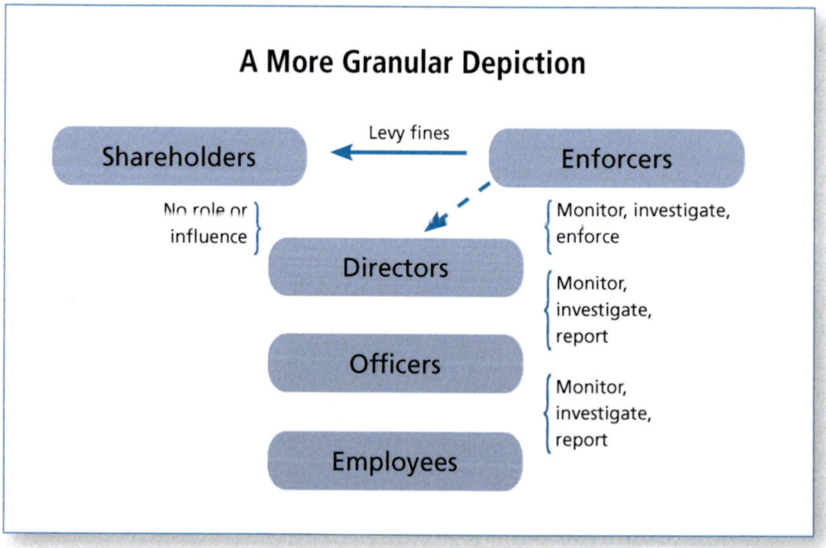

In sum, as matters now stand, neither shareholders nor directors and officers have an incentive to prevent price-fixing as long as it remains profitable for the corporation

ees (at whatever level) who engage in price-fixing is likely to be the more cost-effective way to increase deterrence. Shareholders cannot prevent price-fixing by employees of the corporation. Their options are to hold or to sell their shares and, insofar as possible price-fixing is relevant to their decision, they will choose between holding and selling based upon whether price-fixing is likely to increase the corporation's earnings and hence the market value of their shares.

Corporate officers and directors also reap gains from the corporation's participation in a cartel. They may capture some of the gains in the form of increased compensation and perquisites, and the increased value of shares in the corporation enhances their reputations and career opportunities.

In sum, as matters now stand, neither shareholders nor directors and officers have an incentive to prevent price-fixing as long as it remains profitable for the corporation. And, as we have seen, even at their present enhanced level, corporate fines seem not to take the profit out of price-fixing. The level of corporate fines could, of course, be increased yet again but that makes sense only if it is likely to be the most cost-effective way of achieving an additional quantum of deterrence.

Although imposing a criminal penalty upon a director or an officer would provide him with an incentive to prevent price-fixing, it makes more sense to target the actual employee who fixes prices for two reasons. First, that employee is directly responsible for the price-fixing; sanctioning a director or officer deters price-fixing only if he is able to stop the employee. Second, because an employee has less to gain from price-fixing than does a director or officer, a smaller sanction is required to deter the employee. It is true that price-fixing still occurs in jurisdictions where it is now a criminal offense, but that more likely suggests current penalties are insufficiently severe, not that imposing criminal sanctions upon individuals will have little additional deterrent value.

We assume the probability of detection is relatively fixed for the foreseeable future: Competition agencies have no shortage of resources for uncovering cartels and they have fine-tuned their leniency programs through experience. Still, the evidence suggests that cartel formation is insufficiently deterred. The question how best to increase deterrence therefore comes down to this: Is increasing corporate fines or increasing individual sanctions more likely to increase deterrence by a given amount at a lower cost?

We think it clear the time has come to increase individual sanctions rather than corporate fines. In reality, it is shareholders, not the abstraction called "the corporation," who bear the economic burden—such as it is—of corporate sanctions. It was their agents, however, in management and on the board of directors who violated the law or who may have been in a position to prevent the violation; they should be the focus of the law's efforts to deter price-fixing.[52]

Our more granular depiction of the firm has implications also for the role of compliance programs in evaluating optimal criminal antitrust penalties. If a company has made a reasonable effort to comply with the antitrust law, and an employee nevertheless engages in price-fixing, then it makes no sense to fine the corporation, or to sanction the directors or officers.[53] On the other hand, if the directors or officers were negligent in performing their duty to supervise the employee who actually fixed prices, then they should be held accountable along with the perpetrator. Boards of directors of publicly held companies routinely task a committee of board members—most often the audit committee but sometimes a special committee—with responsibility for corporate legal compliance. Such a committee should and ordinarily does

---

[52] President Woodrow Wilson made the case for shifting penalties from corporations to individuals in his January 20, 1914 remarks to Congress, in which he proposed what later became the Clayton Act:

> We ought to see ... that penalties and punishments should fall not upon business itself, to its confusion and interruption, but upon the individuals who use the instrumentalities of business to do things which public policy and sound business practice condemn. Every act of business is done at the command or upon the initiative of some ascertainable person or group of persons. These should be held individually responsible and the punishment should fall upon them, not upon the business organization of which they make illegal use.

51 Cong. Rec., 1963 (1914).

[53] William Kolasky, when he was a Deputy Assistant Attorney General in the Antitrust Division, said one of the most startling characteristics of cartels "is that they typically involve ... executives who have received extensive antitrust compliance counseling, and who often have significant responsibilities in the firm's antitrust compliance programs." William Kolasky, Deputy Assistant Att'y Gen., Dep't of Justice, Address at the Practising Law Institute Corporate Compliance Conference (July 12, 2009). Kolasky provided a very troubling anecdote about a then-recent DOJ investigation:

> When a top executive at [a] firm arranged a meeting with his chief foreign competitor to discuss exchanging technological information, [the firm's general counsel accompanied him to the meeting as part of the firm's extensive compliance program.] [T]he general counsel must have taken some comfort when [the two executives greeted one another as if they had never met before.] ... Imagine how that general counsel must have felt when he learned, during the course of the [DOJ] investigation, that the introduction ... had been completely staged for his benefit.... In fact, the two executives had been meeting, dining, socializing, playing golf, and participating together and with others in a massive worldwide price-fixing conspiracy for years.

Id. The conspirators even used code names to refer to their general counsels.

insist that management implement an antitrust compliance program. If the board of a corporation that participates in a cartel has failed to do that, or has neglected to monitor management's continued adherence to the program, then it is only sensible to inquire whether the directors were negligent to the point that they, too, should be sanctioned in some way proportionate to their role in the corporation's violation.[54]

In theory at least, the means by which shareholders constrain management is through the oversight provided by the directors, who are fiduciaries and are supposed to act as the shareholders' representatives. That is why a state supreme court recently heard a shareholder's derivative suit against the board of directors of Micron Technology on the theory that the board had failed to prevent known price-fixing by the company's managers.[55] It is notoriously difficult for a derivative suit to succeed, however, and shareholders are rarely able to exert control over their board through the annual election of directors. In short, shareholders simply cannot prevent or deter a corporate employee from price-fixing or a board of directors from negligently failing to notice—but the law, properly targeted, could do so.

With our more granular model of the firm as our foundation, we turn to our proposal for the design of optimal antitrust penalties. Three groups are implicated: the perpetrator, the directors and officers responsible for antitrust compliance, and the corporation (as a stand-in for the shareholders).

Clearly, the actual perpetrator should face the traditional criminal sanctions—jail and fines, to which we would add debarment. There is ample evidence that jail sentences

---

54 See Restatement (Second) of Torts § 317 (Duty of Master to Control Conduct of Servant). For directors,

> no liability exists in the absence of red flags which the exercise of reasonable oversight would uncover. Reasonable oversight entails the creation of reporting systems that provide directors with the information necessary to monitor the corporation and compliance programs that ensure the corporation's adherence to applicable law. The sophistication of any reporting system or compliance program, however, remains a matter of business judgment. ... [O]nce a reporting system or compliance program exists, directors generally bear no liability for losses sustained from any deficiencies absent evidence of gross negligence

Bryan A. McGrane, *The Audit Committee: Director Liability in the Wake of the Sarbanes-Oxley Act and Tello v. Dean Witter Reynolds*, 18 Cornell J.L. & Pub. Pol'y 575, 586–87 (2009) (citing In re Caremark Int'l Inc. Derivative Litig., 698 A.2d 959, 970–71 (Del. Ch. 1996). *Cf.* In re Fed. Nat'l Mortg. Ass'n Sec. Deriv. & ERISA Litig., 503 F. Supp. 2d 25, 37 (D.D.C. 2007) (audit committee liable in private litigation only for extreme recklessness).

55 Orrock v. Appleton, 213 P.3d 398 (Idaho 2009) (holding shareholder insufficiently pled in a case involving a demand by plaintiff that the Board bring suit would be futile).

significantly deter individuals in general and business executives in particular.[56] The deterrent value of a prison sentence is supplemented by the prospect of a decrease in income and in employment opportunities incurred by an individual who has been convicted of price-fixing.[57] Adding debarment to the mix of potential penalties imposes a direct opportunity cost upon the perpetrator and increases both the likelihood and the magnitude of the reputational sanction. It also reduces the length of incarceration required, as well as the amount of the personal fine necessary, to achieve any given level of deterrence. Both debarment and incarceration protect the public from recidivism by a particular individual. Because incarceration involves significant social costs,[58] however, debarment as a complement to incarceration is more likely to achieve the desired level of individual deterrence at a lower social cost than would additional jail time.

To the extent they are culpable, directors and officers responsible for overseeing operations and implementing antitrust compliance programs should also be held accountable for their performance.[59] Of course, those who discharge their responsibility appropriately should not be sanctioned at all. Those who perform these tasks negligently, however, should be fined

---

[56] U.K. Office of Fair Trading, The Deterrent Effect of Competition Enforcement by the OFT 71–72 (November 2007) (survey finding business executives and their lawyers regard criminal penalties as the strongest motivating force for antitrust compliance). Anecdotal evidence also supports the intuitive view that jail sentences are a strong deterrent. *See Hearing on Criminal Remedies Before the Antitrust Modernization Comm'n* (Nov. 3, 2005) (statement of Tefft W. Smith, Partner, Kirkland & Ellis LLP). ("Every antitrust compliance presentation I have seen or delivered begins with the threat of jail for individual executives. It then speaks of 'large' fines and, lastly dwells on the—certain—avalanche of treble-damages and joint and several liability for the sales of all the co-cartelers.")

[57] This effect, which "appears to be based on stigma" is particularly large for "those whose pre-conviction jobs apparently involve trust." Joel Waldfogel, *The Effect of Criminal Conviction on Income and the Trust "Reposed in the Workmen,"* 29 J. Human Resources 62, 75 (1994). *See also* Kent R. Kerley & Heith Copes, *The Effects of Criminal Justice Contact on Employment Stability for White-Collar and Street Level Offenders*, 48 Int'l J. Offender Therapy & Comp. Criminology 65 (2004); John R. Lott, Jr., *The Effect of Conviction on the Legitimate Income of Criminals*, 34 Econ. Letters 381 (1990).

[58] Operating costs for federal prisons are about $75 per inmate per day, or $27,252 per inmate per year. Federal Probation and Pretrial Services System: Reshaping Lives, Protecting Society, Third Branch: Newsletter Of The Federal Courts, May 2010, at 5.

[59] *See* U.S. Sentencing Guidelines Manual § 8B2.1 (describing effective compliance programs). *But see* Amendments to the Sentencing Guidelines (effective Nov. 1, 2010), *available at* http://www.ussc.gov/2010guid/finalamend10.pdf (restricting credit for compliance programs).

The essential tenet of our proposal is that shifting incremental cartel sanctions away from corporations and toward the individuals who engage in price-fixing or are responsible for monitoring antitrust compliance will enhance deterrence

and debarred for a period of years.[60] Similarly, those who are complicit in a price-fixing scheme without rising to the level of a perpetrator—such as an aider or abettor—should also be both debarred and fined.[61]

The essential tenet of our proposal is that shifting incremental cartel sanctions away from corporations and toward the individuals who engage in price-fixing or are responsible for monitoring antitrust compliance will enhance deterrence. The addition of debarment incident to that shift complements the usual antitrust sanctions for individual violators, i.e., a sentence including fines and jail as well as the reputational penalty incurred in the job market. Debarment, moreover, has some unique advantages as an antitrust sanction.

The first advantage is that debarment, like jail, imposes a direct and substantial opportunity cost upon individuals who engage in price-fixing. Indeed, an Office of Fair Trading report presents survey evidence that in the United Kingdom, after criminal penalties, disqualification from serving as a corporate officer or director is the sanction most likely to motivate compliance.[62] Debarment also achieves its deterrent value at a lower social cost because an executive will be equally deterred by a long prison sentence or by a shorter prison sentence (which is less costly to society than is a longer one) and debarment (which is effectively costless to society).[63]

The second and indirect advantage is that debarment enhances the likelihood and magnitude of the reputational sanction imposed by the job market. Increasing reputational penalties

---

[60] Fanean v. Rite Aid Corp. of Delaware, Inc., 984 A.2d 812, 825–26 (Del. Super Ct. 2009) ("An employer [corporation] is liable for negligent hiring or supervision where the employer is negligent ... in the employment of improper persons involving the risk of harm to others or in the supervision of the employee's activities") (quoting Simms v. Christina Sch. Dist., 2004 WL 344015 (Del. Super. Ct. Jan. 30, 2004)). *But see* Stone v. Ritter, 911 A.2d 362, 369 (Del. 2006) ("Generally where a claim of directorial liability for corporate loss is predicated upon ignorance of liability creating activities within the corporation, . . . only a sustained or systematic failure of the board to exercise oversight—such as an utter failure to attempt to assure a reasonable information and reporting system exists—will establish the lack of good faith that is a necessary condition to liability.") (quoting In re Caremark Int'l Inc. Deriv. Litig., 698 A.2d 959, 971 (Del.Ch.1996)).

[61] Current law in both the United States and the United Kingdom allows for the punishment of aiders and abettors in such a situation. See 18 U.S.C. § 2(a) (2006) ("Whoever commits an offense against the United States or aids, abets, counsels, commands, induces or procures its commission, is punishable as a principal"); U.K. Law Commission, Inchoate Liability for Assisting and Encouraging Crime § 1.6 (2006), *available at* www.lawgov.uk/docs/lc300.pdf; Serious Crime Act, (2007) ch. 27, pt. 2, § 44–46.

[62] UK Office of Fair Trading, The Deterrent Effect of Competition Enforcement by the OFT 72 (November 2007).

[63] We think it unlikely that the reputational effect of a jail sentence continues to increase when the sentence exceeds some modest threshold—perhaps the one year that denotes a felony.

would not only enhance deterrence but would also reduce the required level of fines and jail time necessary to achieve any given level of deterrence.[64] To the extent an individual is wealth constrained and therefore unable to pay a large fine, debarment would further improve the efficiency of deterrence.

V. DEBARMENT IN OTHER SETTINGS

Although the United States has relied upon a mix of corporate fines and individual penalties, including fines and incarceration, neither the United States nor the EU has used debarment to deter price-fixing; indeed, as mentioned before, EU competition law does not provide for any sanction against any individual. Several countries, however, either now do or in the near future may debar those persons who engage in antitrust violations. For example, the Competition Commission of South Africa is seeking the authority to apply for a court order barring a person convicted of price-fixing from serving as a corporate director. Similarly, under the 2009 Amendments to the Australian Trade Practices Act, an individual who violates either the competition laws (the Trade Practices Act) or the securities laws (the Corporations Act) may be disqualified from managing a corporation. In Sweden, a law effective since November 1, 2008 authorizes a court to issue a disqualification order (or "trading prohibition") at the request of the Competition Authority. This order bars an individual who has participated in a cartel from managing any business for a specified period.[65]

The United Kingdom appears to be the only jurisdiction that has any experience with debarment as a remedy for an antitrust violation,[66] and that experience is thus far limited to one case.[67] Under the Company Directors Disqualification Act of 1986, a regulator may

---

[64] The deterrent effect of debarment, like that of jail time, will be heterogeneous across individuals. Debarment would weigh more heavily upon individuals with greater firm or industry-specific skills, for example, or with abilities tailored to managing a publicly-traded corporation. At a minimum, debarment will be a more cost-effective deterrent than incarceration in some cases and will, *ceteris paribus*, reduce the level of fines and of jail time necessary to achieve a given level of deterrence.

[65] Swedish Competition Act (2008) ch. 3, art. 24.

[66] The United States has experience with debarring corporations, not individuals, who have been convicted of bid-rigging from bidding again for federal government contracts. *See* 48 C.F.R. §§ 9.406-1 to 9.406-5 (authorizing debarment); *see also, e.g.*, Robinson v. Cheney, 876 F.2d 152 (D.C. Cir. 1989) (affirming debarment order).

[67] The Office of Fair Trading, we note, is considering expanded use of debarment in the form of competition disqualification orders. See U.K. Office of Fair Trading, Competition Disqualification Orders: Proposed Changes to the OFT's Guidance (August 2009).

apply for a court order disqualifying a company director from again acting as a director or participating in the management of any U.K. company for up to 15 years. The OFT acquired this authority in 2002 when the United Kingdom made participation in a cartel a criminal offense.

The Disqualification Act applies to a person if "a company of which he is a director commits a breach of competition law," which means participates in a cartel and "his conduct as a director makes him unfit to be concerned in the management of a company," which means his conduct "contributed to the breach of competition law," "he had reasonable grounds to suspect that the conduct of the undertaking constituted the breach and he took no steps to prevent it," or "he did not know but ought to have known that the conduct of the undertaking constituted the breach."[68]

A disqualification order provides the named individual "shall not be a director of a company ... or in any way, whether directly or indirectly, be concerned or take part in the promotion, formation, or management of a company."[69] The Act has been applied for almost 25 years in contexts other than antitrust, with dozens of disqualification orders issued in 2009 alone,[70] so there should by now be a substantial body of precedent informing terms that are facially unclear, such as what it means indirectly to "take part in the ... management of a company."[71] Thus far, the single example involving debarment of an antitrust violator is the *Marine Hose* case, which is also the only criminal competition case to go to judgment in the United Kingdom. The court sentenced three individuals to jail terms of two to three years for their participation in the cartel and, upon the petition of the OFT, entered disqualification orders of from five to seven years against each of the three defendants.

One need not look only to the United Kingdom for significant experience with debarment as a legal sanction. At least since the early 1980s, the U.S. Securities and Exchange

---

68 Company Directors Disqualification Act of 1986 (as amended in 2002) § 9A. In 1961, then Assistant Attorney General Lee Loevinger testified in favor of punishment for corporate officials who have actual knowledge or "reason to know of an antitrust violation and authority to stop it but who fail to do so." Legislation to Strengthen Penalties Under the Antitrust Laws: Hearing Before the Subcomm. on Antitrust and Monopolies of the S. Comm. on the Judiciary, 87th Cong. 1st Sess., 14 (1961) (statement of Assistant Att'y Gen. Lee Loeringer).

69 Company Directors Disqualification Act of 1986 (as amended in 2002) § 1.

70 *See, e.g.*, Sec. of State for Business, Enter. & Regulatory Reform v. Sainsbury, [2009] EWHC 3456 (Ch.).

71 Company Directors Disqualification Act of 1986 (as amended in 2000) § 1(1)(a). The OFT recently provided guidance indicating directors will be held responsible not only for violations they actually observe but also for those of which they would have had knowledge had they made "reasonable enquiries." *See* U.K. Office of Fair Trading, Company Directors and Competitive Laws: A Consultation on OFT Guidance (October 2010).

Commission has routinely negotiated consent decrees barring a person accused of violating the securities laws from serving as an officer or director of a public company for a stated period of years.[72] Similarly, the Federal Trade Commission has regularly negotiated consent decrees amounting to judicial debarment orders against individuals and businesses accused of violating the consumer protection laws the agency is charged with enforcing.[73]

The U.S. Department of Justice should consider taking a similar approach to sentencing individuals convicted of a criminal violation of § 1 of the Sherman Act. We are aware of no reason for which the Department needs to wait for statutory authority to get started, as did the SEC, by negotiating consent orders providing for debarment.[74] Prosecutors might, for example, if the conditions for leniency are met, agree to allow individual defendants to reduce or avoid jail time, in return for debarring them from working as a manager or director of any publicly traded corporation or for any company in a particular industry if it is either located in or sells into the United States.[75]

---

[72] The SEC has had express statutory authority to seek such an order only since 1990, however, when the Congress authorized the courts to issue an order of suspension or debarment in a securities case—upon finding the defendant, regardless whether he consented to debarment, committed a violation "demonstrating unfitness to serve" as an officer or director of a publicly held corporation. *See* 15 U.S.C. §§ 77t(e), 78u(d)(2) (2006).

[73] *See, e.g.*, Plaintiffs' Motion to Enter Revised Permanent Injunction and Final Order as to Defendant Tarzenea Dixon, FTC v. Your Money Access, LLC., No. 07-CV-05147-ER. at 5 (E.D. Pa. Dec. 22, 2009), 2009 WL 5177847 (permanently enjoining a defendant individual from payment processing, including ACH debits and credit card transactions); Consent Decree, No. 02-5115 at 6 (C.D. Cal. United States v. D.C. Credit Serv., Inc., July 8, 2002), *available at* http://www.ftc.gov/os/2002/07/dcsconsent.pdf (permanently enjoining defendant from debt collection and assisting in debt collection activities); Stipulated Judgment & Order for Permanent Injunction, No. 02-cv-01256 (D. Ariz. FTC v. Corp. Marketing Solutions, Inc., Feb. 6, 2003) (enjoining defendant from telemarketing and assisting or facilitating telemarketing); Stipulated Final Judgment and Order for Permanent Injunction and Other Equitable Relief, FTC v. Universal Greeting Card Corp., No. 02-21753 at 3 (D. Fla. Dec. 17, 2002), *available at* http://www.ftc.gov/os/2003/01/ugccstipruffeino.pdf (permanently enjoining defendant individuals from "[r]eceiving any remuneration of any kind whatsoever from . . . any person engaged in the advertising, marketing, promoting, offering for sale, or sale of any business venture").

[74] It is already clear that unconsented debarment is constitutional. The United States Supreme Court has heard challenges to the constitutionality of debarment as a remedy for bad acts, based upon the due process, ex post facto, bill of attainder, and double jeopardy clauses, and has rejected them all. *See* De Veau v. Braisted, 363 U.S. 144, 157–60 (1960) (rejecting such challenges based upon due process, *ex post facto*, and bill of attainder clauses); Hudson v. United States, 522 U.S. 93, 105 (1997) (rejecting challenges to debarment based upon double jeopardy).

[75] By pursuing a civil case, the DOJ could also seek debarment of individuals whose conduct may not meet the scienter requirements for a criminal charge.

Further, as we have pointed out, debarment would bolster currently weak reputational penalties, thereby reducing the need for individual fines, which are less likely to deter efficiently because of individuals' wealth constraints.

Negotiated orders of debarment would allow the Antitrust Division to accrue much of the benefit of a prison sentence—publicizing the offense and keeping the offender from recidivating—without undertaking the risk and cost of a criminal trial. The period of debarment should be calibrated to have the same average deterrent effect as jail.[76] Further, as we have pointed out, debarment would bolster currently weak reputational penalties, thereby reducing the need for individual fines, which are less likely to deter efficiently because of individuals' wealth constraints.

VI. CONCLUSIONS

The press releases of competition agencies worldwide notwithstanding, we think it is questionable, indeed doubtful that a $100 million fine—or even a fine of over EUR 1 billion[77]—imposed upon a corporation because one of its executives fixed prices serves the primary goal of an antitrust sanction: to deter anticompetitive conduct that injures consumers. When fines are levied against a publicly traded corporation, the persons burdened are consumers and possibly shareholders, two groups almost certainly unable to affect the conduct of the corporation. It was a corporate executive who conspired to fix prices or allocate the market. It was his superiors in management or on the board of directors who failed to ensure the company operated lawfully. These are the individuals we want to deter. But they will not be deterred as long as consumers and shareholders bear the brunt of antitrust penalties while the directors and officers of the company have too little incentive to prevent violations.

---

[76] Because debarment can be imposed at a lower social cost than incarceration, the DOJ should calibrate the length of debarment at which the average defendant slightly prefers debarment to incarceration.

[77] *See* Sigyn Monke et al., *Commission Imposes the Highest-Ever Cartel Fine (More than EUR 1.3 Billion) on Four Car Glass Manufacturers*, Comp. Pol'y Newsletter, 2009, No. 1 at 59, *available at* http://ec.europa.eu/competition/publications/cpn/2009_1_15.pdf.

VII. APPENDIX: PENALTY REGIMES FOR COMPANIES AND INDIVIDUALS

Jurisdiction	Maximum Fines Companies	Maximum Fines for Individuals	Maximum Prison Term	Debarment	Private Action
		European Union			
European Commission[a, b, d, j]	10% of total worldwide turnover; baseline fines of 30% of relevant sales for hard core offenses with no maximum	Not Applicable	Not Applicable	Not Applicable	Not Applicable
		Europe: European Union Members			
Austria[c, gg]	10% of turnover of the preceding financial year	Not Applicable	Not Applicable	Not Applicable	Private actions available; third parties may submit claims; follow-on actions available in theory; no class actions available
Belgium[c, hh]	10% of worldwide turnover for preceding financial year	Not Applicable	Not Applicable	Not Applicable	Private actions available; class actions not yet available[hh]
Bulgaria[c, ii]	10% of total turnover for preceding financial; max suggested to be BGN 300,000[c]	BGN 50,000	Not Applicable	Not Applicable	Private actions available; follow-on actions available; class actions not available
Czech Republic[a, c, d, h]	CSK 10 million or 10% of total worldwide turnover recorded over last calendar year	Up to CZK 10 mil.[h]	5 years	Prohibition on carrying on business activities[c]	Private actions available; class actions not available
Cyprus[c, jj]	10% of combined annual revenue for preceding year or year within which infringement occurred plus €85K/day if infringement continues	Not Applicable	Not Applicable	Not Applicable	Private actions available; follow-on actions available; class actions not available, though representative actions are[jj]
Denmark[a, c, d, i]	Court may impose fine; no maximum though serious cases often warrant a fine >DKK 15 mil.	No maximum	Not Applicable	Not Applicable	Private actions available; follow-on actions available but rare;[i, c] class actions available

Continued on next page

VII. APPENDIX *(continued)*

Jurisdiction	Maximum Fines Companies	Maximum Fines for Individuals	Maximum Prison Term	Debarment	Private Action
Estonia[c, kk]	250 million kroons (€16 million)	500 daily rates/units (calculated by average daily income of offender)	3 years	Not Applicable	Private actions available and follow-on actions available, but not typical; class actions not available
Finland[c, ll]	10% of turnover of the preceding year	Not Applicable	Not Applicable	Not Applicable	Private actions available; follow-on actions available; class actions not available
France[a, c, k, l]	10% of turnover preceding year; €3 mil. if the offender is not a company (i.e., a sole trader)	€75,000	4 years	Not Applicable	Private actions available; follow-on actions available; class actions not available unless brought by consumer ombudsman[ll]
Germany[b, c, m]	(1) 10% of total worldwide turnover, or (2) 5% of total worldwide turnover if infringement is the result of negligence	€1 million (bid-rigging cases only)	5 years	Not Applicable	Private actions available; third parties may submit claims; indirect purchaser standing available
Greece[c, mm]	15% of worldwide turnover preceding financial year	€150,000 or €300,000 (recidivist)	5 years	Not Applicable	Private actions available; follow-on actions available but uncommon; class actions not available
Hungary[a, c, n]	10% of the turnover of preceding financial year[a, c]	Not Applicable	5 years	5 years Applicable Automatic two year debarment for executive officers ruled unconstitutional	Private actions available; follow-on actions
Ireland[a, c, d, o]	Greater of: (1) €4 mil. or (2) 10% of turnover	Greater of: (1) €4 mil. or (2) 10% of turnover	2 years	Not Applicable	Private actions available; follow-on actions available; class actions not available

Jurisdiction	Maximum Fines Companies	Maximum Fines for Individuals	Maximum Prison Term	Debarment	Private Action
Italy[a, c, q]	Fine amount depends on gravity and duration of violation, but no more than 10% of the turnover for each entity during prior financial year from the products forming the subject matter of agreement	Not Applicable	Not Applicable	Not Applicable	Private actions available; follow-on actions available; class action available to consumers only[q] (law amended in 2009 take effect in 2010)
Latvia[c, nn]	10% of the turnover of preceding financial year; not less than €350 for vertical agreements/ €750 horizontal agreements	Not Applicable Fine not exceeding 100× minimum daily wage for failure to comply with decisions	Not Applicable 2 years for failure to comply with lawful demands	Not Applicable 5 years deprivation of right to engage in business activity for failure to comply with lawful demands with 2 year minimum	Private actions available; follow-on actions available when failure to conform with decision; class actions available but rare
Lithuania[c, oo]	10% of gross annual income of preceding financial year	Not Applicable	Not Applicable	Not Applicable	Private actions available but not typical; follow-on actions available but not typical; class actions not available
Luxembourg[c, pp]	10% of highest worldwide turnover realized during preceding financial year during which conduct occurred	Not Applicable	Not Applicable	Not Applicable	Private actions available; follow-on actions available but rare; class actions not available
Malt[ac]	10% of worldwide turnover	10% of world-wide turnover of company	Not Applicable	Not Applicable	Private action available; follow-on actions available; class actions available
Netherlands[a, b, c, d, u]	May not exceed (1) €450,000 or (2) 10% of total worldwide turnover	Administrative: €450,000	Not Applicable	Not Applicable	Private actions available in principle; settlements brought by a group of claimant can be made binding by the courts; indirect purchaser standing available

Continued on next page

VII. APPENDIX *(continued)*

Jurisdiction	Maximum Fines Companies	Maximum Fines for Individuals	Maximum Prison Term	Debarment	Private Action
Poland[a, c, d, w]	Up to 10% of the revenue earned in the preceding accounting year; or, where there is no revenue, fine up to 200 times the average salary	Not Applicable	Not Applicable	Not Applicable	Private actions available; follow-on actions not available; class actions not available
Portugal[c, qq]	10% of turnover in Portugal during previous year	10% of turn-over in Portugal during previous year, subject to special reduction	Not Applicable	Not Applicable	Private actions available; no significant experience with follow-up actions or class actions
Romania[c, rr]	10% of the aggregate turnover of the under taking involved for the preceding financial year	Fines available	4 years	Not Applicable	Private actions available; follow-on actions rare; class actions not available
Slovakia[c, ss]	(1) 10% of the turnover of the undertaking generated in the preceding financial year or (2) €330,000	(1) 10% of the turnover of the undertaking generated in the preceding financial year or (2) €330,000	Not Applicable	Not Applicable	Private actions and follow-on actions available, but rare; class actions not available, but court may join proceedings
Slovenia[c, tt]	10% of the turnover realized the preceding financial year	€30,000	5 years	5 year prohibition from performing occupation	Private actions available; follow-on actions available; class actions not available, but claims may be consolidated
Spain[a, c, y]	Up to 10% of total turnover for the fiscal year preceding the Tribunal's decision	€60,000	Not Applicable	Not Applicable	Private actions available; follow-on actions available class actions in principle not available

Jurisdiction	Maximum Fines Companies	Maximum Fines for Individuals	Maximum Prison Term	Debarment	Private Action
Sweden[a, c, d, aa]	If infringement is intentional or negligent, fine up to 10% of annual turnover	Not Applicable	Not Applicable	Disqualification Orders	Private actions available; follow-on actions available; class actions available
United Kingdom[a,c,d,dd,uu]	10% of total worldwide turnover	Magistrate Court: £5,000 Crown Court: Unlimited	5 years	Competition Disqualification Orders	Private actions available before the Competition Appeals Tribunal (follow-on only) and civil courts representative actions available before specified bodies; indirect purchaser standing available.
Non-European Union Members					
Norway[a, c, d, v]	Fines available up to 10% of worldwide turnover; penalty payments can be imposed while violation persists	Not Applicable	6 years	Not Applicable	Not Applicable
Russia[c, d, x]	15% of company's turnover in market where violation occurred; fine must be at least RUR 100,00 (~$3,400)	1 million rubles or a fine amounting to the convicted person's salary for up to five years	7 years	Prohibition	Not Applicable
Switzerland[a, c, d, bb]	Up to 10% of the three previous years' turnover realized in Switzerland	CHF 100,000	Not Applicable	Not Applicable	Private action available, but not typical; class actions not available
Turkey[a, c, cc]	Fines at least TRL 200 million and up to 10% of the gross income in the prior fiscal year	5% of the fine imposed on the legal entity	Not Applicable	Not Applicable	Private actions available; follow-on actions available; treble damages

Continued on next page

VII. APPENDIX *(continued)*

Jurisdiction	Maximum Fines Companies	Maximum Fines for Individuals	Maximum Prison Term	Debarment	Private Action
			Asia		
Japan[a, d, r]	Administrative surcharge up to 10% of cumulative sales forming the subject of the agreement for the duration of the agreement, up to 3 years; fine up to ¥ 500 million	¥ 500 million	5 years	Not Applicable	Private actions available; follow-on actions available
Korea[a, d, s]	Surcharge up to 10% of the turnover of the relevant product during the relevant period; where there is no revenue, up to KRW 1 billion	If individual engages in cartel activity after agency referral to prosecutor's office, fine up to KRW 200 million	3 years	Not Applicable	Private actions available, no discovery
			Oceana		
Australia[a, b, d]	Greater of (1) AUS $10 million (~ €5 million); (2) if court can determine value of cartel gains attributable to the act or omission then three times the value of that benefit; or (3) if court cannot determine the value of the benefit then 10% of total world-wide turnover during year prior to infringement	Administrative: AUS $500,000 (€251,710) Criminal: AUS $220,000	10 years	Director Disqualification Orders	Class actions and representative actions by the ACCC; private parties may opt-out to pursue own claims;
New Zealand[a, d, vv]	The greater of NZ$ 10,000,000, 10% of corporate turnover, or if court can determine value of cartel gains attributable to the act or omission then three times the value of that benefit	NZ$ 500,000; indemnification is prohibited	Not Applicable	Not Applicable	Private actions available; representative actions available

Jurisdiction	Maximum Fines Companies	Maximum Fines for Individuals	Maximum Prison Term	Debarment	Private Action
			Middle East		
Israel[p, d]	ISL 4 million (~ €700,000) plus ISL 26,000 (~ €4,800) for each day offense persists	ISL 2 million (~ €350,000) plus ISL 13,000 (~ €2,400) for each day offense persists	3 years; 5 years if substantial damage	Not Applicable	Private actions available, class actions available
			Africa		
South Africa[d, z]	No more than 10% of turn-over in South Africa and the firm's exports from South Africa in the preceding year	R 500,000 (proposed)	10 years (proposed)	Proposed Legislation	Not Applicable
			South America		
Chile[g, d]	Up to 30,000 annual tax units (~ US $27 million)	Up to 30,000 annual tax units (~ US $27 million)	Not Applicable	Not Applicable	Private follow-on actions available; class actions possibly available
			North America		
Canada[a, d, e]	Up to CAD 25 million per count (as of March 2010)	CAD 25 million per count	14 years	Not Applicable	Private actions available; class actions available
Mexico[a, d, ff, t]	1.5 million times the minimum general wage prevailing in Mexico City (~ US $6.5 million) for serious offenses, up to 10% of annual sales or 10% of assets whichever is greater	7,500 times the minimum general wage prevailing in Mexico city (~ US $ 30,000)	Not Applicable	Not Applicable	Private follow-on action available

Continued on next page

Jurisdiction	Maximum Fines Companies	Maximum Fines for Individuals	Maximum Prison Term	Debarment	Private Action
United States[a,b, d, ee]	(1) $100 million (~ €76 million), or (2) if authorized by alternative sentencing statute, fines up to twice the gain derived from the criminal conduct or twice the loss suffered by the victims	Criminal: (1) $1 million (€779,277), or (2) twice the gain/ harm	10 years	Not Applicable	Class actions available; private parties may opt-out to pursue own claims; Cartelist faces joint and several liability; treble damages in the event of judgment; indirect purchaser standing not available

Appendix Sources:

a Organisation for Economic Co-operation and Development (OECD), Fighting Hard Core Cartels: Harm, Effective Sanctions and Leniency Programmes (2002), *available at* http://www.oecd.org/dataoecd/41/44/1841891.pdf.

b Office of Fair Trading, An Assessment of Discretionary Penalties Regimes (2009), *available at* http://www.oft.gov.uk/shared_oft/economic_research/oft1132.pdf.

c Antitrust Encyclopedia, *available at* http://www.concurrences.com/rubrique.php3?id_rubrique=512 (last visited April 29, 2010).

d Scott D. Hammond, Deputy Assistant Att'y Gen. for Crim.. Enforcement, Antitrust Div., Dep't of Justice, Presentation at The 24th Annual National Institute on White Collar Crime (Feb. 25, 2010), *available at* http://www.justice.gov/atr/public/speeches/255515.htm.

e Brett Bolton & Kate Williams, *Australia, in* The International Comparative Legal Guide to: Cartels & Leniency 14–21 (2010), *available at* http://www.iclg.co.uk/khadmin/Publications/pdf/3380.pdf

f Barry Zalmanowitz & Susan Paul, *Canada, in* The International Comparative Legal Guide to: Cartels & Leniency 44–49 (2010), *available at* http://www.iclg.co.uk/khadmin/Publications/pdf/3380.pdf.

g José Manuel Bustamante & Nicholas Mocarquer, *Chile, in* The International Comparative Legal Guide to: Cartels & Leniency 50–54 (2010), *available at* http://www.iclg.co.uk/khadmin/Publications/pdf/3380.pdf

h Arthur Braun & Dagmar Bickova, *Czech Republic, in* The International Comparative Legal Guide to: Cartels & Leniency 65–69 (2010), *available at* http://www.iclg.co.uk/khadmin/Publications/pdf/3380.pdf.

i Christian Karhula Lauridsen & Gitte Holtsø, *Denmark, in* The International Comparative Legal Guide to: Cartels & Leniency 70–73 (2010), *available at* http://www.iclg.co.uk/khadmin/Publications/pdf/3380.pdf.

j Simon Holmes & Philipp Girardet, *European Commission, in* The International Comparative Legal Guide to: Cartels & Leniency 83–91 (2010), *available at* http://www.iclg.co.uk/khadmin/Publications/pdf/3380.pdf.

k Natasha Assadi-Tardif & Delphine Cohen, *France, in* The International Comparative Legal Guide to: Cartels & Leniency 98–104 (2010), *available at* http://www.iclg.co.uk/khadmin/Publications/pdf/3380.pdf.

l Natasha G. Assadi-Tardiff & Marc Levy, *France: Cartel Regulations, in* The Eur. Antitrust Rev. 2010, *available at* http://www.globalcompetitionreview.com/reviews/19/sections/ 69/chapters/754/ france-cartels/.

m Alexander Rinne & Tilman Siebert, *Germany, in* The International Comparative Legal Guide to: Cartels & Leniency 105–110 (2010), *available at* http://www.iclg.co.uk/khadmin/Publications/pdf/3380.pdf.

n Judit Budai & Miklos Boronkay, *Hungary, in* The International Comparative Legal Guide to: Cartels & Leniency 117–123 (2010), *available at* http://www.iclg.co.uk/khadmin/Publications/pdf/3380.pdf.

o David Hourihane, *Ireland, in* The International Comparative Legal Guide to: Cartels & Leniency 128–133 (2010), *available at* http://www.iclg.co.uk/khadmin/Publications/pdf/3380.pdf.

p Michal Halperin & Yuval Sasson , *Israel, in* The International Comparative Legal Guide to: Cartels & Leniency 113–118 (2009), *available at* http://www.meitar.com/files/downloads/cartels and leniency2009.pdf.

q Mario Siragusa & Cesare Rizza , *Italy, in* The International Comparative Legal Guide to: Cartels & Leniency 134–141 (2010), *available at* http://www.iclg.co.uk/khadmin/Publications/pdf/3380.pdf.

r Erika Wantanabe, *Japan, in* The International Comparative Legal Guide to: Cartels & Leniency 142–148 (2010), *available at* http://www.noandt.com/publications/pdf/ICLG_Cartels2010_Japan.pdf.

s Sung Born Park & Paul S. Rhee, *Korea, in* The International Comparative Legal Guide to: Cartels & Leniency 149–154 (2010), *available at* http://www.iclg.co.uk/khadmin/Publications/pdf/3380.pdf.

t Jorge A. Sanchez-Davila, *Mexico, in* The International Comparative Legal Guide to: Cartels & Leniency 172–177 (2010), *available at* http://www.iclg.co.uk/khadmin/Publications/pdf/3380.pdf.

u M.J. van Joolingen & S.M.M.C. Vinken, *Netherlands, in* The International Comparative Legal Guide to: Cartels & Leniency 178–182 (2010), *available at* http://www.iclg.co.uk/khadmin/Publications/pdf/3356.pdf.

v Olav Kolstad & Henrik Svane, *Norway, in* The International Comparative Legal Guide to: Cartels & Leniency 183–188 (2010), *available at* http://www.iclg.co.uk/khadmin/Publications/pdf/3380.pdf.

w Aleksander Stawicki & Bartosz Turno, *Poland, in* The International Comparative Legal Guide to: Cartels & Leniency 189–194 (2010), *available at* http://www.iclg.co.uk/khadmin/Publications/pdf/3380.pdf.

x Anna Numerova & Vassily Rudomino, *Russia, in* The International Comparative Legal Guide to: Cartels & Leniency 208–212 (2010), *available at* http://www.iclg.co.uk/khadmin/Publications/pdf/3380.pdf.

y Ramon Garcia-Gallardo Gil-Fournier & Manuel Bermudez Caballero, *Spain, in* The International Comparative Legal Guide to: Cartels & Leniency 230–237 (2010), *available at* http://www.iclg.co.uk/khadmin/Publications/pdf/3380.pdf.

z Daryl Dingley & Martin Versfeld, *South Africa, in* The International Comparative Legal Guide to: Cartels & Leniency 224–229 (2010), *available at* http://www.iclg.co.uk/khadmin/Publications/pdf/3380.pdf.

aa Eva-Maj Muhlenbock & Martin Karlsson, *Sweden, in* The International Comparative Legal Guide to: Cartels & Leniency 238–243 (2010), *available at* http://www.iclg.co.uk/ khadmin/Publications/pdf/3380.pdf.

bb Jurg Borer & Michael Vleck, *Switzerland, in* The International Comparative Legal Guide to: Cartels & Leniency 244–249 (2010), *available at* http://www.iclg.co.uk/khadmin/Publications/pdf/3380.pdf.

cc Gonenc Gurkaynak, *Turkey, in* The International Comparative Legal Guide to: Cartels & Leniency 250–256 (2010), *available at* http://www.iclg.co.uk/khadmin/Publications/pdf/3380.pdf.

dd Simon Holmes & Philipp Girardet, *United Kingdom, in* The International Comparative Legal Guide to: Cartels & Leniency 257–264 (2010), *available at* http://www.iclg.co.uk/khadmin/Publications/pdf/3380.pdf.

ee Ray V. Hartwell, III & David Higbee, *USA, in* The International Comparative Legal Guide to: Cartels & Leniency 265–272 (2010), *available at* http://www.iclg.co.uk/khadmin/Publications/pdf/3380.pdf.

ff Jens Erik Gould & Crayton Harrison, *Mexico's Calderon Seeks Stronger Antitrust Law, Fines*, Bloomberg Businessweek, April 5, 2010, *available at* http://www.businessweek.com/news/2010-04-05/mexico-s-calderon-seeks-stronger-antitrust-law-fines-update1-.html.

gg Dieter Hauck & Esther Hold, *Austria, in* The International Comparative Legal Guide to: Cartels & Leniency 22–26 (2010), *available at* http://www.iclg.co.uk/khadmin/Publications/pdf/3380.pdf.

hh Jules Sturck & An-Marie Vandromme, *Belgium, in* The International Comparative Legal Guide to: Cartels & Leniency 27–32 (2010), *available at* http://www.iclg.co.uk/khadmin/Publications/pdf/3380.pdf.

ii Vladimir Penkov & Svetlin Adrianov, *Bulgaria, in* The International Comparative Legal Guide to: Cartels & Leniency 38–43 (2010), *available at* http://www.iclg.co.uk/khadmin/Publications/pdf/3380.pdf.

jj Olga Georgiades, *Cyprus, in* The International Comparative Legal Guide to: Cartels & Leniency 60–64 (2010), *available at* http://www.iclg.co.uk/khadmin/Publications/pdf/3380.pdf.

kk Ants Mailend & Valdo Poldoja, *Estonia, in* The International Comparative Legal Guide to: Cartels & Leniency 74–82 (2010), *available at* http://www.iclg.co.uk/khadmin/Publications/pdf/3380.pdf.

ll Iikka Leppihalme, *Finland, in* The International Comparative Legal Guide to: Cartels & Leniency 92–97 (2010), *available at* http://www.iclg.co.uk/khadmin/Publications/pdf/3380.pdf.

mm Stamatis Drakakakis, *Greece, in* The International Comparative Legal Guide to: Cartels & Leniency 111–116 (2010), *available at* http://www.iclg.co.uk/khadmin/Publications/pdf/3380.pdf.

nn Liga Mence & Janis Loze, *Latvia, in* The International Comparative Legal Guide to: Cartels & Leniency 155–160 (2010), *available at* http://www.iclg.co.uk/khadmin/Publications/pdf/3380.pdf.

oo Lina Daruliene & Andrius Bambalas, *Lithuania, in* The International Comparative Legal Guide to: Cartels & Leniency 161–166 (2010), *available at* http://www.iclg.co.uk/khadmin/Publications/pdf/3380.pdf

pp Patrick Santer & Leon Gloden, *Luxembourg, in* The International Comparative Legal Guide to: Cartels & Leniency 167–171 (2010), *available at* http://www.iclg.co.uk/khadmin/Publications/pdf/3380.pdf.

qq Mario Marques Mendes & Pedrio Vilarinho Pires, *Portugal, in* The International Comparative Legal Guide to: Cartels & Leniency 195–201 (2010), *available at* http://www.iclg.co.uk/khadmin/Publications/pdf/3380.pdf.

rr Ramona Lie & Cristina Voevodschi, *Romania, in* The International Comparative Legal Guide to: Cartels & Leniency 202–207 (2010), *available at* http://www.iclg.co.uk/khadmin/Publications/pdf/3380.pdf.

ss Alena Cernajova & Juraj Steinecker, *Slovakia, in* The International Comparative Legal Guide to: Cartels & Leniency 213–217 (2010), *available at* http://www.iclg.co.uk/khadmin/Publications/pdf/3380.pdf.

tt Natasa Pipan Nahtigal & Ziva Juznic, *Slovenia, in* The International Comparative Legal Guide to: Cartels & Leniency 218–223 (2010), *available at* http://www.iclg.co.uk/khadmin/Publications/pdf/3380.pdf.

uu ABA, Antitrust Law Developments, vol. I (6th ed. 2007).

vv Phil Taylor, Simon Ladd & David Blacktop, *New Zealand, in* Private Antitrust Litigation, 116–120 (2009), *available at* http://www.bellgully.com/resources/pdfs/Private_Antitrust_Litigation09.pdf.

INTERVIEW:
UPDATE ON "ANTITRUST CRIMINAL SANCTIONS: THE EVOLUTION OF EXECUTIVE PUNISHMENT"

Scan our QR code with your mobile device to listen to the recorded interview. Note: you must have a scanner app or installed software to read the QR code.

As part of our Spring 2012 issue, CPI is presenting a retrospective of our best articles in the past and providing updates. One of our selections is "Antitrust Criminal Sanctions: The Evolution of Executive Punishment," originally appearing in the Fall 2010 issue of the Journal. With me today is the author, Donald Klawiter.

Don is a partner in the Antitrust and Trade Regulation practice group of Sheppard Mullin's DC office. His practice focuses on international cartel investigations and litigation. Don has defended corporations and executives from around the world in a number of different sectors. He chaired the ABA's Section of Antitrust Law from 2005 to 2006, and he is the current chair of the Section's International Cartel Task Force.

In your article, you write that, "the clear enforcement trend in the United States in its fight against cartels is to focus on punishing the defendant executive." You note that this trend can also be observed in the U.K., Australia, Brazil, Canada, and Japan. What can you say about how this trend has developed in the two years since the article was published?

One of the interesting things is that the trend has actually been developed further in the United States in those past two years, and before getting to the other countries, let me just make a quick comment about that. In 2011, with the first of the cases involving the auto parts industry, the Department of Justice has actually increased the prison terms that it has recommended for executives who are defendants in various cases. It's interesting because, until that time, the prison sentences for executives who are outside the United States and had to subject themselves to the jurisdiction of the United States in order to be convicted, those individuals always had a lower sentence than someone who was resident in the United States would have. In recent years, that has been in the range of six to eight months, for the most part. With the newest cases within the last year, the Antitrust Division has actually gotten sentences that are much higher, beginning at a year and a day and going to a range of about two years. This basically puts the non-U.S. executives in a similar range of sentences as the U.S. resident executives, and that is a major change and development in United States antitrust enforcement.

This basically puts the non-U.S. executives in a similar range of sentences as the U.S. resident executives, and that is a major change and development in United States antitrust enforcement

As to the other countries, there has been much interest in all of the jurisdictions you mentioned in pursuing criminal cases. The United Kingdom was very successful in the first case it pursued, and it did it in conjunction with the Antitrust Division of the United States Department of Justice. By having individuals convicted in both the U.K. and in the U.S. and having comparable prison sentences for them, they would only have to serve one of the prison sentences, but it had to be of similar duration to the U.S. sentence in order for the U.S. to sign off on a U.K. prison sentence. That was the *Marine Hose* case. It is interesting to note that since that case, and the great success of it, the U.K. has been stalled in terms of bringing further cases. The one that they brought, involving the airline industry, and British Airways executives in particular, actually went to trial and the case had to be dismissed early in the trial for lack of evidence and other procedural issues. So that was not a great success at all, but the U.K. vows that they will continue to bring these cases as criminal prosecutions.

Canada is an interesting example as well. There is new legislation in Canada which actually made conviction for an antitrust criminal case easier than it had been. There had been a standard known as "undueness" that the Canadian law required, and that standard has been repealed now, and the prosecution standard in Canada is quite similar to that in the U.S.

Brazil is another jurisdiction that has moved to increased use of criminal penalties and bringing cases as criminal cases. It's been slow in coming, but they are certainly committed to significant criminal cases in the future.

Japan, similarly, has opened several investigations, and noted that they were criminal investigations, but we haven't seen the outcome of those yet. Time will tell whether that is an enforcement trend in Japan, and in other places.

Would you be able to speak more on the tension between leniency and imprisonment? Do you think they can work together as complementary tools of enforcement?

I think leniency and prison are the carrot and stick of antitrust enforcement. It was very interesting in the 1990s—and this was not imprisonment, but it was higher fines—but the leniency policy that was implemented by the U.S. Department of Justice in 1993 took a few years to become popular and be used by companies and individuals, in part because until 1996 or so, the penalties were lower than they are today.

For example, on the side of the fines, the highest fine the U.S. recommended to a court before 1996 with the ADM case was a fine of $10 million. Companies did not seem to think of that as a high number, and hence there were very few people who felt motivated to come in and obtain leniency because they would take their chances with the current system. After the fine level went up to $100 million and higher with the ADM case, we saw a flurry of companies going in for leniency, and I think the same principle applies to individual leniency. Individuals, if they see the likelihood that they would spend one, two, or three years in jail, they would be more likely to go in and try to get leniency. Similarly, companies would go in on behalf of the company itself and its executives, and the executives who cooperate with the leniency program would receive a free pass and would not go to jail, and that is certainly a big deal. So I think the two are very complementary and work well together on the enforcement side. The penalties over the past ten years have gotten higher both for corporations and for individuals, and I think that has really fueled the leniency program and made it so successful.

You cite to Doug Ginsburg and Josh Wright's article, "Antitrust Sanctions," which actually appears in the same issue of the Journal as your article. Ginsburg and Wright call for not just imprisonment as a deterrent, but they also endorse debarment. What are your thoughts on this? Does debarment go too far if the carve out designation is also a significant deterrent, especially for non-U.S. executives?

I think that's exactly right. I think that in the United States, as I mentioned in the section of the paper entitled "Maintaining Employment is Very Difficult," that in the United States, by virtue of the Sarbanes-Oxley legislation of several years ago, in the midst of a lot of corporate misconduct, it has become very, very difficult for an executive in the United States to keep his job if he is convicted of a violation of the antitrust laws or even if he is carved out, as part of the company's plea agreement. So I think that that issue, with respect to U.S. companies and U.S. citizens, pretty much takes care of itself without the need for a separate debarment procedure.

With respect to other countries, there is no trend that is yet formed, in terms of either terminating people or keeping them on. In many countries, there is still a culture that they would keep the individuals on after they serve their sentence. That is largely the rationale in many of the Asian countries that we're seeing with companies under prosecution right now. But I think the simple fact is it would be hard to reach those companies under U.S. law if the individuals and the corporations are outside the United States. But I think that in those situations, especially if you are talking about not a conviction, but a carve out, that that carve out has no impact other than to say that the Department of Justice lawyers believe that that individual is subject to prosecution or could be prosecuted. Many of the individuals on the carve out list are never prosecuted, and if they are subject to debarment without any court proceeding to find them guilty or not guilty, that, I think, would be a serious violation of due process.

Many of the individuals on the carve out list are never prosecuted, and if they are subject to debarment without any court proceeding to find them guilty or not guilty, that, I think, would be a serious violation of due process

So I think we should keep thinking and talking about what the penalties are, and whether debarment is a good step or a necessary step, but I think as to the U.S. citizens, Sarbanes-Oxley and the general corporate environment take care of that already. That's probably the extent of the reach of U.S. antitrust law for U.S. companies and U.S. citizens, and that's just the situation.

You highlight the role compliance programs must play in informing executives of criminal behavior and penalties. What is your idea of an ideal compliance program that is fully transparent and communicative?

I think, as I noted in the article, that most companies still do not do compliance programs very well. Some are terrific, but most will focus on what I refer to as "reading people the Ten Commandments"—you shall not fix prices, you shall not rig bids, that sort of approach; or, just giving out a written statement to people or asking them to do a little compliance training on the computer. I don't think any of those give the individual any indication of what it is like to face questions about whether you are colluding with a competitor, whether you're fixing prices, or whether you're coordinating anything with a competitor.

most companies still do not do compliance programs very well

So being prepared for the investigation is, I think, akin to being prepared for a fire in any major building, where there would be specific things you need to know in order to keep yourself safe

What we like to do is to have a very intensive session, especially with the senior management of the company, and we try to do four different things:

The first is to work through a series of case studies of conduct where you're in a situation and here's what a competitor says, here's what you say, here's what happens: are you violating the antitrust laws? Those are much more nuanced, they are much more focused, and we are told by many of the executives who sit through them that it is much more of a real-life situation where they can see where something they may think is not at all a problem turns out to be a criminal violation of the antitrust laws. So, that's number one, and that's really the focus of the compliance program.

The second thing we do is we actually take people through the different things that will happen during the course of an antitrust investigation, particularly looking at things like a dawn raid, a drop-by visit by the FBI to an executive's home—which is a common occurrence in the U.S.—being stopped at the border if you're a non-U.S. citizen and asked questions about the investigation, those sorts of things, so that executives know that if there is an investigation, this will happen, and they should not panic. And, most importantly, they should not lie to the officials because that can only cause them greater trouble in the future. So being prepared for the investigation is, I think, akin to being prepared for a fire in any major building, where there would be specific things you need to know in order to keep yourself safe. I think that that is true in training people on how to deal with an investigation.

The third one is to talk to people about using certain words and phrases that typically end up being important words and phrases in antitrust cases. The fact that people are talking about "coordinating," they're talking about "respecting each other's customers," they're talking about "collaboration" of one kind or another, but they are all things that, at the end of the day, will create words and phrases that not only are suspicious to the Department of Justice, but in this era of electronic discovery, are key words that will be searched to determine if people are using them and then to read into those words some more nefarious meanings. So it's good for people to learn to communicate with each other in a way that does not use those words or phrases and thus would get them in trouble if they tended to communicate that way. Emails are a notorious problem because people write what they would normally say—they don't think about it, they don't edit, and there are often things in emails that would come back to haunt people in a criminal antitrust investigation.

And finally, the last part of what we do is explain the context of how the Antitrust Division, the European Commission, and other agencies around the world work. There are criminal fines for corporations, there is imprisonment, and we essentially make them familiar with what they may occasionally read in the *Wall Street Journal* but with which they may not understand fully what is going on. We give them a little more perspective on what the government is looking to investigate, and how, so they know that if they do have a problem, they can come back to the company and bring it to the company's attention and be saved or exempted from prosecution because they would probably, in that instance, be the leniency candidate.

Procedures of that kind are very, very important so they know where to report, who to talk to, who to discuss these matters with—either within the company or with outside counsel—so we see compliance as really being very comprehensive and taking more than one or two hours. It is really something where you need to sit down and work through these issues and get input from the executives. But most importantly, a corporation should know what is legal and illegal and how to deal with investigations when they come. We found that to be a very effective means of training people and keeping them out of harm's way.

Don, thank you so much for this update, and for sharing your insights into antitrust penalties, deterrence, and compliance. This has been a terrific discussion.

ANTITRUST CRIMINAL SANCTIONS: THE EVOLUTION OF EXECUTIVE PUNISHMENT

Donald C. Klawiter *

ABSTRACT

Judge Douglas H. Ginsburg and Professor Joshua D. Wright's excellent study of antitrust sanctions for corporations and individuals concludes with a strong recommendation that individual penalties, specifically incarceration, will be the most appropriate and effective penalties for antitrust violations.[1] *This article will analyze the punishment of defendant executives as it has evolved during the era of international cartel enforcement (1995 to 2010) and will conclude that, although it was slow to get there, the current enforcement policy and practice focuses much more directly on the defendant executive that if ever has and is approaching the Ginsburg-Wright model as the major deterrence factor. The article also argues that both the Antitrust Division and corporate compliance training must inform the corporate executives much more effectively of the harsh penalties executives will face if they violate the law. Finally, the article reviews several activities that may cause defendant executives greater risk during an antitrust investigation and provides important advice to the executives, counsel, and board members to navigate around those serious risks.*

I. INTRODUCTION

Despite the continuing assessment of huge corporate fines, and the seeming competition between the United States and the European Commission to achieve the highest corporate fines, the clear enforcement trend in the United States in its fight against cartels is to focus on punishing the defendant executive. There are strong proponents for this trend: Senior enforcement

---

* Donald C. Klawiter is a partner in the Antitrust Practice Group at Sheppard Mullin Richter & Hampton LLP's Washington, D.C. office. His practice focuses on antitrust investigations, litigation, and compliance, with special emphasis on defending corporations, senior corporate executives and corporate boards in international cartel criminal investigations and antitrust damage cases.

[1] Douglas H. Ginsburg & Joshua D.Wright, Antitrust Sanctions, 6(2) Competition Pol'y Int'l, (Autumn 2010).

officials at the Antitrust Division of the U.S. Department of Justice have long argued that incarceration for senior executives is the greatest deterrent to antitrust violations. More specifically, Judge Douglas H. Ginsburg and Professor Joshua D. Wright's excellent study of antitrust sanctions for corporations and individuals, included elsewhere in this journal, presents a strong recommendation that jail sentences for defendant executives are the most appropriate and effective penalties for antitrust violations.[2] The increased focus on the defendant executive also raises a number of problems that will keep company counsel, as well as targeted executives and their independent counsel, awake at night.

Thus began the era when the shock and trauma of $100 million corporate fines became the rule and, for the next fifteen years, the calculation of $100 million fines became the essential boast of the Antitrust Division utilizing graphs and charts to display the success of the Division's program, including $1 billion in corporate fines in 2009

The shift to focusing more intensively on the actions of the defendant executive, not only in the United States, but also in the United Kingdom, Australia, Brazil, Canada, and Japan, is creating greater risks and will require more intensive and sophisticated compliance training. The identification of these issues provides the opportunity to limit the risk that the defendant executive may face by being implicated in a cartel enforcement action.

The United States has, in fact, been moving slowly but consistently in the direction that Judge Ginsburg and Professor Wright suggest with respect to executives, although the enforcers continue to pursue steadfastly the corporate monetary penalties that Judge Ginsburg and Professor Wright would challenge and eliminate. Over the past fifteen years, corporate fines have increased dramatically. With the first of the blockbuster corporate fines of the international cartel era, the $100 million Archer-Daniels-Midland ("ADM") fine, the Antitrust Division shifted its corporate fine methodology completely away from the old standard of a $10 million statutory maximum and, in effect, warned that the $100 million fine would be far more common than the $10 million one.[3] Thus began the era when the shock and trauma of $100 million corporate fines became the rule and, for the next fifteen years, the calculation of $100 million fines became the essential boast of the Antitrust Division utilizing graphs and charts to display the success of the Division's program, including $1 billion in corporate fines in 2009.[4]

[2] *Id.*

[3] United States v. Archer-Daniels-Midland, CR No. 96-CR-00640 (N.D.Il, October 15, 1996).

[4] According to the Antitrust Division's fine chart, 18 companies have been fined $100 million or more and 57 have been fined between $10 million and $100 million.

II. THE DEVELOPMENT OF THE ANTITRUST DIVISION'S CRIMINAL PENALTIES FOR DEFENDANT EXECUTIVES

This problem was highlighted by the utter disaster of the industrial diamonds case, where the Division could not gain jurisdiction over its defendants and its witnesses

It has taken a very long time for the incarceration of corporate executives, especially corporate executives from outside the United States, to become the standard penalty for antitrust misconduct. The Sherman Act was a criminal statute from the outset and individuals were prosecuted from the earliest days of the law when Sherman Act violations were criminal misdemeanors. In 1921, four contractors were first sentenced to jail—but only for a total of ten months. The next jail sentences—90 days—came in the hand tool investigation in 1959. They were followed by the great electrical equipment conspiracy cases where seven executives were sentenced to two to six months each, still under the misdemeanor statute.[5] When the Sherman Act was made a felony in 1974—and the maximum prison sentence was increased to three years—the Antitrust Division still had very limited success in convincing judges to send convicted antitrust felons to jail, even for a few months. It was only with the creation of the U.S. Sentencing Commission in 1984 and the implementation of the Sentencing Guidelines in 1987 that a consistent and transparent process of calculating antitrust sentences for executives emerged. Even with the Guidelines, however, only 37 percent of convicted antitrust felons served any jail time during the 1990s. That was certainly not the type of deterrence that Judge Ginsburg and Professor Wright are contemplating in their analysis.

As the cartel enforcement program became more targeted on global cartels, not simply U.S. cartels, the use of imprisonment as a powerful deterrent began to develop—although it did not develop quickly. In the early 1990s, the Antitrust Division had the interest and the resolve to tackle international cartels, but it did not have the ability to obtain the evidence of witnesses outside the United States. This problem was highlighted by the utter disaster of the industrial diamonds case, where the Division could not gain jurisdiction over its defendants and its witnesses. The Court dismissed the ill-fated case at the close of the government's case. This was, indeed, a major setback to the Division's enforcement program.[6] After the trial, the Antitrust Division analyzed its mistakes and developed a strategy to obtain the evidence it needed in international cartel cases.

---

[5] *See generally* Donald C. Klawiter & Jennifer M. Driscoll, Sentencing Individuals In Antitrust Cases, 23 ANTITRUST MAG. 75 (Spring 2009). For a more detailed history of criminal sentencing, see Gregory J. Werden, Sanctioning Cartel Activity: Let the Punishment Fit the Crime, Eur. Competition J. (2009), *available at* http://www.usdoj.gov/atr/public/articles/240611.htm.

[6] United States v. General Electric Co., No CR-2-94-019 (S.D. OH, Feb. 17, 1994).

A. 1996—Non-U.S. Executives Do Not Go to Jail

With the guarantee of no jail and a friendly immigration decision, many non-U.S. executives took on the mantle of cooperating witnesses and helped the Division build a strong record of enforcement success

In the aftermath of the industrial diamonds case, the Division opened a substantial number of international cartel investigations. The focus was clearly on criminally charging large corporations with substantial volumes of commerce in the United States and assessing huge corporate fines. This is obviously not consistent with the Ginsburg-Wright thesis which asserts both that prison sentences are the strongest deterrent and that high fines for corporations have little deterrent effect, inasmuch as high fines punish the shareholders and consumers. The Division, however, did not have the luxury of compelling witnesses and documents from the rest of the world. The Division at this time had to focus on obtaining the evidence from the non-U.S. executives and, as a result, had to offer them more lenient treatment. Except for the three ADM executives—all U.S. citizens—who were indicted, went to trial, and were convicted, non-U.S. corporate executives took advantage of an Antitrust Division policy that encouraged their cooperation.

Non-U.S. executives who cooperated with the Division were required to surrender to U.S. jurisdiction, plead guilty to a felony, and pay an individual fine. For their cooperation, often against the U.S. executives with whom they conspired to fix prices, they were given no-jail deals and their immigration status as felons was pre-adjudicated so they could travel to the United States freely even though they were convicted of a felony. This was, indeed, an excellent deal for the globetrotting non-U.S. executives, and it provided the necessary incentives to persuade reluctant executives to surrender to U.S. authorities and cooperate fully. With the guarantee of no jail and a friendly immigration decision, many non-U.S. executives took on the mantle of cooperating witnesses and helped the Division build a strong record of enforcement success.

As time went on, however, there were serious inequalities in the sentences different executives received. In the graphite electrode case, the non-U.S. chief executive, who created and operated the cartel with his U.S. chief executive counterpart, pled guilty, was assessed a significant fine that was paid by the company, and received an immigration "all clear." Meanwhile, his counterpart, who lived in the United States, was sentenced to seventeen months incarceration and fined $1.25 million that, by statute, he had to pay out of his own resources. This is the starkest example of the sentencing disparities caused by this otherwise brilliant idea of motivating non-U.S. defendants to cooperate with the U.S. investigation. The no jail policy got the international cartel enforcement program off to a strong start in the United States by building strong cases quickly.

B. 1998—The New Leniency Policy Takes Hold

The Division could now say it did not need the non-U.S. executive as critically as it needed him in 1996, thus the need for the generous no jail plea agreements decreased in importance and the Division became much more aggressive with non-U.S. executives

The perfect complement to the no jail policy was the new U.S. leniency program. Announced in August 1993, the program expanded the opportunity to obtain leniency by making leniency available after an investigation had started, assuming that the Antitrust Division did not yet have sufficient evidence to establish a case.[7] While it is hard to believe today, the 1993 leniency policy was slow to gain traction. It was only after the dramatic announcement of the $100 million fine assessed on ADM in 1996, and the assurances by Division officials that this was how the Division would calculate sentencing recommendations in the future, that companies appreciated the value of the leniency program.

The Antitrust Division, which three years earlier believed that it needed to give no jail deals to non-U.S. executives who were seriously culpable, now saw the increasing number of leniency and leniency plus candidates as providing more than significant evidence of global antitrust violations. The necessary evidence of cartel behavior formerly provided by the non-U.S. executive was now increasingly provided by leniency applicants. The Division could now say it did not need the non-U.S. executive as critically as it needed him in 1996, thus the need for the generous no jail plea agreements decreased in importance and the Division became much more aggressive with non-U.S. executives.

C. 1999—The Vitamins Era: Incarceration for All Defendants

The massive vitamins cartel was a picture-perfect opportunity to bring about the change the Division's policy regarding non-U.S. executives in cartel cases. The vitamins cartel had a leniency applicant who did not surface until the investigation was ongoing for some time. During that investigation, the Antitrust Division negotiated a plea agreement with a Swiss vitamins executive who agreed to plead guilty and serve a jail term of four months in the United States.[8]

---

[7] The original U.S. leniency policy was announced in 1978 by then-Assistant Attorney General John H. Shenefield. It provided that the first company to report its illegal conduct before any investigation was initiated would not be prosecuted criminally nor would its cooperating executives. A small number of companies took advantage of the program. The new leniency policy was announced in 1993 by then-Assistant Attorney General Anne Bingaman. That policy maintained most of the initial program but added the opportunity to seek leniency after an investigation had begun. Leniency was available to the first company in and all of its cooperating executives if the Division did not yet have evidence sufficient to establish a case.

The Division announced that it would no longer agree to a "no jail" deal with such key executives. While the Division would continue to pre-adjudicate the immigration status of convicted executives to make it easier for them to continue to travel to the United States, it would insist that they go to jail for limited sentences. This was a major shift in policy.

What incentives do the Antitrust Division provide for these executives to leave their homes and families to go to a foreign country and give up their liberty

Looking back to this policy shift, many practitioners believed that non-U.S. executives would never agree to surrender to U.S. jurisdiction and voluntarily agree to go to jail. Yet, a substantial number of non-U.S. executives implicated in these cases have submitted to U.S. jurisdiction and have agreed to serve jail time in the United States. Between 1999 and today, over 45 executives from France, Norway, the Netherlands, Germany, Switzerland, Sweden, the United Kingdom, Japan, Korea, and Taiwan[9] have submitted to U.S. jurisdiction. A review of Antitrust Division press releases and plea agreements confirm that while the initial sentences in 1999 were in the range of three- to six-months, sentences had increased to the nine-month range by 2009.

What incentives do the Antitrust Division provide for these executives to leave their homes and families to go to a foreign country and give up their liberty? Discussions with Division officials and with affected executives suggest that there are generally three incentives. First, if an executive cooperates and serves his sentence, he will be able to travel freely to the United States and continue his career as an international businessman—effectively, his career will continue as it was after this short interruption. While most U.S. companies terminate their convicted executives, this is not often the case in Europe or Asia. Second, the executive makes the sacrifice for his company and his job. The executive understands that the company must cooperate with the Antitrust

Division and his lack of cooperation could harm the company's deal with the Division. Since he wants to continue his employment, he will do what the company wishes him to do. He believes his job security is better if he is a good corporate citizen and "takes one for the team." Finally, the executive understands the perils of being what the Antitrust Division calls an "international fugitive" who is on the INTERPOL Red Notice and is subject to being detained as he enters many countries around the world. He also worries about the risk of his

---

8 United States v. Kuno Sommer, CR 3:99 CR 201-R (N.D. Tx, May 20, 1999). Scott D. Hammond, Deputy Assistant Attorney General, Antitrust Division, The Evolution of Criminal Antitrust Enforcement Over the Last Two Decades, Feb. 25, 2010, at 7, *available at* http://www.justice.gov/atr/public/speeches/255515.htm.

9 *Id.* at 7.

government cooperating with the United States at some future time regarding extradition or other attempts to expedite his surrender. The executive does not want to be hunted and constantly look over his shoulder for antitrust enforcement officials. If the sentence is short enough, the incentive to cooperate is strong; if the sentences are too long, the non-U.S. executives will simply stay home.

For about ten years, the Division and defense counsel have struggled to develop the correct balance between negotiating plea agreements that place non-U.S. executives in prison and non-U.S. executives deciding to stay out of the United States and other countries that may cooperate with the United States. Many of these executives are at the end of their careers and do not put a premium on international travel, particularly to the United States. This is a clear option for the executive—and each needs to determine what is right for him and his family.

If an executive decides to submit to U.S. jurisdiction, enters a plea agreement, and pleads guilty, that individual will be required to report to a prison facility in the United States. In almost all cases these facilities are minimum security camps such as Lompac (California) or Morgantown (West Virginia). He will be housed in a dormitory setting with other inmates, will be required to work in the prison community, and will have limited opportunities to talk to or visit with friends and relatives.

The ability of non-U.S. executives to have an alternative to not surrendering to U.S. authorities undoubtedly affects the deterrence calculation of the Ginsburg-Wright analysis. As sentences proposed for non-U.S. executives get longer, many more non-U.S. executives will opt to stay in their homelands. Longer sentences will shift the costs and benefits of surrender significantly towards staying home.

D. The Concept of the "Carve Out"

Since the late 1990s, the Division has entered into plea agreements with corporate defendants that specifically define the scope of cooperation that the corporate defendant will provide, but expressly exclude certain corporate executives from the cooperation provision of the plea agreement. This list of excluded executives has come to be known as "carve outs." If an executive is "carved out," it means that the Division will not, at the time of the plea agreement, consider the executive to be a cooperating witness and he will be a potential candidate for indictment. All other cooperating employees receive a non-prosecution promise that provides some certainty as to their futures. In early plea agreements, the Division would also enumerate those individuals whose cooperation they expressly required. In recent times, the Division has not listed the required cooperators; it has only listed the "carve outs."

The Division has made much of the designation of "carve outs." On one hand, it has used the growing number of "carve outs" to indicate that the Division is pursuing more and more executives, noting that the later a company seeks cooperation, the more executives will be on the "carve out" list. In some of the more recent cases, as many as seven or eight executives have been listed as potential defendants—a long way from the single executive charged in the late 1990s.

The Division has made much of the designation of "carve outs."

While the Division uses the "carve out" list to press its aggressive pursuit of corporate executives, a careful comparison of the carve out lists against the list of executives actually charged seems to reveal that only a limited percentage of "carved out" executives are actually prosecuted. In fairness, the Division does not represent that all "carve outs" will be prosecuted, but the simple fact is that the Division wants the world to know that these are people who are at great risk of being prosecuted.

Being "carved out," in many respects, is a significant form of punishment in itself. The executive is placed on a very public list that will be known to the executive's employer, to his customers, to his family and friends, and to his financial advisors and creditors. If the executive resides outside of the United States, he is unlikely to be able to travel to the United States or to any country with an extradition treaty with the United States unless or until his status is changed. There is no time limitation to the "carve out" designation, so the executive does not know if and when he can resume his business career. While the executive can negotiate a plea agreement with the enforcers, it is virtually certain that a plea agreement will require the executive to serve jail time. Many "carve outs" have been living under these conditions for several years. That, itself, is real punishment and limits the executive's career and travel opportunities substantially.

E. 2004-05—Tougher Maximum Sentences Focus on Executives

In June 2004, the Antitrust Criminal Penalty Enhancement and Reform Act of 2004 went into effect. The Act increased the maximum corporate fine from $10 million to $100 million or "twice the gain or twice the loss." More importantly, it increased the maximum penalties for corporate executives from three to ten years imprisonment and from $350,000 to $1 million in individual fines. Since the Antitrust Division already had the ability to obtain fines of $100 million and more through the alternative fine provision, 18 U.S.C. 3571(d), the major impact of the legislation was the ten-year maximum prison sentence.

As a result of the new legislation, the U.S. Sentencing Commission held hearings designed to amend the Sentencing Guideline for antitrust violations, consistent with the higher penalties. The entire hearing focused on the issue of longer prison sentences and de-

The enhancements to the Guidelines, however, raised the stakes considerably

terrence. The Sentencing Commission revised the Antitrust Guideline to a higher starting point for guidelines calculation and established a larger number of enhancements for the volume of commerce affected. The Commission showed considerable restraint in amending the Antitrust Guideline, U.S.S.G. 2R1.1, understanding that sentences that are too harsh will affect the incentives for defendants to cooperate.

The enhancements to the Guidelines, however, raised the stakes considerably. As in any negotiation, if the Antitrust Division presses too hard and increases its sentencing recommendations too aggressively, the result may be that more defendants go to trial, which uses a significant amount of scarce prosecutorial resources. It may also mean that more and more non-U.S. executives will stay in their homelands and refuse to surrender to U.S. jurisdiction. Neither of these alternatives is very satisfying or valuable to the Antitrust Division.[10] Restraint and balance should guide the Antitrust Division. Excessive sentencing recommendations will weaken the Division's program substantially.

F. 2007—Using Leniency Applicants to Conduct A Covert Investigation

In several investigations, the Antitrust Division has asked leniency applicants to continue to participate in the conspiracy that they reported while the Division gathers more and better evidence. This "covert" investigation often takes the form of telephone conversations that are recorded by the FBI, but the most successful operation to date is the Division's video surveillance in the *Marine Hose* investigation. Representatives of the major competitors in the marine hose business—virtually all of whom were non-U.S. citizens living abroad—traveled to Houston, Texas to attend the Offshore Technology Conference, the major annual conference of the offshore oil and gas businesses. Executives from companies in France, Italy, Japan, and the United Kingdom organized a meeting of the competitors at the conference and the leniency applicant, who had been covertly working with the Division, provided the location so the Division could place a video camera in the room and record the meeting. At the meeting, the paid organizer of the cartel made a presentation of how successful the cartel had been for the members, stating that this was not the time for the group to disband.

Armed with a video recording of this meeting, the Antitrust Division obtained arrest warrants and executed them on the participants in their hotel rooms in the early morning hours

10 For a more expansive discussion of these strategy considerations and the likely results of aggressive sentences, see Klawiter & Driscoll, *supra* note 5.

of the next day. They were arrested and sent to the Houston lockup where they were housed with very dangerous inmates awaiting hearings and trials. They were released on bond, but the court took their passports and limited their ability to travel. They could not return home until they pled guilty and served their sentences or went to trial. Not only were they held in the United States for many months while they negotiated their plea agreements (the "shortest" was over eight months from arrest to incarceration), but because the enforcers caught them on U.S. soil, they were treated for sentencing purposes like U.S. citizens and were not given the usual sentencing discount for submitting to U.S. jurisdiction. Rather than the six to eight month sentences that were common for non-U.S. executives at that time, the sentences ranged from a low of fourteen months to a high of thirty months.

The Marine Hose matter changed the focus and the equation for sentencing in U.S. antitrust cases

The *Marine Hose* matter changed the focus and the equation for sentencing in U.S. antitrust cases. Because the executives were arrested and held in the United States absent their passports, time became an important condition for the executives. There was a great incentive to cooperate and negotiate a plea agreement because any delay meant a longer time away from their homes and families. Importantly, the Division made the executives the focal point of the investigation and the plea negotiations of the executives took precedence over the corporate plea process, a considerable change in Division focus.

One of the interesting dynamics that took place in *Marine Hose* was that the Division first received detailed information about the conduct from the proffers and interviews of the executives, rather than the proffers that are usually controlled by company counsel. Indeed, this reverse process made the "omnibus question" (the inquiry of whether the individual is aware of any anticompetitive conduct in other products) much more of a threat against the company's opportunity to receive "leniency plus" credit. In this setting, it can be quite easy for the executive to provide evidence of other violations on his own—preempting the company from obtaining "leniency plus" credit. As such, astute counsel for the company and the executive have to plan strategies to make certain that both the company and the executive received proper credit under the leniency policy for information first provided by the executive.

The *Marine Hose* investigation changed the dynamic of criminal prosecutions and made the executive the focal point of the race to the courthouse and the plea agreement process. Obviously, a *Marine Hose*-type case replete with video surveillance is an infrequent occurrence, but it does underscore the far greater interest in pursuing executives rather than corporations in major global cases.

G. The Defendant Executive Has Become More Central and More Visible as the International Cartel Era Has Matured

The prosecution of senior executives has evolved and matured since the first international cartel cases in the mid 1990s. From the decision to seek jail for cooperating non-U.S. executives, to the proliferation of "carve outs," to the arrested executives who were center stage in the marine hose investigation, the Antitrust Division is moving much more in the direction of the Ginsburg-Wright analysis. Other jurisdictions, from Australia to the United Kingdom, from Brazil to Japan, are also shifting their enforcement efforts to the executives. All of those jurisdictions are just beginning serious pursuit of the executives, which will undoubtedly complicate the process for enforcers and defenders alike. Enforcers are not completely there yet, but the focus on executives is certainly evolving—and quickly. The next five years will be a very interesting time for anti-cartel enforcement and for continuing to apply the Ginsburg-Wright thesis.

III. KNOWLEDGE OF ILLEGAL ACTIVITY: WHAT SHOULD KEEP IMPLICATED EXECUTIVES AND THEIR COUNSEL AWAKE AT NIGHT?

Neither the Antitrust Division nor corporate compliance programs have been aggressive enough at imparting information that will literally keep executives and their counsel up at night

One of the major difficulties in deterring corporate executives from violating the antitrust laws is the lack of knowledge executives have about antitrust enforcement. How can they be deterred if they do not understand that executives just like them are going to jail regularly for cooperating with their competitors? Without greater knowledge of the enforcement environment, executives will continue to find ways to justify their illegal conduct, believing that they are helping their companies, preventing unemployment, and generally not harming anyone. Neither the Antitrust Division nor corporate compliance programs have been aggressive enough at imparting information that will literally keep executives and their counsel up at night. In the deterrence analysis at the core of the Ginsburg-Wright thesis, a fundamental element is that executives must know and understand the great risk of cartel behavior, as well as the array of dangers that continue even after the investigation begins. Within the current enforcement cycle of fifteen years, executives and their lawyers have seen every danger and many of them have made executives' personal exposure even greater.

A. Judicial and Enforcement Attitudes Are Much More Aggressive than Ten Years Ago

The evolution of the criminal enforcement of the antitrust laws against executives has been dramatic—and very successful. In the United States and throughout the world, the judiciary and the bar have defined this business conduct as "fraud" and "stealing." That perception was clearly expressed in the Sentencing Commission hearings on the Guidelines revisions, and resulted in the enhanced penalties. Undoubtedly, the ADM and *Marine Hose* videotapes, and the realization that very senior corporate executives could conduct themselves with complete disregard of the law, changed the perception of judges, enforcers, and consumers alike. The blatant conduct played out on the ADM tapes brought a very strong judicial reaction which obviously affected sentencing decisions. The opening paragraph of Judge Kanne's opinion in Andreas[11] conveys the shock and disgust of the judiciary after seeing the conduct played out on a video screen:

> For many years, Archer Daniels Midland Co.'s philosophy of customer relations could be summed up by a quote from former ADM President James Randall. "Our competitors are our friends. Our customers are the enemy." This motto animated the company's business dealings and ultimately led to blatant violations of U.S. antitrust law, a guilty plea and a staggering criminal fine against the company. It also led to the criminal charges against three top ADM executives that are the subject of this appeal. The facts involved in this case reflect an inexplicable lack of business ethics and an atmosphere of general lawlessness that infected the very heart of one of America's leading corporate citizens. Top executives at ADM and its Asian co-conspirators throughout the early 1990s spied on each other, fabricated aliases and front organizations to hide their activities, hired prostitutes to gather information from competitors, lied, cheated, embezzled, extorted and obstructed justice.

Executives in companies around the globe need to understand that this judge was not overreacting. To a court that viewed the videos and heard the testimony, the reaction was a strong one. Making this understanding a serious part of antitrust compliance is the first step to demonstrating to the executives that the judiciary will react strongly. If they are participating in similar conduct, they should be terrified.

The first step in antitrust compliance is to teach the executives that prosecutors and courts view this conduct as theft, not as normal business practice, and that if the executive is involved, he is in very serious trouble.

---

[11] United States v. Andreas, 216 F.3d 645 (7th Cir. 2000).

B. An Executive Should Be Trained to Understand that His Conduct During the Investigation Can Have Serious Consequences

What do senior executives need to know about antitrust investigations? Senior executives are almost always ill prepared for an investigation. Many of the critical pressure points of the antitrust investigation are dangerous for senior executives because they are simply untutored about investigations—they do not understand law enforcement rules and procedures. For example, senior executives are often visited at their homes by the FBI and Antitrust Division on the day before a formal criminal investigation begins. The enforcers exploit the element of surprise and are often highly successful at getting the executive to provide significant information, including information that will implicate the executive in criminal conduct. Because many executives believe they will look guilty if they do not talk to the enforcers, and because they truly believe they have nothing to hide, executives often provide substantial incriminating information to enforcers at these meetings. In the worst case, executives believe they can persuade the enforcers to go away by minimizing the impact of the conduct, leaving out important details, or just straight out lying to the enforcers.

It is for these reasons that executives should receive compliance training to understand the rationale for these interviews and think of the consequences carefully. The executive will not fully understand the implications of illegal antitrust behavior unless he receives careful and detailed training on a regular basis.

C. Actions in the Boardroom Can Also Have Serious Consequences

Independent counsel representing corporate executives in international cartel investigations not only represent their clients in the courtroom; they represent them in the boardroom as well. To be effective, independent counsel must advise their clients carefully to avoid additional—and far greater—criminal risk once the antitrust investigation begins.

Imagine a corporate CEO or other high level executive who was involved directly in cartel meetings and, therefore, is completely aware of the cartel activity when the investigation starts. The day that the investigation begins the CEO may receive inquiries from the Chair of his Board's Audit Committee about the investigation and the CEO decides he must meet with the entire Board immediately. The CEO is contacted by major customers who want an explanation, as do securities analysts with significant investments in the company. Further, the analysts wish to have a videoconference and record the meeting, as is their standard procedure. And while all of these meetings are being scheduled, the CEO invites the General Counsel and those assisting in the investigation to brief him on the evidence and the investigative strategy.

All of these are normal activities that the CEO is expected to perform, but they become minefields when the CEO or other senior executives are implicated in the illegal conduct. Independent counsel for the CEO is the person who is most likely to succeed in moving the CEO away from all of these activities. Even the General Counsel, who probably serves at the pleasure of the CEO and is a close friend of the CEO, will have a difficult time moving the CEO away from these "normal" duties. Yet, moving the CEO away from these normal activities is essential to keeping the CEO out of serious trouble—the analysts videotape is perhaps the most dangerous evidence imaginable, and such videotapes have been used effectively in past Antitrust Division trials.[12]

All of these are normal activities that the CEO is expected to perform, but they become minefields when the CEO or other senior executives are implicated in the illegal conduct

The only way the executive will become aware that these normal duties are dangerous is through careful and detailed compliance training and the strong advice of independent counsel who can guide the executive through this very dangerous time.

D. Maintaining Employment is Very Difficult

In the age of Sarbanes-Oxley and corporate ethics reform, the fate of a senior executive who is charged with antitrust misconduct is perilous—and often very complicated. Many U.S. corporations have zero tolerance for executive misconduct and termination is often viewed as the only appropriate action. In other parts of the world, procedures are not as well defined. There have been examples of European companies that have terminated senior executives, while others have not. The issue is still a new and undefined one in Asia.

One of the major issues that confronts a company when one of its senior executives is a target of the investigation is how the executive's removal affects the company's ability to defend itself in the investigation and subsequent litigation. The company that wishes to cooperate with the Division's investigation and obtain the maximum credit for cooperation needs the cooperation of its executives who were involved in the conduct. An involved executive, at the same time, knows that he will likely be terminated if he pleads guilty or goes to trial, yet he knows that his continued income stream is entirely dependent on the company's good will towards him. The result is often a very nuanced dance among the parties.

12 For a more detailed discussion of these difficult activities see Donald C. Klawiter, Please Show This To Senior Executives: Risks of Antitrust Investigations in the Courtroom and the Boardroom, COMPETITION L. INT'L (October 2006) at 32.

Without such an arrangement, the executive and the company may each act against the other's interests, often triggering even more litigation, which could be helpful only to the enforcers and the private plaintiffs

The principal issue is often not salary and benefits; it is the continued advancement of legal fees under an indemnification agreement.[13]

In practice, it is in the company's best interest to pay these fees so that the executive and his counsel maintain a dialogue—and a joint defense agreement—with the company so that the company obtains helpful evidence from that executive. The company will likely need his evidence to assist with the Division investigation and in the private damage litigation that follows.

In addition to the legal fees, there is often an opportunity to negotiate a severance agreement that will move the executive out of the company but provide him with some income that will be helpful as he serves a jail term and then begins to rebuild his life. Whether there is a settlement or not depends on a number of special circumstances in the case as well as the executive's value to the company in resolving the case. Without such an arrangement, the executive and the company may each act against the other's interests, often triggering even more litigation, which could be helpful only to the enforcers and the private plaintiffs.

IV. WORKING TO KEEP THE EXECUTIVES OUT OF HARM'S WAY

Executives need to be tutored regularly on the perils and consequences of antitrust misconduct. Deterrence cannot be successful unless the stark reality of criminal enforcement and the likelihood of jail are known to the executive. This tutoring is the only way to drive home the impact of a criminal investigation, the trauma of going to jail, and the horror of job removal. By making these events real, deterrence has a chance to work. That is what corporate counsel should highlight and reinforce. Such effective compliance training—not the lecture or slide show, but a candid meeting that examines the subtle issues—ultimately focuses on the corporate executive and the similarity of circumstances between him and those who serve terms in jail and it brings home the tragic consequences of enforcement actions. Only in that environment can Judge Ginsburg and Professor Wright's concept of deterrence have a fighting chance to be successful.

---

[13] At the beginning of an investigation, senior executives that may be involved in the conduct under investigation are asked to execute an undertaking by which the company agrees to advance them their legal fees and the executive agrees that if he is determined to have acted contrary to the company's interests he commits to repaying the advanced fees. The fees in these cases may add up to hundreds of thousands or millions of dollars and are thus substantial revenues for the executive.

COLLUSION THEORIES IN MERGER ANALYSIS: STILL ALIVE AND KICKING*

*Malcolm B. Coate**

I. INTRODUCTION

In a 2008 paper published in this journal, I described the continuing success of coordinated interaction (hereinafter, collusion) theories in maintaining their role as an alternative analytical technique to the unilateral effects theories used in Federal Trade Commission ("FTC") merger reviews.[1] While recent Agency commentary and guidelines have suggested a further shift in policy towards unilateral effects analysis,[2] collusion analyses remain entrenched in the internal files. Staff appears to apply the theory most compatible with the available facts.

After an overview of developments in merger policy, this paper compares the level and outcome of collusion and unilateral effects analyses over the 1993-2010 time period. Remarkably little change in relative activity is observed and challenge rates remain relatively constant once the samples are standardized for entry impediments.[3] Focusing on the counts

---

* Federal Trade Commission, mcoate@ftc.gov. The analyses and conclusions set forth in this article are those of the author and do not necessarily represent the views of the Commission, any individual Commissioner, or any Commission Bureau.

[1] Malcolm B. Coate, *Alive and Kicking: Collusion Theory in Merger Analysis at the Federal Trade Commission*, 4(2) COMP. POL'Y INT'L., 3 (2008). The paper studied the application of collusion analysis to a sample of investigations undertaken by the FTC between 1993 and 2005. The results identified structure, homogeneous nature of the good, lack of buyer power, presence of evidence for the competitive concern and lack of efficiencies as the key factors in the FTC's decision on the ease of collusion.

[2] Federal Trade Commission and U.S. Dep't of Justice, *Commentary on the Horizontal Merger Guidelines*, (2006), *available at* http://www.ftc.gov/os/2006/03/CommentaryontheHorizontalMergerGuidelinesMarch2006.pdf [hereinafter *Merger Commentaries*; U. S. Dep't of Justice and Federal Trade Commission, *Horizontal Merger Guidelines*, Aug.19, 2010 *available at* http://www.ftc.gov/os/2010/08/100819hmg.pdf [hereinafter *2010 Merger Guidelines*].

[3] The Commission decides to challenge a merger at the end of an investigation when it has the required reason to believe that the merger is likely to substantially lessen competition. Most challenged mergers settle, while a few are litigated, and still others are abandoned by the parties.

Facts, not theory, appear to affect FTC evaluations

of significant rivals, the data shows that both four-to-three and three-to-two mergers tend to end in challenges when entry evidence is strong. Moreover, a reasonable case can be made that the challenge rates are higher in homogeneous goods markets when five or more premerger rivals exist, although the small sample size limits this conclusion. Thus overall, facts, not theory, appear to affect FTC evaluations.

II. DEVELOPMENTS IN MERGER ANALYSIS

Introduced in the 1992 Merger Guidelines, unilateral effects analysis generally applies models of Bertrand competition to differentiated product markets and models of Cournot competition to homogeneous goods markets.[4] In either situation, key facts (lack of close competition between the products of the merging firms in Bertrand competition and substantial supply elasticities for non-merging firms in Cournot competition) mandate the rejection of the unilateral concern, leaving the analyst to apply a traditional collusion analysis. These concepts were explained in more detail in the 2006 Merger Commentaries[5] and the 2010 Merger Guidelines.[6]

Commentators suggest unilateral concerns became the dominant theory of concern, an assertion that tracks the common understanding of the Merger Guidelines.[7] This hypothesis is compatible with evidence from a review of the text dedicated to either unilateral effects or collusion theories in three merger guidance documents issued during the last 20 years. The 1992 Merger Guidelines led with a discussion of collusion, allocating it almost four pages of text,[8] then followed with unilateral effects analysis, presented in a little over three pages.[9] The 2006 Commentaries on the Merger Guidelines reverse the emphasis, with unilateral concerns addressed first, with 11 pages used to explain the analysis.[10] Collusion concerns followed with about 7 pages.[11] This preference for unilateral concerns continued into 2010, as the revised

---

[4] U. S. Dep't of Justice and Federal Trade Commission, *Horizontal Merger Guidelines*, ANTITRUST TRADE REG. REPORT 1559 (1992).

[5] Merger Commentaries, *supra* note 2.

[6] 2010 Merger Guidelines, *supra* note 2.

[7] *See, e.g.*, Jonathon B. Baker, *Why Did the Antitrust Agencies Embrace Unilateral Effects?* 12(1) GEO. MASON L. REV. 31 (2003). Baker noted a recent (2002-03) revival in interest for collusion.

[8] U. S. Dep't of Justice and Federal Trade Commission, *Horizontal Merger Guidelines*, ANTITRUST TRADE AND REGULATION REPORT, NO. 1559, 1992 at section 2.1.

[9] *Id.*, at section 2.2.

[10] Merger Commentaries, *supra* note 2, at 25-36.

[11] Id., at 18-25.

Guidelines allocated 6.5 pages to unilateral concerns,[12] while the collusion analysis was limited to 3.5 pages.[13] To summarize the trend, the percentage of pages dedicated to collusion issues can be shown to decline continuously from 59 percent to 39 percent to 35 percent. If the emphasis of the documents offers any insight, some movement in the investigational approach should be observed in the files.

In addition to the shift in emphasis, the rise in the importance of unilateral effects analysis also had an impact on market definition. Joseph Farrell & Carl Shapiro advance an Upward Pressure on Price ("UPP") methodology for evaluating the competitive effect of a merger from information on diversion ratios, margins, and efficiencies.[14] This model is integrated into the 2010 Merger Guidelines and serves to support the suggestion that market definition could be an after-thought in a merger review. Louis Kaplow puts forth an even more radical idea – unilateral analysis eliminates the intellectual viability of market definition.[15]

These concepts have not remained unchallenged. Joseph Simons & Malcolm Coate contend that Farrell & Shapiro need a benchmark for their analysis to differentiate substantial from insubstantial effects.[16] Benchmarking may require market definition. Dennis Carlton raises a more serious problem, questioning the intellectual distinction between the unilateral and collusive concerns that underpins the entire analysis.[17] Carlton observes that the standard Bertrand and Cournot models represent applications of static game theory, and this assumption gives rise to the firm's unilateral ability to raise price.[18] If the game is generalized to allow dynamic play, then, abstracting from the monopoly issue, collusion concerns are relevant.

Lost in the theoretical disputes, but clearly relevant to the policy analyst, is the question of monopoly. To the extent that the merger creates a single firm able to set price and restrict output, the core monopoly model of antitrust predicts the merger is likely to substantially lessen competition in all but the most extraordinary situations. Thus, in any study of competition policy,

---

12 2010 Merger Guidelines, *supra* note 2, at section 6.

13 *Id.*, at section 7.

14 *See* Joseph Farrell & Carl Shapiro, *Antitrust Evaluation of Horizontal Mergers: An Economic Alternative to Market Definition*, 10(1) B. E. J. of Theoretical Econ. 1 (2010).

15 *See* Louis Kaplow, *Why Ever Define Markets?*, 124 Harv. L. Rev. 437-516 (2010). For an alternative view, see Malcolm B. Coate & Joseph J. Simons, *In Defense of Market Definition*, Antitrust Bulletin (forthcoming). The working paper version is available at http://ssrn.com/abstract=1967208.

16 *See* Joseph J. Simons & Malcolm B. Coate, *Upward Pressure on Price Analysis: Issues and Implications for Merger Policy*, 6(2) Eur. Competition J. 377 (2010). This paper simulates the effect of an UPP policy and finds it would be much more aggressive than the status quo.

17 *See* Dennis Carlton, *Revising the Horizontal Merger Guidelines*, 6(3) J. Comp. L. & Econ. 619 (2010).

18 *Id.*, at 627-29.

To the extent that unilateral effects analysts have been counting monopoly concerns as unilateral issues, they have been over-counting the success of their innovative theories

it is necessary to first put aside the transactions that create or enhance a pure monopoly position. To the extent that unilateral effects analysts have been counting monopoly concerns as unilateral issues, they have been over-counting the success of their innovative theories. As seen in the next section, two-to-one mergers play a large role in FTC merger reviews.[19]

III. EMPIRICAL EVIDENCE AT THE FEDERAL TRADE COMMISSION

The most recent research file contains 333 market analyses associated with a sample of mergers filed under the Hart-Scott-Rodino Act[20] from fiscal year 1993 to 2010.[21] To ensure data on a wide range of variables, only mergers with three or fewer competitive overlaps are studied. The 2008 study was based on a sample of 75 merger reviews undertaken with a collusion analysis after a clear finding of entry impediments.[22] To compare the FTC's treatment of collusion investigations with its treatment of unilateral concerns analyses, the collusion sample was updated in 2010 to obtain a data set of 90 market studies.[23] The unilateral sample started with 192 market-level evaluations and deleted 92 two-to-one markets and 21 matters in which the evidence of substantial entry impediments could not be established.[24] This left a sample of 79 market studies for review. The two research objectives were to (1) shed light on any change in policy over the 1993-2010

---

[19] Most of the two-to-one mergers represent small competitive overlaps associated with conglomerate transactions. Thus, these challenges almost always settle. In a few cases, the two-to-one merger is the core of the transaction, with the parties claiming easy entry, a broad market (hence to them, the merger is not two-to-one) or buyer power. A few such transactions are allowed, as the evidence shows the merger is not likely to substantially lessen competition.

[20] Hart-Scott-Rodino Antitrust Improvements Act of 1976, 15 U.S.C. § 18(a).

[21] The sample was collected for a study of the effect of natural experiments, along with customer complaints and hot documents, on the merger challenge decision. For more details on the study, see Malcolm B. Coate, The Use of Natural Experiments in Merger Analysis (Nov. 17, 2011) (working paper, available at http://ssrn.com/abstract=1853705). While this data set is based on historical information, anomalies in the data are corrected and therefore various samples will not be perfectly backward compatible; instead, they represent the best available evidence at the time they were collected.

[22] Coate, *supra* note 1.

[23] Following the procedure in the 2008 paper, three collusion matters were excluded because the merger raised strong failing firm/division concerns.

[24] In some cases, the memos suggested enforcement action could occur under both theories and the wording of the documents was reviewed to determine which theory would be the primary basis for a merger challenge. Because merger policy is law enforcement, the legal considerations were considered controlling. It is certainly possible that an economist looking at the same factual evidence would suggest certain matters be recoded from collusion to unilateral for differentiated goods and from unilateral to collusion for homogeneous goods.

TABLE 1 Theories of Concern by Era for FTC Merger Reviews (1993-2010)

	Unilateral Theory Cases	Win Rate	Collusion Theory Cases	Win Rate
Steiger Era	15	80%	19	47%
Pitofsky Era	31	71%	34	67%
Muris + Era	16	69%	20	80%
Commentaries Era	17	88%	17	82%
Overall	79	76%	90	69%

time period and (2) identify the key considerations that appear to drive differences in the relevant analyses. Because the focus of the study is on the effect of the analyses given substantial evidence on impediments to entry, the results may not fully apply to the universe of mergers reviewed.[25]

Four time periods were defined for the initial analysis. The earliest sub-sample (named after Chairman Steiger) was comprised of the investigations reviewed between the 1993 start of the data set and the April 1995 arrival of Chairman Pitofsky. The second sub-sample tracked the Pitofsky administration from April 1995 through May 2001. The third sub-sample included the Muris administration (starting in June 2001) and extended beyond his term to the late March 2006 issuance of the *Commentaries on the Merger Guidelines* (labeled Muris+). The final sub-sample focused on the additional mergers filed through the end of fiscal 2010. Empirically, the first three sub-samples approximate the data from the earlier paper. While the samples generally link to political administrations, the tested hypotheses are apolitical—a slow movement towards unilateral effects cases starting in 1992 and possibly continuing through 2010, coupled with higher challenge rates for the unilateral concerns. The alternative hypotheses postulate no change in the ratio of collusion to unilateral cases and comparable challenge rates for the two theories.

Table 1 provides information on case count and win rate for the four time periods. In each period, collusion cases make up between 50 and 56 percent of the overall sample, thus no evidence

[25] While unilateral analysis is not rejected due to entry considerations, the theories are rejected in favor of collusion analysis based on repositioning arguments (which are likely to be correlated with ease of entry). Hence the collusion sample would be likely to contain more matters in which the standard for entry imposed on the data cannot be met. In particular, 48 matters were deleted for lack of strong entry evidence for the collusion sample, while only 21 were for the unilateral effects sample. Some of these matters were still challenged, if the totality of the evidence tended to raise competitive concerns. (Evidence on ease of entry was not dispositive in all 68 excluded matters.)

TABLE 2 Theories of Concern and Modeling Assumptions by Structure (1993-2010)

	Unilateral	Effects	Coordinated	Effects
Rivals	Homogeneous Goods Markets	Heterogeneous Goods Markets	Homogeneous Goods Markets	Heterogeneous Goods Markets
Three-to-Two	6 (100%)	38 (89%)	14 (100%)	12 (100%)
Four-to-Three	3 (100%)	13 (92%)	14 (93%)	17 (65%)
Five-to-Four	2 (50%)	6 (17%)	9 (33%)	8 (25%)
Six-to-Five +	1 (100%)	10 (20%)	8 (75%)	8 (12%)
Total	12 (92%)	67 (73.1%)	45 (80%)	45(58%)

+ signifies the classification also includes all matters with more the six pre-merger rivals.

exists to suggest that the FTC prefers unilateral theories of violation once the (two-to-one) monopoly cases are deleted from the sample. Win rates show some random variation for the unilateral matters with a range from 69 percent to 88 percent in the most recent interval. Collusion matters show more change, with the win rate increasing from 47 percent to 82. However, the 47 percent win rate turns out to be an anomaly, driven by the inclusion of matters with 9 or 10 rivals in the sample; in later time periods, such cases are closed with a quick look. Thus, for both the case count and the win rate, the samples are compatible over the four time periods.[26]

Table 2 provides a summary of the case counts, with win rates in parentheses, for the full sample of investigations exhibiting clear evidence on entry impediments. The tabulation compares challenge rates for various rival counts using both competitive theories of concern and two modeling structures for the relevant product (here, either homogeneous or differentiated goods). Theories of unilateral effects are generally applied for differentiated goods, with merger challenges likely in four-to-three and three-to-two market situations, but not likely in the less concentrated markets such as five-to-four transactions.[27] This result implies that findings of unilateral con-

[26] Unilateral investigations dominate for three to two mergers, with collusion investigations making up between 36 percent and 41 percent of the investigations in each period.

[27] For more details on unilateral effects cases, see Malcolm B. Coate, *Benchmarking the Upward Pricing Pressure Model with Federal Trade Commission Evidence*, 7(4) J. of Competition L. & Econ. 825 (2011). Of particular interest is the list of findings that preclude unilateral effects analysis in differentiated products.

cerns are heavily dependent on structure whenever the relevant products appear differentiated. For homogeneous goods markets, the outcome of the unilateral effects investigation appears much less dependent on structure, but the small sample size limits the interpretation of that result.[28]

Collusion theories are more likely to be applied in homogeneous goods markets, with the challenge rate very high for either three-to-two or four-to-three mergers. Differentiated goods also exhibit a high rate in the three-to-two sample, but a statistically lower (t-statistic 1.96) rate for four-to-three mergers. Combining the rest of the data also shows challenge rates are higher (t-statistic 2.06) when the product market is relatively homogenous. Tabulating the data across the entire sample for the marginally concentrated markets also shows homogeneous goods markets exhibit higher challenge rates: 55 percent for the 20 homogeneous goods cases versus 19 percent for the 32 differentiated goods cases, t-statistic 2.64.

While unilateral concerns are more likely than not in differentiated product markets, collusion theories remain relevant and support a wide range of enforcement when the staff cannot substantiate sufficient head-to-head competition to apply unilateral effects analysis

IV. CONCLUSION

The data suggests that collusion theories continue to represent a viable alternative line of analysis at the Federal Trade Commission. While unilateral concerns are more likely than not in differentiated product markets, collusion theories remain relevant and support a wide range of enforcement when the staff cannot substantiate sufficient head-to-head competition to apply unilateral effects analysis. For homogeneous goods markets, a surprising number of matters are reviewed with unilateral concerns, a result compatible with an implicit application of a Cournot-style model. Challenge rates are clearly affected by market structure, with mergers in homogeneous goods markets more likely to raise concerns than mergers in differentiated goods when five or more pre merger rivals exist.

It remains to be seen if the 2010 revision of the Merger Guidelines will have a material effect on enforcement at the FTC. A reasonable case can be made that unilateral concerns are clearly the primary choice for a competitive challenge under the new Guidelines, although an equally good case can be made that the courts remain unconvinced and thus the FTC staff might prefer the status quo.[29]

---

[28] Roughly half of these investigations are related to health care, with most in the two recent periods.

[29] *See, e.g., FTC v. Swedish Match* 131 F. Supp 2d 151 (D.D.C. 2000); *U.S. v. Oracle*, 331 F. Supp. 2d 1098 (N. D. Cal. 2004); and *FTC v. CCC Holdings* 605 F. Supp. 2d 26 (D.D.C. 2009).

ALIVE AND CLICKING: COLLUSION THEORIES IN MERGER ANALYSIS AT THE FEDERAL TRADE COMMISSION

*Malcolm B. Coate**

ABSTRACT:
This paper explores the use of collusion theories in merger analysis at the U.S. Federal Trade Commission ("FTC"). The 1992 Merger Guidelines ("Guidelines") focused more on unilateral effects concerns, relegating collusion analysis to a second-tier theory. That said, both structural and behavioral conditions conducive to establishing or maintaining an arrangement to restrict competition were listed in the Guidelines to structure collusion analysis. This paper undertakes a systematic review of 75 merger decisions to identify the conditions that increase the likelihood of a collusion finding. Standard structural concerns are readily identified, while behavioral factors defy characterization. The results of the analysis also support a Folk Theorem in which structural concerns are validated with some type of performance evidence. Further work finds that allegations of maverick conduct add little to the analysis, while the Bush administration appears to have been slightly more likely to identify a collusion problem than the Clinton administration.

I. INTRODUCTION

The 1992 revision of the *Merger Guidelines*[1] accepted the burden to move beyond a structural checklist and tell a logical story that links a competitive effect of concern to the consummation

* Malcolm Coate is an economist with the Federal Trade Commission. The analyses and conclusions set forth in this paper are those of the author and do not necessarily represent the views of the U.S. Federal Trade Commission. The author would like to thank Jeff Fischer and Seth Sacher for helpful comments.

1 U.S. Department of Justice and Federal Trade Commission, *Horizontal Merger Guidelines*, ANTITRUST TRADE REG. REPORT 1559 (1992).

of a proposed merger.[2] Two lines of analysis were given, one based on a traditional collusion theory (re-branded as "coordinated interaction") and the other tied to anticompetitive activity that the merged firm could undertake independently ("unilateral effects"). This evolution was inevitable in light of the continual decline in the breadth of the *Philadelphia National Bank* ("PNB") structural presumption.[3] In 1990, the appellate court in Baker Hughes concluded that the PNB presumption could be offset with evidence on a wide range of pro-competitive considerations.[4] Once the respondent presented some evidence compatible with a pro-competitive outcome for the merger, the plaintiff had to prove a likely competitive concern stemming from the merger. Thus, to prevail on the merits, the plaintiff needed evidence. To structure this evidence, it needed a story.

A careful review of Guidelines-based enforcement would conclude that the new unilateral effects theory defined the enforcer's leading story

A careful review of Guidelines-based enforcement would conclude that the new unilateral effects theory defined the enforcer's leading story.[5] For a unilateral effects theory, the government only had to introduce evidence on a unique similarity for the merged firm's products, given a limited number of rivals. If this information was lacking, simple market share evidence could establish a presumption. In effect, unilateral effects might end up as nothing more than a structuralist model underpinned with a veneer of economic authority.[6] Collusion analysis was demoted to a second-tier theory, as that analysis was

---

[2] Paul Denis, *Advances of the 1992 Horizontal Merger Guidelines in the Analysis of Competitive Effect*, 38(3) ANTITRUST BULL. 479-515 (1993).

[3] U.S. v. Philadelphia National Bank, 374 U.S. 321 (1963). For a useful commentary on the decline of the Philadelphia National Bank presumption, see Jonathan Baker, *Mavericks, Mergers, and Exclusion: Proving Coordinated Effects Under the Antitrust Laws*, 77 NYU L. REV. 135-201 (2002).

[4] U.S. v. Baker Hughes Inc., 731 F.Supp. 3 (D.D.C. 1990), *aff'd* 908 F.2d 981 (D.C. Cir. 1990).

[5] *See, e.g.*, Robert Lande & James Langenfeld, *The Evolution of Federal Merger Policy*, 11(2) ANTITRUST 5-9 (1997); or Jonathan Baker, *Why Did the Antitrust Agencies Embrace Unilateral Effects?*, 12(1) GEO. MASON L. REV. 31-37 (2003).

[6] *See, e.g.*, Robert D. Willig, *Merger Analysis, Industrial Organization Theory and Merger Guidelines, in* BROOKINGS PAPERS: MICROECONOMICS 281-332 (Brookings Institution, 1991); or Gregory J.Werden & Luke M. Froeb, *The Effects of Mergers in Differentiated Products Industries: Logit Demand and Merger Policy*, 10(2) J.L. ECON. & ORG. 407-26 (2004). These models link structure to performance by assuming away a wide range of real-world complications. The models may be appropriate in special case situations, but fall short of general models of the competitive process. For example, the models require the producing firm to post price, rather than negotiate on terms of trade. Likewise, the models presume the firms are locked into a specific product portfolio. For a critical overview, see Malcolm B. Coate, *Efficiencies in Merger Analysis: An Institutionalist View*, 13 GEO. MASON SUP. CT. ECON. REV. 189-240 (2005).

generally qualitative, often discussing factors summarized in Posner (1976) and (2001).[7] While the maverick model had long been mentioned as a viable empirical structure for the coordinated interaction analysis, the bulk of the Guidelines focused on generic models of coordination. Without a clear model of collusion, it was hard to know when one had "enough" evidence.

With roughly 15 years of experience under the 1992 *Merger Guidelines*, it is possible to study the implementation of the coordinated interaction policy with a systematic review of the relevant enforcement decisions undertaken for a set of mergers filed between 1993 and 2005. By limiting the study to coordinated interaction cases, it is possible to build on a 2007 paper by Davies, Olczak, and Coles, and use the enforcement decisions to create a model of coordinated interaction.[8] As long as the investigations with easy entry are deleted from the sample, the enforcement decision and the conclusion on the ease of collusion are the same. A number of structural variables are readily available to build a Posnerian model of collusion. Moreover, the structural model can be supplemented with a performance-based effects variable to test the importance of evidence related to various explicit or implicit natural experiments. If the natural experiment evidence matters, then theoretical analysis of ease of collusion may take a back seat to natural experiments in predicting merger effects. Finally, the model can be expanded to (1) determine if claims of maverick status are relevant and (2) identify any political influence on the analysis.

Overall, the results are broadly compatible with Posner's structural theory and support the importance of natural experiment evidence. A small positive effect for the Bush administration is identified, but no pure maverick effect appears to exist. In court, natural experiment evidence should assist a plaintiff in meeting its burden of proof, a task that has been difficult in recent unilateral effects cases.[9] Section II of this paper provides an introduction to early oligopoly (collusion) theory, with a specific focus on Stigler's contribution. It also introduces concepts from modern game theory. Section III presents an overview of the impact of economics on the *Merger Guidelines*. A review of the FTC's case files highlights the role of natural experiment evidence in the enforcement process. The basic modeling is presented in section IV, with the statistical results in section V. Section VI concludes.

---

[7] Richard A. Posner, Antitrust Law: An Economic Perspective (1976) (2nd ed. 2001).

[8] Stephen Davies et al., Tacit Collusion, Firm Asymmetries and Numbers: Evidence from EC Merger Cases (unpublished manuscript) (2007).

[9] *See, e.g.*, U.S. v. Sungard 172 F. Supp. 2d 172 (D.D.C. 2001); or U.S. v. Oracle, 331 F. Supp. 2d 1098 (N.D. Cal. 2004).

II. ECONOMICS OF OLIGOPOLISTIC COLLUSION

Oligopoly has a long history, predating the formalization of economics. Schumpeter traced the term "oligopoly" to Saint Thomas Moore's 1516 book, Utopia.[10] Cournot structured the oligopoly concept by postulating firms simply assumed their rivals would hold output fixed, regardless of what the firm in question did.[11] This assumption allowed market equilibrium to be computed at a price between the monopoly and competitive level. Chamberlin linked the oligopoly market equilibrium to "recognized mutual dependence."[12] After first touching on the Cournot and Bertrand structures, Chamberlin posited oligopolists would assume their actions affect the responses of their rivals and that they take that conclusion into account in setting price. When this interdependence was completely recognized, profit-maximization behavior generated a monopoly outcome.[13] Uncertainty could generate less perfect recognition and thus lower prices, although this tacit coordination would generally allow oligopolistic (collusive) firms to raise price well above the competitive level. Market concentration, on its own, seemed problematic. Stigler's model of collusion showed how market interactions were really much more complex, with a wide range of factors affecting the likelihood of collusion. Modern game theory formalized the basic Stigler insights.[14] These developments are discussed below.

A. Chicago Analysis

Stigler's 1964 analysis represented a huge innovation in collusion (oligopoly) theory as the model detailed various conditions that made interdependent pricing more or less likely. After making the initial point that product homogeneity plays an important role in the development of a collusive pricing scheme, Stigler advanced the idea that cartel participants can track changes in sales patterns to detect (and thus deter) competitive pricing in the marketplace. Stigler's model suggests that detection of competitive conduct is easiest when information on prices and sales is readily available. It is also possible to infer competitive conduct from the totality

---

[10] Joseph Schumpeter, History of Economic Analysis (1954); and Thomas Moore, Utopia (1516). Thomas Moore was sainted as he died a martyr for the Catholic Church in 1535. Reading a few pages of the English translation of the book, Utopia, clearly suggests that the book has little to do with neoclassical economic theory. Adam Smith's position as the first modern economist appears secure.

[11] Augustin Cournot, Researches into the Mathematical Principles of the Theory of Wealth (1838) (Eng. trans. 1971).

[12] Edward Chamberlin, The Theory of Monopolistic Competition (1933).

[13] *Id.* at 54.

[14] George Stigler, *A Theory of Oligopoly*, 72(1) J. Pol. Econ. 44-61 (1964).

Game theory offers a mathematical characterization for the oligopolistic interactions among firms

of the evidence. Such an inference is more likely when the number of buyers served by each competitor is relatively large (numerous customers switching leads to inference of discount pricing, even though little market share is lost), the market is relatively stable (buyers grow or shrink slowly, so they are less likely to switch suppliers for reasons unrelated to discounts), and the industry is relatively static (few new buyers exist to disrupt historical business relationships). If competitive conduct is readily identified, it is less likely to occur.

Stigler's theory clearly identified the two considerations associated with coordinated interaction concerns. First, the incumbents must be able to converge to a joint course of conduct to elevate price above the competitive level. Second, the incumbents require a mechanism to detect (and then punish) deviations from the arrangement to increase the probability that all participants abide by the chosen course of conduct. Understanding the structure of the firms, the fundamentals of the market transaction, and the information available to competitors is shown to be necessary to model the ease of collusion. Finally, the model retains a dynamic flavor as conditions that upset the collusive equilibrium (e.g., entry, growth, and innovation) are thought to make persistence of non-competitive pricing less likely. These core ideas are repeated in more modern characterizations of the collusion problem.

B. Post-Chicago Game Theoretic Analysis

Game theory offers a mathematical characterization for the oligopolistic interactions among firms.[15] Before providing an overview, it is necessary to introduce the models through which game theory represents the competitive process. The standard competitive baseline for both homogenous and differentiated goods is the one-shot Nash-Bertrand price-setting game. In a homogeneous market, with comparable cost conditions, the perfectly competitive equilibrium is generated as firms simply cannot raise price above the marginal cost, while in a differentiated goods market, firms unilaterally price above marginal costs to cover the fixed costs associated with the differentiation. Supra-normal profits are eliminated by entry.[16] The Cournot

[15] Carl Shapiro, *Theories of Oligopolistic Behavior, in* Handbook of Industrial Organization (Schmalensee & Willig, eds. 1989); and Dennis Carlton & Jeffrey Perloff, Modern Industrial Organization (2000).

[16] Mergers that fall short of monopoly may have no effect for the homogeneous goods market, but may allow a material price increase for a differentiated good. This non-cooperative price increase for differentiated goods markets represents the core of the unilateral effects concern introduced in the 1992 *Merger Guidelines*, although more detailed analysis must ensure (1) the model actually represents reality, (2) the price effect is material, and (3) repositioning of other rivals is unable to offset the price increase.

regime represents a secondary structure relevant to situations in which the firms (with homogenous goods) compete by setting output levels. Under these conditions, firms would restrict output below the competitive level and force price up. Again, entry could eliminate the supra-normal profits.[17]

Game theory illustrates just how difficult collusion is to prove

The possibility for collusion is usually modeled through the use of punishment strategies integrated into infinitely repeated games ("supergames") in which oligopolists compete in period after period. Technically, the strategies remain noncooperative as each firm unilaterally chooses to implement the punishment tactics. However, the interactive process implicit in the supergame represents almost a textbook characterization of tacit collusion (or mutual dependence recognized), so economists cannot help but characterize these non-cooperative games as collusive. Supergames allow for an infinite number of equilibriums, and lead to the Folk Theorem of Oligopoly: collusive equilibriums are sustainable for some set of parameters. Of course, competitive equilibriums are also possible, leading to another characterization of the Folk Theorem: competitive equilibriums are sustainable for some set of parameters. While economists could add complexities to try to eliminate the plethora of equilibriums, the problem remains that games could also be restructured to generate any desired theoretical equilibrium.[18] Game theory illustrates just how difficult collusion is to prove.

Game theoretical analysis remains useful, because the models highlight the discount rate that links the periods of the supergame together. Minimal discounting of the next period's returns (which implies rapid reactions to precompetitive price reductions) makes less than competitive equilibriums more viable. In effect, the ability of the collusive suppliers to respond quickly to competition means precompetitive behavior is less likely. While it is well understood that this speed of adjustment is related to the ability to quickly detect competitive conduct in a "spot" market, it is less obvious how to model speed of detection when customer-supplier commitments are relevant. If a firm can establish a long-term relationship with a large customer by cheating on

---

[17] Mergers may generate price effects in Cournot games, although the model would rarely be useful, as most firms set price and not output. Without some institutional restriction on output expansion to match a rival's action, the Cournot structure is not viable. The Cournot game may be more useful as a collusion model, assuming some exogenous agreement on the "rules of the game" has created the artificial incentive for firms to hold output fixed. Given an agreement to fix output via the Cournot structure, a merger would tend to make the market less competitive. *See* Malcolm Coate & Mark Williams, *Generalized Critical Loss for Market Definition,* 22 Research in L. & Econ. 41-58, note 4 (2007).

[18] For an analysis of the problems with real world applications of Post-Chicago economics, see Malcolm Coate & Jeffrey Fischer, *Daubert,* Science, and Modern Game Theory: Implications for Merger Analysis (unpublished manuscript) (September 2008), *available at* http://papers.ssrn.com/sol3/papers.cfm?abstract_id=1268386.

a cartel, then it may be impossible for its rivals to respond quickly even if the competitive conduct can be detected immediately. In effect, cheating on the collusion may allow the independent firm to lock up new business for a long period of time (this implies the need to use a high discount rate in the mathematical model). Understanding how market processes work should enable an analysis of the extent of vertical customer-supplier relationships. While game theory leaves a role for structural checklists, it significantly increases the level of detail required to undertake competitive analysis.

III. APPLICATION OF ECONOMICS TO MERGER ANALYSIS

Over the years, economic theory has generated a number of insights for the merger review process. The 1968 *Guidelines* focused enforcement on very small changes in market share, but noted that a more detailed analysis should be undertaken when share appeared to be a poor predictor of competitive effect. More aggressive enforcement was warranted when the target firm was likely to be a disruptive force in the market (this "disruptive force" concept was later remarketed as the "maverick" firm). The 1982 *Guidelines* added a set of "other factors" relevant to oligopoly analysis.[19] Structure, conduct, and performance considerations were all mentioned and the discussion generally tracked Posner's oligopoly checklist. The 1992 *Guidelines* presented a more complex economic analysis that separated the discussion associated with reaching an agreement from the commentary on policing an agreement. The importance of a sophisticated understanding of information structures, along with knowledge of the basic institutional mechanisms of a market, was also stressed. However, the importance of performance evidence was limited to a comment on explicit price-fixing and a couple of footnotes.[20]

As the foundation for the 1982 *Guidelines*, Posner's checklist is addressed in sub-section A, while the 1992 *Guidelines* material is discussed in more detail in sub-section B. A final sub-section, which focuses on performance evidence, is included to introduce the "Folk Theorem of Merger Enforcement." This concept, implicit in the staff applications of the *Guidelines*, suggests that structural collusion models should be tested with exogenous evidence.

---

[19] *See* U.S. Department of Justice, *Merger Guidelines*, ANTITRUST TRADE REG. REPORT 1069 (1982); and U.S. Department of Justice, *Merger Guidelines*, 2 Trade Reg. Report (CHH) ¶ 4510 (1982).

[20] The 1992 *Merger Guidelines* note that market conditions are likely to be conducive to coordinated interaction when firms in the market have (1) engaged in express collusion and (2) salient characteristics of the market have not changed. Implicit performance evidence may also be addressed. *See, e.g.,* § 2.1 (focuses on consumer harm) and note 22 (mentions the use of normal course of business documents) of the *Guidelines*.

A. The 1982 *Guidelines* and Posner's Checklist

Richard Posner created a classic checklist of characteristics associated with oligopolistic interdependence as part of his ambitious attempt to expand the reach of the antitrust laws to encompass tacit collusion.[21] These structural conditions are listed below.[22]

- High market share: The Herfindahl statistic (defined by the sum of the square of the market shares held by the firms in the market) is a generally accepted proxy for impact of market share on the probability of less than competitive conduct. While higher values for the Herfindahl statistic tend to increase the likelihood and duration of competitive problems, the magnitude of the effect must be evaluated on the basis of industry-specific evidence. High values of the Herfindahl are correlated with relatively few significant competitors (firms required to participate in the cartel), but the Herfindahl is able to proxy the relative size of the firms.
- No fringe: Fringe firms are price takers and thus unlikely to participate in any arrangements to raise price. Collusion is more likely to evolve or persist, the smaller the fringe (and the more limited its ability to expand output).
- Inelastic demand at competitive price: The market elasticity measures the loss of sales associated with customers substituting away from the market. If a price increase leads to a small reduction in output (inelastic demand), then the significant firms need only to

[21] In contrast to most scholars who consider pure tacit collusion to be legal (due to the lack of an agreement), Posner looked at the effects of the tacit collusion (usually higher prices) and found price-fixing. He proposed a more aggressive style of analysis in which the pricing in a less than competitive manner would be illegal. *See* Posner (1976), *supra* note 7. To promote this outcome, Posner listed a number of factors that make markets relatively more susceptible to tacit collusion and introduced conduct and performance factors that were potentially compatible with collusion. While this style of price-fixing analysis never had much support, it became the standard for merger analysis in the 1980s.

[22] Two conditions (local markets and cooperative practices) are not listed here, because they seem more related to reaching an illegal price-fixing agreement than coordinated interaction. Posner also added one characteristic of conduct (antitrust record) to his list of conditions favorable to collusion and four examples of problematic conduct (exchange of price information, industry-wide resale price maintenance, base point pricing, and exclusionary conduct) as examples of economic evidence of less than competitive behavior. These conduct considerations were also mentioned in the 1982 *Guidelines*, along with the 1968 *Guidelines'* concept of the disruptive firm. Finally, Posner's analysis included a list of performance conditions suggestive of less than competitive behavior. Evidence associated with current less than competitive performance is useful to test the implications of the structural analysis.

reduce their production slightly to force price up. Thus, coordinated interaction is more likely to occur.

- Entry takes a long time: Collusion to restrict competition is more likely to evolve and persist when entry takes a long time, as the potential returns to less than competitive behavior are higher.
- Buying side of market is unconcentrated: Arrangements to restrict competition are more likely to persist when the buyer side of the market is relatively atomistic. Large buyers may be able to threaten the stability of a cartel by shifting significant purchases to suppliers willing to price competitively.
- Standardized product: Firms generally find it easier to agree on the terms of coordination and ensure all significant rivals participate in the arrangement when the product is standardized. Also, standardization makes it easier to detect deviations from any collusive agreement.
- Non-durable product: Non-durable goods are not relevant for market competition in future periods, because customers cannot invest in maintenance to extend the life of the good. Thus, markets with nondurable goods are more likely to suffer from collusion than markets with durable goods.
- Principal firms sell at same level of distribution: Coordination interaction is simpler to establish and maintain when it is operationalized at one vertical level.
- Similar cost structures and production processes: Some form of collusion is more likely to evolve and persist when all the significant competitors share the same cost structure and technology.
- Demand is static or declining: Firms are more likely to sustain a policy of less than competitive behavior when the market is static or declining, because the oligopolists do not have to deal with a constant flow of new customers and products into the market.
- Prices can change quickly: The ability to adjust price in a timely manner makes punishment strategies more effective and hence tends to make coordinated interaction more successful.

---

[23] The 1982 *Guidelines* generalize this point to focus on the supplier's ability to obtain detailed information on prices, outputs, or specific transactions. Sealed bidding is simply one example in which good information is available.

- Sealed bidding: The use of sealed bidding makes it easier to identify competitive pricing, as the winning bid must be published. As secret price discounts are impossible, collusion is more likely to be sustained over time.[23]

The fundamental problem with a structural Posnerian merger analysis is the lack of a general theoretical analysis to facilitate the evaluation of the relevant factors. Empirical information on the structural factors can be tabulated and some broad-based observations derived, but balancing the impact of the factors to evaluate the likely competitive effect of a merger is purely subjective.[24] Moreover, it is unclear how to work the structural effect of the merger into the analysis. As Scheffman and Coleman note, checklists "are too crude to provide much assistance in determining whether a coordinated interaction theory is relevant."[25]

In its defense, Posner's collusion presentation moves beyond structure and includes market performance evidence. Generalizing Posner's price-fixing analysis to address merger enforcement would therefore trigger a search for performance evidence compatible with the structural competitive concern. Hence, a complete Posnerian study of a merger in an oligopolistic industry could generate useful results, as the implications of the structural analysis would be validated with performance evidence.

B. The 1992 *Merger Guidelines* Characterization

The 1992 *Merger Guidelines* address the limitation of the structural analysis first by sub-dividing the coordinated interaction issue into its constituent parts (predicting (1) whether a post-merger arrangement is likely to evolve and (2) if that arrangement is likely to persist), and then by insisting that the analysis provides an explanation of how prices could be elevated above the competitive level. By concentrating on the need to tell a story, the revised *Guidelines* are better able to focus the analysis on the relevant informational and institutional structures in the market. While informational issues underlie a number of the Posnerian conditions, the *Guidelines* stress the importance of information as a stand-alone structural characteristic. The institutional details of the competitive process within a market must also be evaluated to determine if

[24] The standard Posnerian checklist could be used to conclude a merger is not likely to enhance collusive pricing if the review identified few factors suggestive of concern. Alternatively, if enough assumptions are made, then a mathematical model could be parameterized and used to estimate the price effects of a merger. *See, e.g.,* Janusz Ordover et al., *Herfindahl Concentration and Mergers*, 95 Harv. L. Rev. 1857-73 (1982).

[25] David Scheffman & Mary Coleman, *Quantitative Analysis of Potential Competitive Effects from a Merger*, 12(2) Geo. Mason L. Rev. 319-69, 327 (2003).

However, a more detailed collusion model could suggest price agreements are less likely to form in static markets, because the potential profit from collusion is lower

post-merger collusion is likely. For example, generic information on the business conditions facing rivals may increase the probability of some form of agreement, while the availability of information on specific transactions or individual prices and output levels may make the detection of price discounting more likely, all else equal. On the other hand, customer-supplier relationships might moot the importance of information, because once the customer switches, the new vertical relationship is established. This relationship may possibly be immune to short-run offers of discounts.

The basic Posnerian considerations generally point in the same direction for the two 1992 *Guidelines* questions.[26] For example, high market share is considered to make an agreement on price more likely to occur, because fewer firms need to be involved in the understanding. Likewise, an agreement is easier to monitor and police when it is only necessary to follow the actions of a few competitors. Arguments can also be made that certain conditions support one oligopoly task, while making the other less likely. Either effect could dominate, given specific market conditions. For example, Stigler's model shows agreements are easier to monitor in a static market. However, a more detailed collusion model could suggest price agreements are less likely to form in static markets, because the potential profit from collusion is lower.

A few of Posner's factors are generalized by the *Guidelines*. Posner considers collusion more likely when demand is static or declining. The *Guidelines* expand this concept to address any dynamic change in the market. Maintaining a collusive agreement is simply more difficult when market conditions (e.g., demand curves, cost conditions, or innovation) are changing rapidly. Second, Posner observes collusion is more likely when prices can change rapidly. The *Guidelines* also generalize this issue to focus on the characteristics of the typical transaction. The speed associated with changing any detail in the representative transaction could also affect the ease of collusion.

---

[26] Three of Posner's characteristics are not explicitly mentioned in the *Guidelines'* competitive effects section, but remain relevant to the overall analysis. Inelasticity of demand is not noted, although the factor is important in the market definition analysis. Likewise, the relevance of ease of entry for the likelihood of coordinated interaction is not explained, although it is obviously covered in the entry section. Finally, the durable nature of the good is not highlighted as relevant to collusion, but is touched on in the entry discussion.

[27] In a recent commentary, Dick (2003) suggested that the *Guidelines'* analysis should focus on two questions to address this concern. First, what constrains the suppliers' pre-merger incentive or ability to coordinate their actions? In effect, the merger review must discover what drives the pre-merger pricing decisions. This understanding leads to the second question: How will the proposed merger change the existing constraints on competition? This approach would also link the *Guidelines'* analysis to a specific economic theory. *See* Andrew Dick, *Coordinated Interaction: Pre-merger Constraints and Post-merger Effects,* 12(1) Geo. Mason L. Rev. 65-88 (2003).

While the *Guidelines'* structure offers insight into the issue of collusion, it must link the analytical structure to the merger in question to be useful for antitrust policy.[27] In the overview to the coordinated interaction section, the *Guidelines* state: "A merger may diminish competition by enabling the firms selling in the relevant market more likely, more successfully, or more completely to engage in coordinated interaction that harms consumers."[28] The term "more likely" implies the merger causes some type of regime shift in which the merger changes the market from competitive to collusive (the maverick model explicitly mentioned in the *Guidelines'* text is simply an example of a regime-shift model) and the phrase "more completely" suggests that some type of structuralist model is relevant (as the market is currently less than competitive, and the merger worsens the situation). "More successfully" implies some effect on the durability of the coordinated interaction process (regime shift becomes more likely to persist given the fixed probability it will occur or the structuralist effect becomes more long-lasting).

Coate & Ulrick discuss three styles of coordinated interaction analysis (maverick, general regime shift, and structuralism) that are found in FTC staff analysis.[29] Maverick analysis applies when one of the merging parties has a relatively unique and significant incentive to deviate from the terms of the collusive consensus. Under certain conditions, the maverick firm ensures that the market remains competitive and its loss through merger leads to some form of collusion. In the standard maverick theory, facts are used to identify and prove the specific characteristics of the maverick and its loss is then considered likely to trigger collusion.[30] Mathematical precision is possible if the compatible oligopolists are considered to act in a

---

[28] *See* 1992 *Merger Guidelines*, at § 2.1.

[29] *See* Malcolm Coate & Shawn Ulrick, *Influential Evidence in Merger Enforcement at the Federal Trade Commission, in* Issues in Competition Law & Policy (W.D. Collins, ed. 2008). The three theories are also mentioned in Malcolm Coate, *Economic Models in Merger Analysis: A Case Study of the Merger Guidelines,* 2(1) Rev. L. & Econ. 53-84 (2006). Moreover, Scheffman & Coleman (2003), *supra* note 25, at 328-29, without benefit of the systematic review of the files, define three comparable theories (evidence of existing effective coordinated interaction, removal of a maverick, and removal of other impediments to coordination).

[30] Baker & Shapiro (2007) also posit a more generic maverick model to be applied when specific facts are not available. This model simply assumes that the merger partners have a significant probability of being the maverick when the number of significant competitors is small. Thus, the merger is likely to lead to the loss of this hypothetical maverick. This second "theory" simply appeals to structuralism, as specific facts supporting the maverick hypothesis are not required. *See* Jonathan Baker & Carl Shapiro, Reinvigorating Horizontal Merger Enforcement (unpublished manuscript) (June 2007), *available at* http://faculty.haas.berkeley.edu/shapiro/mergerpolicy.pdf.

[31] The analysis could start with the classic Landes & Posner (1981) model and generalize the monopolist to represent the set of collusive firms and the fringe to include the maverick. The model would be calibrated to generate a competitive equilibrium when the maverick prices as a fringe firm. *See* William Landes & Richard Posner, *Market Power in Antitrust Cases,* 94(5) Harv. L. Rev. 937-96 (1981).

less than competitive manner, but coordinated pricing is not profitable in light of the competition from the maverick firm (in combination with the fringe entities). Parameterizing a complex model should allow the calculation of a competitive equilibrium.[31] Then the analyst could adjust the model to transform the maverick from an independent competitor to a cartel participant and compute the merger-related price increase. Baker (2002) and Baker & Shapiro (2007) appear to advance the maverick model as the only relevant model of collusion for antitrust policy.[32]

The staff also considers a general "regime-shift" model in which the pre-merger structure gives rise to a competitive outcome, while the post-merger structure is conducive to some form of collusion. Modeling the regime shift is limited only by the imagination of the merger analyst. For example, mergers that created or enhanced the power of a leading firm could be problematic as price leadership could facilitate both establishing and policing an agreement. Moreover, the concern with the leadership would be heightened if the leader actively supported conduct (e.g., product standardization or information exchanges) that appeared to reduce the costs of coordinated interaction. Mergers may also create more symmetry in the market. When few rivals exist, increasing the product, marketing, distribution, and cost symmetries in the market could make a collusive equilibrium more likely. Concerns would be enhanced when market structures ensure that rivals understand their mutual interdependence. More generic models of competition could also give rise to collusive concerns when the number of firms in the market is reduced. These regime shift models can also be quantified by modeling the shift from competition to some form of collusion.[33]

Structuralism is also anticipated in the *Guidelines*, as the pre-merger structure could support a small collusive surcharge, while the post-merger structure could enable a higher collusive price. Structural evidence may suggest that at least weak coordinated interaction is likely pre-merger. Post-merger, the structure will become much more compatible with less than competitive behavior and the market price may rise. While theorists consider Cournot to represent unilateral behavior, the single shot Cournot game could be used to give a mathematical veneer to a structural coordinated interaction model, as prices rise with a reduction in the number of independent competitors, holding costs constant. The analyst need only parameterize the model for the current market conditions and compute the effect associated with deleting a rival. Interested analysts could generalize the simple model to allow for fringe competition, differentiation, or cost asymmetries.

---

32 *See* Baker (2002), *supra* note 3; and Jonathan Baker & Carl Shapiro, *supra* note 30.

33 Fisher et al. (1988), for example, used a Cournot structure for the collusive regime, while a Bertrand structure illustrated the pre-merger competition. *See* Alan Fisher et al., *Price Effects of Horizontal Mergers*, 77 CAL. L. REV. 777-827 (1988).

Building a theoretical foundation for coordinated effects concerns appears to move the analysis beyond the checklist stage and creates a road map for economic analysis. The analyst can review the record of the investigation and collect evidence to parameterize the relevant theory in much the same way as unilateral effects analysis. Scheffman & Coleman detail a number of studies that can be undertaken as part of the analysis.[34] Facts must determine which of the many oligopoly theories are appropriate for the specific merger. In effect, this analysis can appeal to the timeless Friedman commentary on methodology in economics.[35] The analyst can infer the market behaves "as if" competition follows a model of collusion whenever the collusion model generates testable implications for competition in the particular market that are not falsified by the evidence. If multiple models survive the testing process, the choice between the models is based on a balancing of simplicity and fruitfulness considerations. Mathematical derivation from stylized facts may be helpful, but it is not necessary. In the next subsection, details on how this testing process appears to have played out are given.

Building a theoretical foundation for coordinated effects concerns appears to move the analysis beyond the checklist stage and creates a road map for economic analysis

C. Folk Theorem of Merger Enforcement

In reviewing FTC enforcement activity, it is clear that the *Guidelines'* analyses define testable hypotheses for the competitive effects of mergers.[36] The structural analysis explains the effect of the merger-related change in structure on the competitive environment. Competitive concerns are raised when the merger is likely to generate an adverse effect on consumers in a relevant market. While the bulk of the coordinated effects analyses remain qualitative, mathematical

---

[34] *See* Scheffman & Coleman (2003), *supra* note 25.

[35] Milton Friedman, Essays in Positive Economics 3-43 (1953).

[36] Scheffman et al. (2003) note that evidence on customer concerns and hot documents have always been used to support inference of coordinated interaction in the modern Guidelines era. Natural experiments were also noted as relevant to the study of likely competitive effects. See David Scheffman et al., *Twenty Years of Merger Guidelines Enforcement at the FTC: An Economic Perspective,* 71(1) Antitrust L.J. 277-331, 304 (2003). The FTC-DOJ merger commentaries also detail situations in which evidence is used to support inferences of less than competitive behavior stemming from a merger. *See* U.S. Federal Trade Commission & U.S. Department of Justice, Commentary on the Horizontal Merger Guidelines (2006), at 22-23, *available at* http://www.ftc.gov/os/2006/03/CommentaryontheHorizontalMergerGuidelinesMarch2006.pdf. *See also* Malcolm Coate, *Empirical Analysis of Merger Enforcement under the 1992 Merger Guidelines,* 27 REV. INDUS. ORG. 279-301 (2005); and Coate & Ulrick (2008), *supra* note 29.

collusion models can be designed to predict less than competitive outcomes that can then be balanced against efficiencies. Any type of economic analysis actually generates a testable hypothesis for the effect of the merger.

From reviewing the case files, it is clear that a "Folk Theorem of Merger Enforcement" exists. Simply put, this theorem observes that whenever pre-merger evidence suggests a causal relationship between structure and performance exists, then a merger materially affecting structure is likely to substantially lessen competition. Theory is needed to give context to the evidence and evidence is needed to test the implications of the theory. As Friedman observes, economic science is hypothesis testing. Of course, testing does not guarantee success in court, because the defendants might also advance a validated economic theory suggestive of continued competition. The legal process sorts out the valid evidence and reaches a decision on the merits.

In another article, three types of evidence used by FTC staff for "testing" coordinated interaction theories are discussed.[37] In the best case scenario, evidence of natural experiments is found in which a structural change, comparable to the merger in question, generated anticompetitive effects. This evidence is likely to be more available for the very explicit theories of concern (maverick and structuralist), because the search for evidence can be focused. Natural experiment evidence may also be inferred from evidence on hot document or customer complaints. In this instance, the idea is that the hot document or customer complaint is based on a firm's or customer's recollection of a natural experiment (or series of natural experiments), that leads to the conclusion memorialized in the specific evidence. The reviews of the FTC analyses show some form of evidence is regularly found in the investigations, although actual evidence is not a necessary condition for an enforcement action.[38] In the next section, econometric analysis checks for the link between natural experiment evidence and coordinated interaction findings.

[37] Coate (2005), *id.* It is also possible to consider natural experiment evidence that supports a pro-competitive theory of the merger. Initial analysis shows this pro-competitive evidence variable does not have a significant effect on the enforcement decision.

[38] In addition to explicit or implicit natural experiments, it is possible to test theories of competitive concern with general economic evidence. The anticompetitive effects associated with merger to monopoly are the best example of such an analysis, because economic science has systematically found monopolies behave in a less than competitive manner. The structure-conduct-performance model also provided the scientific basis for merger enforcement until the general version of the theory was falsified. *See* Coate & Fischer (2008), *supra* note 18. A recent study by Kovacic et al. (2005) suggests that mergers to duopoly are problematic, at least in homogeneous (chemical) industries. *See* William Kovacic et al., Lessons for Competition Policy from the Vitamins Cartel (unpublished manuscript) (Sep. 2005), *available at* http://ssrn.com/abstract=818744.

IV. AN ENFORCEMENT MODEL FOR COORDINATED INTERACTION

The background on economic theory will serve to structure the search for an empirical model of coordinated interaction. Statistical analysis should highlight relationships between structural characteristics and FTC enforcement policy (this paper's proxy for a collusion concern), as well as identify the impact of the natural experiment effects evidence or any other explanatory variable. One limitation must be discussed. The 1992 *Guidelines* propose a case-specific study of coordinated interaction, with the analyst required to obtain data on information structures and institutional realities. This style of analysis is not easily quantified and thus must be left out of this study. However, this search for informational structures and institutional realities is (1) based on structural considerations and (2) would be expected to affect the collection of effects evidence. Thus, the formal *Guidelines* style of analysis may be implicit in the modeling. In the following two subsections, the data collection process is reviewed first, followed by a discussion of model specification.

A. Data On Collusion Analysis in Merger Enforcement

The merger enforcement decision at the FTC has been studied in a number of recent papers[39] While these papers estimate the probability of a merger challenge, the basic data can also be used to evaluate the likelihood of a subsidiary finding that the merger makes collusion "more likely, more successful, or more complete." This subsidiary finding will drive the enforcement decision if (1) coordinated interaction is the appropriate theory, (2) barriers to entry are present, and (3) efficiencies are integrated into the analysis to account for the overall effect (if any) of cost savings. Thus, to transform a dataset focused on the enforcement decision into a dataset addressing the likelihood of coordinated interaction, it is only necessary to delete all the unilateral effects cases, remove the matters in which ease of entry is dispositive on the issue of competitive concern, and incorporate evidence on efficiencies into the model. Of course, such an analysis is only able to identify the interpretation of coordinated interaction that appears in FTC enforcement decisions. To the extent the agency's interpretation is not

---

39 *See* Mats Bergman et al., Comparing Merger Policies: the European Union versus the United States (unpublished manuscript) (March 2007), *available at* http://ssrn.com/abstract=975102; Malcolm Coate & Shawn Ulrick, *Transparency at the Federal Trade Commission: The Horizontal Merger Review Process*, 73(2) ANTITRUST L.J. 531-570 (2006); and Coate (2005), *supra* note 36. For an overview of all the recent papers using FTC data, see Malcolm Coate, An Overview of Transparency at the Federal Trade Commission: Generalities and Innovations in Merger Analysis (unpublished manuscript) (September 2008), *available at* http://ssrn.com/abstraxt=1111687.

consistent with an economic evaluation of the coordinated interaction concerns, the analysis may draw incorrect conclusions.[40]

The data collection process started with the 166 merger investigations identified in Bergman et al. exhibiting between one and three markets potentially affected by the merger and added twenty-one new matters reviewed in 2004 and 2005 to the dataset.[41] The 108 unilateral effects cases were deleted to focus purely on the collusion investigations. A further 19 files were deleted as the staff attorneys concluded entry was easy. This left a total of 60 collusion cases. To increase the sample, additional markets associated with the 187 matters were coded, whenever (1) the theory of concern was oligopoly and (2) the legal staff found barriers to entry. By looking at every market studied in the 187 investigations, it was possible to increase the sample to 76 investigations. One case had to be deleted, because the decision to close was intertwined with the failing-firm analysis. This left a sample of 75 collusion merger investigations undertaken during the 1993 to 2005 period.

Figure 1 defines the structural and evidence variables collected from the FTC files and provides the ranges and summary statistics.[42] In addition to the standard information on the Herfindahl (HHI), the detailed review of the files identified the number of firms in the market with an ability to materially affect the outcome of the competitive process (defined as significant rivals and measured prior to the merger) as well as raw market share data. This share information allowed the calculation of two additional explanatory variables: fringe share and leadership ratio. The fringe variable was computed by summing the shares attributed to the significant rivals and then subtracting that number from one. It ranged from 0 to over 40 percent. The leadership proxy was calculated by dividing the share of the leading firm by the share of the second largest firm in the market. This variable ranged from one (for numbers equivalent situations in which no firm leads the market) to over five. It was calculated for the post-merger environment to incorporate the change in structure caused by the merger.

Five binary variables were coded to capture insights associated with market structure. A homogeneous goods index was derived based on a staff finding of relative similarity for the products in the market.[43] If the staff reported the specific good was customized to the buyer's

[40] Of course, the study would remain useful as an evaluation of the internal review structure even if it could be shown that some enforcement decisions were not consistent with standard economic theory.

[41] *See* Bergman et al. (2007), *supra* note 39.

[42] The raw structural information (market concentration, theories of concern, and product homogeneity) are based on the attorney analyses. More complex variables (not necessarily addressed in every attorney memo) are based on findings by either attorneys or economists.

[43] *See* Coate (2006), *supra* note 29.

FIGURE 1 Overview of the Explanatory Variables

Variable	Definition	Range	Mean Enforced	Mean Closed
Herfindahl (HHI)	Herfindahl Index computed by summing the square of market share held by each firm in the post-merger market	1437-7008	3727*	2990
Significant Rivals	Number of pre-merger "significant" rivals in market affected by merger	3/10	4.02*	5.85
Fringe Share	Market share held by firms not considered significant in the analysis.	0/43.6	9.20*	12.3
Share Ratio	Ratio of share of largest post-merger firm to share of second largest entity	1/5.8	1.91	1.76
Homogenous Good	Indicator variable for homogeneous goods finding in attorney data	0/1	.521	.370
Buyer Sophistication	Indicator variable to identify cases in which buyer power was found by either attorneys or economists	0/1	.188*	.370
Inelastic Demand	Indicator variables for market in the hospital, oil, or drug industry	0/1	.417	.370
Vertical Issues	Indicator variable to identify cases in which vertical aspects of merger were considered by attorneys or economists	0/1	.125*	.370
Efficiencies	Indicator variable for efficiency finding by either attorneys or economists	0/1	.438*	.741
Evidence	Index of anti-competitive findings associated with customer complaints, hot documents or historical natural experiments by either attorneys or economists; 0 implies no such findings, 3 means all three factors reported.	0-3	1.17*	.407
Maverick Firms	Indicator variable for Maverick firm finding in the attorney files	0/1	.270	.111
Administration (Bush)	Indicator variable for control of FTC by Chairman appointed after June 2001	0/1	.333	.185
Cases	Number of matters reviewed		48	27

*The sample mean for the enforced cases is significantly different from the mean for closed cases.

specification, this was also coded as homogenous when the bulk of the firms in the market were able to meet consumer demand on relatively equal terms. Buyer sophistication signaled a staff observation that customers had some ability to negotiate with their suppliers.[44] Having a large buyer implied sophistication, but no clear buyer share cutoff existed. The vertical variable identified mergers in which the staff investigation identified some vertical relationship affected by the merger.[45] For example, if a large upstream firm with a horizontal presence in a downstream market bought a competitor, the vertical relationship would be found. A fourth variable attempts to proxy the elasticity of demand with information on the industry involved in the merger.[46] Finally, an efficiency index was assembled.[47] It takes on the value one whenever either the attorneys or economists report evidence of merger-specific efficiencies. As the FTC often stops short of formally endorsing the efficiency claims, language suggestive of merger-specific savings was taken as relevant.[48] Figure 1 reports that the enforced matters were statistically likely to exhibit different findings for sophistication, vertical issues, and efficiencies.

Performance evidence associated with natural experiments was also collected.[49] Simply put, each file was reviewed for hot documents, validated customer complaints, and economic effects compatible with the theory of concern. The evidence on hot documents and customer concern was relatively easy to obtain from the files.[50] FTC staff generally highlighted these "legal" findings and explained their importance relative to the rest of the information in the file. Thus, it was possible to separate the relevant from the irrelevant information.[51] The economic effect variable required more creativity, because economic facts must be interpreted in light of a theory of concern. In this instance, the analysis first identified the theory of concern at the core of the investigation and then evaluated any natural experiment supportive of the predictions of that theory. For example,

---

43 *See* Coate (2006), *supra* note 29.

44 Buyer sophistication was borrowed from Coate & Ulrick (2008), *supra* note 29. In effect, the variable flagged markets in which the staff recognized that the institutional arrangements associated with market competition allow complex bilateral negotiations.

45 The vertical variable is lifted from Bergman et al. (2007), *supra* note 39.

46 Hospital, oil, and drug industry matters are assumed to exhibit relatively inelastic demand

47 *See* Coate (2005), *supra* note 36.

48 The level of verification memorialized in the file varied from case to case, thus conclusionary language was used to code the index.

49 *See* Coate (2005), *supra* note 36.

50 This is detailed in Coate & Ulrick (2006), *supra* note 39.

51 Customers complain about all sorts of things, sometimes related to the likely competitive effect of the merger on competition and other times linked to the effect of the merger on their business. FTC staff reviews identify the complaints associated with a loss of competition. Likewise, a range of documents can be identified as "hot." The review only flags the claims when the document links an adverse effect on competition to the consummation of the merger.

FIGURE 2 Types of Collusion Investigations with Barriers to Entry[a] (percentage in parenthesis is enforcement rate)

Market Conditions	Matters	Homogeneous Sophisticated	Homogeneous Not Sophisticated	Not Homogeneous
One Merger Partner is Industry Leader	36 (66.7%)	6 (50%)	13 (92.3%)	17 (52.9%)
Together Merged Firm Becomes Industry Leader	22 (63.6%)	0 (NA)	10 (70.0%)	12 (58.3%)
Together Merged Firm Becomes Second Firm	8 (62.5%)	1 (0%)	0 (NA)	7 (71.4%)
Number Equivalent Analysis	5 (60.0%)	0 (NA)	3 (100%)	2 (0%)
Together Merged Firm Becomes Third Firm	4 (50.0%)	1 (0%)	1 (0%)	2 (100%)
Total	75 (64.0%)	8 (37.5%)	27 (81.5%)	40 (57.5%)

[a] Number of Cases for each structural regime listed in Figure.

economic evidence that the acquired firm had behaved as a maverick in the past and protected competition would be considered supportive of the implications of a maverick theory of violation.[52]

Two other variables ("maverick" and "administration") were recovered from the files. The maverick variable flags the cases in which the staff simply reported a claim of maverick status for one of the merging parties, but failed to present natural experiment evidence supportive of the maverick model. Thus, this indicator flags the cases in which the investigation identified unsubstantiated allegations of maverick status. The second variable, administration, identified the cases filed after June 2001. These matters were all decided under a chairman appointed by U.S. President George W. Bush.

Figure 2 presents some initial information on the data. As a first analysis, the shares of all of the significant competitors were identified and analyzed. The first row summarizes results

[52] Posner's list of performance characteristics could be useful to show the market is currently performing in a less than competitive manner, a result supportive of a structural model of concern. See *Posner* (1976), *supra* note 7.

for 36 matters in which one of the two merging firms holds the largest share in the market. By definition, these firms would obtain an even larger lead on their rivals if the merger was consummated. However, it is important to note that the merger would not allow the new firm to dominate the market, because that concern would have triggered a unilateral effects analysis. The second row focuses on transactions in which a larger leading firm was created by the merger. Here, another 22 matters are flagged, although in some matters, the post-merger share would barely exceed that of the previous market leader. The next row provides information for mergers that create a larger number two firm. Only eight cases are found. The fourth row reports on five numbers-equivalent cases. In these matters, the staff weights all the significant competitors equally; hence, a merger would reduce the number of players by one, but have no other effect on structure. The last row counts the mergers that create stronger number three competitors, where a total of four cases are noted.

In theory, structural analysis should differ for each type of case, probably leading to significant differences in enforcement probabilities. In fact, this does not occur as the enforcement rates vary only slightly (50 percent to 66.7 percent) over the sample. The rest of figure explores this result, disaggregating the cases by a combination of homogeneous goods and buyer sophistication status. Although the sample of homogeneous goods with sophisticated buyers is small, these matters show relatively low enforcement (37.5 percent), especially when compared to the rate associated with homogeneous goods with unsophisticated buyers (significantly higher at 81.5 percent). Moreover, the homogeneous goods markets without sophisticated buyers are statistically more likely to end in enforcement action than the differentiated goods.[53] In light of these complex interrelationships in the data, econometric analysis is required to sort out the regularities in the data.

B. Modeling Merger Enforcement

In theory, it would be desirable to separately model what appear to be the FTC's three collusion theories (maverick, regime shift, and structuralist). However, this approach is precluded by data limitations. Instead, it is necessary to aggregate all the data together and explore two general models, one that focuses purely on structural considerations and the other that adds an evidence variable to the analysis. If evidence matters, then the variable would take on a significant positive sign. If the structural variables also matter, then they will retain their statistical significance (and signs). Within this approach, it is possible to model market concentration in more detail, investigate the scope of customer sophistication, and explore the impact of the

[53] Interestingly, buyer sophistication does not appear to affect enforcement probability in the differentiated goods sample.

maverick theory. Finally, it is possible to see if the Bush administration changed the decision-making process for coordinated interaction investigations.

Finally, it is possible to see if the Bush administration changed the decision-making process for coordinated interaction investigations

The basic structural model focuses on a concentration index (e.g., the Herfindahl index) and five control variables (homogeneous good, buyer sophistication, inelastic demand, vertical considerations, and merger-related efficiencies). The market share data available in the files allows the analysis to move beyond the Herfindahl index and explore market structure in more detail. Three variables are considered. First, the number of significant competitors is included, because the coordinated interaction would require cooperation from all significant players. Second, the size of the fringe could matter, because a substantial fringe might be able to undermine the collusion. Third, the potential for leadership might be important, because a relatively large firm could set the terms for coordination. Leadership is defined as the post-merger ratio of the share of the leading firm to its largest competitor. These three variables are used to replace the Herfindahl index in some of the specifications.

The five control variables all represent standard structural considerations. First, it is generally considered easier to coordinate price when the product is relatively homogeneous. Therefore, a positive sign is expected for this index. Buyer sophistication tends to make coordinated interaction less likely, as sophisticated buyers are able to negotiate with the various competitors in the market and possibly undermine collusive prices. In this instance, a negative sign is expected. Inelastic demand is generally thought to make collusion more likely as output restrictions needed to support higher prices would be relatively low. A positive sign is likely. The vertical indicator identifies markets in which firms interact at various vertical levels. In general, this observation would suggest that less room exists for collusive behavior. Moreover, the merger supposes a change in this vertical relationship, a change that would tend to reduce vertical transaction costs. These vertical efficiencies also make cartelization less likely. Overall, a finding of vertical ramifications implies a negative relationship with a finding of coordinated interaction.

The final variable addresses efficiency considerations. Findings of efficiencies imply an effect on the cost structure of some of the market competitors. Cost differentials can affect the probability of coordinated interaction in two ways. First, cost differences make it more difficult to coordinate on price, hence collusion is less likely. Second, even if some coordination can occur, the price could be lower. Both considerations point to a negative effect on coordinated interaction. One generalization of the basic model is considered, as customer sophistication is interacted with the homogeneous good variable. Basically, sophistication would be expected to have a much greater effect when the market is homogeneous and customers could more easily pit suppliers against each other and undermine any collusive agreement.

The structural model is complemented with the evidence index. This variable serves to identify the degree of exogenous support for the relevant theory of coordinated interaction. Logically, the more evidence supporting a competitive concern, the more likely a collusion finding will be made. Hence, a positive coefficient is expected for the evidence variable. The other structural variables may retain their significance, or become statistically indistinguishable from zero, depending on whether evidence supplements or trumps market structure.

Next, an indicator for a claim of maverick status is added to the model. If the maverick status mattered, it would make a finding of collusion more likely whenever a maverick firm is identified.[54] Note the analysis is only testing for the importance of a maverick allegation, because natural experiment evidence related to a maverick effect is already included in the model through the evidence index.

Finally, an indicator for Bush administration control of the FTC is included in the model. The shift parameter indicates whether the Bush administration revitalized coordinated effects analysis.[55] This data is unable to determine if the administration was more aggressive overall, because it would require a joint study of entry and coordinated effects analysis.

V. ESTIMATION OF THE MODELS

The statistical analysis is undertaken in a series of twelve probit regressions, presented in Figures 3, 4, and 5.[56] The discussion in this section will track the visual presentation of the models, although the bulk of the analysis will be focused on the last model in each figure. Examples of the impact of various structures on the probability of a concern will be given.

Figure 3 presents a standard Herfindahl-based model of coordinated interaction.[57] In all the specifications, the Herfindahl index is positively related to a concern, suggesting market shares matter. In model 3-1, customer sophistication, inelastic demand, and vertical issues also affect the collusion finding, with the expected signs. Efficiencies exhibit the expected negative effect, but tests slightly below conventional levels of statistical significance. A finding of homogeneous goods

---

[54] *See* Baker (2002), *supra* note 3.

[55] *See* Darren Tucker & Bilal Sayyed, *The Merger Guidelines Commentary: Practical Guidance and Missed Opportunities,* Antitrust Source 1-13, 8 (May 2006).

[56] Both the continuous and discrete variables are transformed with the natural logarithm function to allow for more nonlinear effects (one is added to the evidence index to enable the transformation). A clustered errors technique is used to address the fact that some mergers are represented by two or three analyses of different markets of concern.

[57] The change in Herfindahl along with the interaction of the change and the Herfindahl can be included in the model, but proved to be statistically insignificant and thus are not reported.

FIGURE 3 Standard Oligopoly Model[a]

	3-1 (Structure)	3-2 (Structure)[b]	3-3 (Evidence)	3-4 (Evidence)[b]
HHI	2.756*** (5.11)	2.864*** (4.32)	2.588*** (4.55)	2.665*** (3.66)
Homogenous Good	.3813 (.92)	1.054** (2.18)	.4563 (1.02)	1.358** (2.13)
Buyer Sophistication or Sophistication *Homogeneous	−1.480*** (−2.85)	−2.10** (−2.51)	−1.452*** (−2.77)	−2.522*** (−2.81)
Inelastic Demand	.8416* (1.91)	.3398 (.83)	1.058** (2.23)	.5889 (1.32)
Vertical Issues	−.9773** (−1.98)	−.5562 (−1.12)	−1.388*** (−3.34)	−1.105*** (−2.57)
Efficiencies	−.5945 (−1.43)	−.7982* (−1.95)	−.6931 (−1.34)	−.9962* (−1.70)
Evidence	–	–	1.253*** (2.86)	1.603*** (2.80)
Constant	−20.97*** (−4.89)	−22.05*** (−4.17)	−20.08*** (−4.51)	−20.94*** (−3.61)
Predictions (percentage)	80.0	82.7	84.0	86.7
Pseudo-R-square	.4296	.4505	.5015	.5489
Log Pseudo-likelihood	−27.95	−26.93	−24.43	−22.11

a. t-statistic in parentheses; * significant at 10%; ** significant at 5%; *** significant at 1%.
b. Buyer sophistication is interacted with homogeneous good index.

increases the chance of enforcement, but the effect is not significant. Looking back at Figure 2, this result is not surprising, because customer sophistication appears to interact with product homogeneity. Re-estimating the model with the buyer sophistication variable interacted with homogeneity (model 3-2) generates the expected effect.[58] On its own, a homogeneous good facilitates coordinated interaction. However, when customer sophistication is relevant, a competitive problem is less likely, as sophisticated consumers have an ability to protect themselves from collusive overcharges. In this second regression, the other control variables retain their signs, but now only the efficiency variable is statistically different from zero.

The next two regressions (models 3-3 and 3-4) repeat the two initial specifications, but add the evidence variable to the regressions. Here, evidence suggestive of a competitive concern has the expected positive effect on the probability of a coordinated interaction finding. This result serves to confirm the importance of testing structural oligopoly models with natural experiment-related evidence. The structural variables retain their signs and all but one achieves statistical significance in model 3-4.[59] The final model correctly predicts 87.5 percent of the 48 collusion findings, and 85.2 percent of the 27 no-effect conclusions.

The magnitude of the coefficients cannot be directly compared across the models. Instead, any comparison must evaluate the standard normal function given values for all of the other variables in the model. For example, consider an efficient merger in a homogeneous goods market. Using model 3-2, the probability of a collusion concern moves from 15 to 87 percent, as the Herfindahl increases from 1,400 to 3,000. Switching the focus to model 3-4 generates marginal reductions in the enforcement probability when no evidence is available, but a single finding of evidence causes the probability to jump to a range of 44 to 97 percent. Other information can significantly change these probabilities. Holding the structure and evidence variables at fixed values, the direction of the effect for the five remaining structural variables can be computed by just summing up the relevant coefficients. For example, in the last situation mentioned, findings of buyer power and inelasticity will create a probability of collusion ranging from almost 0 to 87 percent. Overall, it is clear that both structural findings and evidence matters.

Figure 4 repeats the analysis in Figure 3, but replaces the Herfindahl index with three parameters designed to offer a more detailed structural analysis. The count on the number

58 An alternative specification in which the buyer sophistication index was interacted with both the homogenous and differentiated good variables was also estimated. The interaction of buyer sophistication and differentiation was not significantly different from zero in any of the models, and it was removed from the model for expositional ease to obtain the specifications presented in the text.

59 The five structural indictor variables test jointly significant. (The Chi-square statistics are 19.26, 12.65, for models 3-3 and 3-4, respectively. Both models' results are above the cutoff for five degrees of freedom of 11.07.)

FIGURE 4 Complex Oligopoly Model[a]

	4-1 (Structure)	4-2 (Structure)[b]	4-3 (Evidence)	4-4 (Evidence)[b]
Significant Rivals	–4.320*** (–3.83)	–5.787*** (–5.29)	–4.857*** (–3.70)	–8.100*** (–3.92)
Share Ratio	.5422 (1.62)	.5529 (1.57)	.7673** (1.96)	.9379** (2.01)
Fringe	–.3339 (–1.58)	–.0890 (–.44)	–.4607* (–1.95)	–.2319 (–.65)
Homogenous Good	.6109 (1.34)	1.939*** (3.46)	.6445 (1.30)	3.209*** (3.29)
Buyer Sophistication or Sophistication *Homogeneous	–1.547*** (–2.77)	–3.227*** (–3.48)	–1.893*** (–2.90)	–5.488*** (–3.77)
Inelastic Demand	1.002* (1.93)	1.222** (2.12)	1.352** (2.50)	1.953** (2.29)
Vertical Issues	–1.321** (–2.28)	–1.109* (–1.74)	–1.959*** (–3.47)	–2.295*** (–3.53)
Efficiencies	–.5485 (–1.32)	–.7694 (–1.54)	–.9883* (–1.95)	–1.867** (–2.51)
Evidence	–	–	1.661*** (3.14)	2.773*** (2.80)
Constant	7.075*** (4.10)	8.362*** (4.95)	7.532*** (3.69)	11.30*** (3.56)
Predictions	81.33	84.0	85.33	89.3
Pseudo-R-square	.4735	.5530	.5670	.6902
Pseudo Log-likelihood	–25.80	–21.91	–21.21	–15.18

a. t-statistic in parentheses; * significant at 10%; ** significant at 5%; *** significant at 1%.
b. Buyer sophistication is interacted with homogeneous good index.

of significant competitors is inversely related to the likelihood of coordinated interaction in all the specifications. The ratio of the share of the leading firm to its closest competitor takes on the expected positive sign, but its significance level is marginal in the first two specifications. Fringe share is significant in only one specification.[60] It is possible to nest the models in Figures 3 and 4 by adding the Herfindahl index to the Figure 4 specification.[61] In the (unreported) regressions, the Herfindahl index never becomes statistically significant, while the joint hypothesis setting the coefficients of three new concentration variables to zero cannot be rejected for the first two specifications. Thus, it is impossible to distinguish between the first two sets of share-based parameters. Once the evidence variable is added, it is possible to conclude that, when taken together, significant rivals, ratio of shares of leading firms, and fringe share are statistically different from zero.[62] Thus, when data is available, the user has a reason to prefer models 4-3 and 4-4 over models 3-3 and 3-4.

Adding the evidence variable in models 4-3 and 4-4 increases the level of significance of the other control variables. The results for buyer sophistication match those found in Figure 3, in which the sophistication effect is basically focused in homogeneous goods industries. Elasticity and vertical ramifications remain significant in the new specifications, while the pure efficiency effect becomes significant. Thus, in all the specifications, the structural variables remain important when the model is generalized to address explicit or implicit natural experiment evidence.[63] Model 4-4 correctly predicts 91.7 percent of the findings of collusion and 85.2 percent of the no effect matters.

Predictions for the probability of a collusion finding would generate similar results to those discussed above, although now the structural parameters would focus on significant competitors: the leadership share ratio and fringe share. As noted above, models 4-3 and 4-4 appear preferable to the simple Herfindahl models 3-3 and 3-4. Of course, for any

---

[60] Interacting fringe share with product homogeneity does not improve the results. Possibly fringe firms face expansion constraints in the real world, or customers require partnership relationships with their core suppliers even when the good is homogeneous. Thus, industry-specific facts may limit the importance of the fringe.

[61] As the three new structural variables explain 84 percent of the variance in the Herfindahl, multicollinearity may limit the results of the testing.

[62] The Chi-square statistics needed to reject a zero effect for rivals, share ratio and fringe share are 14.4 and 13.86 for models 4-3 and 4-4, respectively. Both are greater than the relevant Chi-square cutoff of 7.81. For models 4-1 and 4-2, the test statistics are insignificant, at 4.56 and 4.51, respectively.

[63] Given that the t-statistics already highlight the significance of the five structural indictor variables, it is not surprising that the joint Chi-square test also generates highly significant results (17.7 for model 4-3 and 19.22 for model 4-4).

particular merger, it is straightforward to compute a fitted value for any probit equation and use the standard normal function to generate the probability of a collusion finding that ranges from zero to one. While the models in Figure 4 do a better job of predicting than those in Figure 3, the difference is small (1 to 2.5 percentage points). A more sophisticated analysis would look at each prediction. The review of the fitted probabilities shows the more complex model (model 4-4) predicts the correct outcome within ten percentage points of the actual outcome (over 90 percent for concern and under 10 percent for no concern) in 69.3 percent of the cases. In contrast, the standard Herfindahl model (model 3-4) only achieves this success in 52 percent of the transactions. Overall, the more detailed model appears to perform better, although the model requires a complex understanding of market structure. Without access to all the market share data, the complex model cannot be used.

Figure 5 explores two special considerations, one that turns out interesting and one that does not. The models in model 3-4 and 4-4 were recycled into Figure 5, with models 5-1 and 5-3 focus on maverick firm findings, while models 5-2 and 5-4 search for a change in understanding of oligopoly associated with the Bush administration.[64]

The maverick results are anticlimactic, as the index associated with maverick-based analysis is insignificant (although the coefficient takes on the expected positive sign). The results on the other variables are robust, suggesting that exclusion of this effect does not impact the analysis. While maverick-based analysis remains a theory of collusion and finding natural experiment evidence on real-life maverick behavior would generally support a competitive concern, speculation on maverick status adds nothing to the likelihood of a coordinated interaction finding. These statistical conclusions are not compatible with the Baker-Shapiro hypothesis that the maverick model is the single theory of collusive oligopoly.

The results associated with the Bush administration variable are much more interesting. In model 5-2, the dummy variable exhibits a positive effect and the test statistic approaches conventional levels of significance. While the coefficients on the other variable jump around a little, the results do not strongly support inclusion of the administration effect. In contrast, model 5-4 identifies a significant administration effect, suggesting that the Bush enforcers were more likely to infer coordinated interaction. While the magnitude of the coefficient is smaller than those associated with the other binary variables, the effect is still substantial. Adding this

[64] For the 1993-2005 sample, the Bush administration investigated 45.9 percent of their cases with a collusion theory, while the earlier administrations studied 41.8 percent of their cases with collusion analysis. The similarity in these two figures suggests the Bush administration did not systematically reclassify matters from unilateral to collusion.

FIGURE 5 Oligopoly Model with Maverick or Administration Variables[a]

	5-1 (Maverick)	5-2 (Admin)	5-3 (Maverick)	5-4 (Admin)
HHI	2.630*** (3.61)	2.521*** (3.58)		
Significant Rivals			−7.943*** (−3.90)	−8.535*** (−4.13)
Share Ratio			.9416** (2.00)	1.134** (2.38)
Fringe			−.2420 (−.65)	−.04312 (−.16)
Homogenous Good	1.376** (2.09)	1.283* (1.84)	3.170*** (3.23)	3.398*** (3.40)
Sophistication *Homogeneous	−2.519*** (−2.77)	−2.763*** (−2.98)	−5.414*** (−3.73)	−6.588*** (−3.97)
Inelastic Demand	.6989 (1.43)	.7376 (1.48)	1.938** (2.31)	2.877*** (3.07)
Vertical Issues	−1.104*** (−2.60)	−1.544*** (−2.98)	−2.258*** (−3.46)	−3.012*** (−3.74)
Efficiencies	−.9937* (−1.71)	−.7700 (−1.33)	−1.843** (−2.48)	−1.844** (−2.41)
Evidence	1.668*** (2.79)	1.773*** (2.84)	2.773*** (2.72)	3.098*** (2.94)
Maverick Firms	.7195 (1.00)	–	.3225 (.38)	–
Administration	–	.9384 (1.62)	–	1.446** (2.04)
Constant	−20.80*** (−3.55)	−20.18*** (−3.53)	11.02*** (3.42)	10.69*** (3.90)
Predictions	84.0	82.7	88.0	89.3
Pseudo-R-square	.5572	.5741	.6911	.7265
Pseudo Log-likelihood	−21.70	−20.87	−15.14	−13.41

a. t-statistic in parentheses; * significant at 10%; ** significant at 5%; *** significant at 1%.

variable allows the model to explain 93.8 percent of the collusion findings and 88.9 percent of the matters in which the theory was rejected.

Further analysis addressed the question of how big a shift in policy is suggested by the data. A simple split of the sample showed an enforcement probability of 59.3 percent prior to June 2001 and 76.2 percent after. Without statistical decomposition, it is impossible to tell how much difference is due to the change in understanding and how much is related to the specific sample.[65] Data limitations (there are only 21 Bush administration cases) preclude this analysis. However, it is possible to simulate the pre-Bush situation that would have occurred had the Bush administration merger been filed prior to June 2001. Focusing on the 16 collusion findings, the data suggest that the Bush effect is responsible for 3 of the conclusions. Of course, it is impossible to draw any overall conclusions without an analysis of entry barriers. If the Bush administration also made it easier to reach an ease of entry finding, the two effects could cancel out.

VI. CONCLUSIONS

FTC enforcement policy allows the analyst to draw insights into the agency's best understanding of coordinated interaction in oligopolistic industries. By focusing on the sub-sample of collusion cases and excluding the matters in which entry is easy, the enforcement decision effectively proxies a finding on ease of collusion. Statistical results are broadly consistent with economic theory. Concentration-related variables like the Herfindahl, a count of the number of competitors, the homogeneity of the market, and the sophistication of the customer base for homogeneous goods all have strong and expected effects on the outcome. Proxies for inelasticity, vertical relationships, and changes in cost caused by efficiencies also have expected effects in some specifications. A leadership variable appears to contribute to the analysis, while no consistent effect for the size of the fringe can be found.

This structural model retains some explanatory power when a variable associated with exogenous evidence (natural experiments, validated customer concerns, and hot documents) is added to the model. This test of the Folk Theorem of Merger Enforcement (if evidence supports a structural problem, then it is reasonable to infer a competitive concern from a relevant change in structure) confirms the importance of the natural experiment evidence. Other results note a maverick theory of violation does not add to the concern associated with the structure and the

---

65 For an example of decomposition, see Bergman et al. (2007), *supra* note 39.

Finally, well-done coordinated interaction analyses are simply more likely to prevail in court, because these studies will provide a link to real-world evidence

Bush administration was more aggressive in its analysis of coordinated interaction.

A number of practical implications are obvious. First, market definition must remain the first step in merger analysis. Coordinated interaction only makes sense if the rivals that the merged firm is expected to coordinate with can be identified. Second, market shares can be integrated into the analysis in a sophisticated manner when the detailed data is available. Third, natural experiment evidence can be very useful in confirming the implications of a structural model. Thus, the *Guidelines'* focus on market institutions remains highly relevant, because understanding the competitive dynamics of the market is likely to aid the search for natural experiments. Fourth, customer concerns and hot documents should be analyzed in great detail in an attempt to isolate the natural experiments that underpin these concerns. While some facts may be lost to history, the reconstruction of even a qualitative natural experiment could serve to confirm a coordinated effects theory. Fifth, it appears customer sophistication serves to reduce the likelihood of collusion. This observation also implies a need to understand how the market of interest actually performs. Finally, well-done coordinated interaction analyses are simply more likely to prevail in court, because these studies will provide a link to real-world evidence. While it is possible to ground unilateral effects analyses in fact, it is also possible to become captured by the deductive logic that builds from the profit-maximization assumption to the theoretical conclusion on a price increase. In court, assumptions are not proof.

WELFARE STANDARDS AND MERGER ANALYSIS REVISITED

*Ken Heyer**

In 2006, Competition Policy International published my article "Welfare Standards and Merger Analysis: Why Not the Best?" in its Fall issue. In the article, I presented arguments for employing a total, rather than a consumer welfare standard for evaluating and determining whether to challenge proposed mergers. Prior to the article being accepted, I learned that its publication would likely be contingent upon the editors finding an author willing to take an opposing side of the issue. Appropriately, they wanted to provide the journal's readership with competing views on a relevant and controversial topic.

Although I was very much hoping to see my article in print, my pleasure in learning of its acceptance was short-lived. This is because the journal had managed not only to find one outstanding author to write a dissenting piece, but two. The co-authors, to my dismay, were Joe Farrell and Mike Katz. These two exceptional economists are not only ones for whom I have the greatest respect and admiration, but also former bosses of mine who served with distinction as chief economists at the Antitrust Division of the Justice Department.

Fortunately, from my perspective at least, the companion piece written by Joe and Mike was less a frontal assault on my primary premises and analytics, and more a thoughtful analysis of a broader issue: how the goal of maximizing total welfare might be better served by having decision makers employ a consumer welfare standard when evaluating mergers.[1]

Six years later: What more is there to say?

Since the time the article was published, it is hard to think of major theoretical advances that merit serious reconsideration of the core arguments. With one possible exception, discussed below, the issues and our knowledge of them are much the same now as

* This article was written while Ken Heyer was Chief, Competition Policy Section, Antitrust Division of the United States Department of Justice. In June of this year Ken joined the Federal Trade Commission as Deputy Director for Antitrust in its Bureau of Economics. The views expressed herein are his alone, and do not purport to represent those of either the Department of Justice or the Federal Trade Commission.

[1] Their finding flows from an analysis of how the competition authority's standard for challenging mergers may affect the universe of mergers that end up being proposed. When faced with a decision maker who expressly employs a consumer rather than a total welfare standard, the mergers proposed by profit-maximizing firms might, somewhat counter-intuitively, do a better job of maximizing total welfare.

The welfare effects from enhanced buyer power are readily analyzed under a total welfare standard. On what basis would mergers that enhance buyer power be challenged under a consumer welfare standard?

they were then. Still, there have been some relevant developments worth noting. In particular, the Antitrust Division, jointly with the Federal Trade Commission, issued revised Horizontal Merger Guidelines in 2010.[2] These include some new discussion of how the Agencies may deal with specific fact patterns. In particular, the revised Guidelines' discussion of mergers of competing buyers and the potential these may have to enhance monopsony power bears on the welfare standard likely to be applied.[3]

A "consumer welfare standard" focuses on the effects that a merger is likely to have on those who purchase the relevant product (or service). In cases where those proposing to merge are substantial buyers, however, the competitive concern is that those potentially affected adversely are sellers, not purchasers. Indeed, in such cases it is the customer who is likely to benefit from a diminution in competition. The welfare effects from enhanced buyer power are readily analyzed under a total welfare standard. On what basis would mergers that enhance buyer power be challenged under a consumer welfare standard?

One answer is that the exercise of buyer power by an intermediate firm may, by depressing the price that sellers receive, lower total output in the marketplace. Doing so would, in turn, harm final consumers, and it is the welfare of final consumers that a consumer welfare standard is designed to protect.

This line of argument is correct as far as it goes, but it goes only so far. For one thing, if sellers are currently exercising market power, enhanced power on the buying side may (but will not invariably) result in greater output for final consumers if the prices of sellers are moved closer to the competitive level. In addition, even where at-risk sellers are exercising no market power pre-merger, a merger-generated exercise of monopsony power will not necessarily lower the total quantity supplied to, or raise the prices paid by, final consumers. This can easily be the case when buying markets are relatively local, but selling markets are much broader.

Consider a hypothetical merger to monopsony in the purchase of some agricultural or mineral product. The merger might, for example, involve two railroads who compete to transport goods from the production site, or two grain elevators who aggregate grain and store it, or any two intermediate purchasers or processors whose facilities happen to be located especially close to the potentially at-risk producers. If the prices at which the relevant product is sold to

---

2 U.S. Dep't of Justice & Federal Trade Commission, Horizontal Merger Guidelines (2010), *available at* http://www.justice.gov/atr/public/guidelines/hmg-2010.pdf.

3 *Id.*, at Section 12.

final consumers are set in a world market, final consumers are protected from an exercise of market power by the merged firm. Nevertheless, those from whom the merging parties purchase--perhaps farmers in the Midwest—may be at risk.[4]

Despite such predictions, there remains for many an open empirical question as to whether firms actually do treat fixed cost savings according to the predictions of microeconomic theory

Notably, the revised Guidelines contain an explicit statement that expresses concern over exactly this possibility. *Example 24* in Section 12 "Mergers of Competing Buyers" depicts a hypothetical merger in which monopsony power may be enhanced—and be of concern to the competition authority—even where there will be no harm to final consumers of the product. "These [harmful] effects," it states in relevant part, "can arise even if the merger will not lead to any increase in the price charged by the merged firm for its output."

It is not obvious why such mergers would be objectionable under a consumer, rather than a total, welfare standard.

Finally, in my original article I gave as one reason for adopting a total welfare standard the difficulties competition agencies can face in determining the extent to which claimed efficiencies involve incremental cost savings or fixed cost savings (the second of which, according to conventional microeconomic theory, would not be expected to lower prices). Despite such predictions, there remains for many an open empirical question as to whether firms actually do treat fixed cost savings according to the predictions of microeconomic theory.

I attended a year or two ago one of the many panel discussions that have sprung up in the wake of the growing interest in behavioral economics. While there, I had occasion to speak with one of the panelists, Professor Steve Salop, about some of the issues it raised for antitrust policy. We speculated as to how, when evaluating merging parties' claims of demonstrable and merger-specific *fixed* cost savings, the competition authorities would respond to strong evidence that the firms in their normal business practice actually do set prices partly as a function of the level of their fixed costs. If, for whatever combination of reasons, they behave in this way, it would imply that even fixed cost savings—those entirely acceptable as a defense under a total welfare standard—might in part help firms satisfy a consumer welfare standard as well.

The jury is still out on whether evidence will ever confirm persuasively this possibility. Should it do so, however, supporters of a total welfare standard would not be displeased. After all, it is not only the welfare of the economy's entrepreneurs, investors and manufacturers that we believe should be valued. Consumers are people too.

---

[4] If those selling to the merging firms face an upward sloping marginal cost curve of producing and selling their product, and supply from other sources is elastic at current prices, monopsony power could profitably be exercised over the former despite the fact that their reduced output would be completely offset by greater output from others.

WELFARE STANDARDS AND MERGER ANALYSIS: WHY NOT THE BEST?

*Ken Heyer**

ABSTRACT:
Over the past several decades, there has emerged a rough consensus among professional antitrust practitioners, and within the law and economics community generally, that the "competition" referred to in our antitrust statutes is not to be interpreted simply as pre-merger rivalry among entities. Rather, it is best viewed as a process, the outcome of which is welfare, with welfare—not rivalry—being the object of interest. Consistent with this interpretation, scholars, competition authorities, and the courts have come to treat antitrust law as condemning only those mergers whose effect may be substantially to reduce welfare.

In this paper, I argue for using the total welfare standard, rather than the more commonly employed consumer welfare standard. In doing so, I respond to three broad objections that have been raised. One is that use of a total welfare standard conflicts with antitrust law, or at least with legal precedent. A second is that employing a total welfare standard would clearly be more costly for antitrust agencies than employing one or another flavor of a consumer welfare standard. A third is that the total welfare standard ignores important distributional considerations—considerations that are better treated under some form of consumer welfare standard. Each of these objections is evaluated, and ultimately found unpersuasive.

* The author is the Economics Director of the Antitrust Division, U.S. Department of Justice. The views expressed in this article are his alone, and do not represent the views of the U.S. Department of Justice. He would like to thank Doug Melamed, Sheldon Kimmel, Dan O'Brien, Dennis Carlton, Carl Shapiro, Ralph Winter, Mark Frankena, Tim Brennan, Craig Conrath, and Nien-Huei Jiang for their comments on an earlier draft of this article. He would like also to acknowledge the excellent research assistance provided by Gillian Oak. An earlier version of this paper appeared as Economic Analysis Group Discussion Paper EAG 06-8, March 2006.

I. INTRODUCTION

Antitrust agencies in the United States, and increasingly around the world, have adopted what has been termed the consumer welfare standard for analyzing proposed mergers. For example, in a recent article, the then-Deputy Assistant Attorney General, and currently Assistant Attorney General of the U.S. Department of Justice's Antitrust Division stated, "Today, most would agree that proper enforcement of the antitrust laws focuses on consumer welfare." He added that "the enforcement authorities in the United States look most frequently at the question of what is best for consumers."[1] And, in a speech given shortly after succeeding Mario Monti as EC Competition Commissioner, Neelie Kroes observed that:

> "Consumer welfare is now well established as the standard the Commission applies when assessing mergers and infringements of the Treaty rules on cartels and monopolies. Our aim is simple: to protect competition in the market as a means of enhancing consumer welfare and ensuring an efficient allocation of resources."[2]

Under the consumer welfare standard, if a merger appears likely to harm consumers as a result of a reduction in competition—some would add significantly, or substantially—in any relevant market, the merger is illegal.[3] This article considers the basis for applying a consumer welfare standard, and examines the arguments for instead employing a total welfare standard (i.e., a standard that considers a merger's likely effect on all members of society, not simply the consumers of products produced by the merging firms).[4]

---

[1] Thomas O. Barnett, *Substantial Lessening of Competition-The Section 7 Standard*, 2005 COLUM. BUS. L. REV. 293, 295-298. Barnett states explicitly that "The views and opinions expressed herein are those of the author and do not necessarily represent the official position or policies of the U.S. Department of Justice."

[2] Neelie Kroes, European Competition Policy – Delivering Better Markets and Better Choices, Presentation at European Consumer and Competition Day (Sep. 5, 2005).

[3] As discussed later in this paper, U.S. competition agencies will at times consider efficiencies "not strictly in the relevant market, but so inextricably linked with it that a partial divestiture or other remedy could not feasibly eliminate the anti-competitive effect in the relevant market without sacrificing the efficiencies in the other market(s)."

[4] This article does not address the proper welfare standard to apply in the case of civil non-merger investigations, such as those implicated by Section 2 of the Sherman Act or Article 82 of the EC's competition law. While, in principle, the economic case for a total welfare standard would seem to be equally applicable outside the narrow setting of merger policy, issues such as ease of application, among others, distinguish the two situations. For discussions of the appropriate standard to apply outside the merger setting, see Gregory Werden, *Identifying Exclusionary Conduct under Section 2: The 'No Economic Sense' Test*, 73 ANTITRUST L.J. 413 (2006), Steven C. Salop, *Exclusionary Conduct, Effect on Consumers, and the Flawed Profit-Sacrifice Standard*, 73 ANTITRUST L.J. 311 (2006) and A. Douglas Melamed, *Exclusive Dealing Agreements and other Exclusionary Conduct – Are There Unifying Principles*, 73 ANTITRUST L.J. 375 (2006). Neither, I would note, proposes that total welfare maximization be the test.

As an initial matter, it is quite clear that the relevant sections of U.S. antitrust law say nothing about welfare—consumer or otherwise. Rather, they state that mergers are illegal when their effect "may substantially reduce competition in any line of commerce."

Over the past several decades, there has emerged a rough consensus among professional antitrust practitioners, and within the law and economics community generally, that the competition referred to in our antitrust statutes is not to be interpreted simply as pre-merger rivalry among entities. Rather it is best viewed as a process, the outcome of which is welfare, with welfare—not rivalry—being the object of interest. Consistent with this interpretation, scholars, competition authorities, and the courts have come to treat antitrust law as condemning only those mergers whose effect may be substantially to reduce welfare.

That having been said, there remains a question of which welfare standard to use, and exactly whose welfare to consider. Several candidates suggest themselves. One is the welfare of consumers in each of the markets potentially impacted by the merger. Under this standard, a merger is permissible if (and only if) consumers in each and every one of the markets at issue are likely to be at least as well off after the merger as they were before it. One might call this an actual Pareto consumer welfare standard, though for reasons explained later in this paper, applying even this standard does not necessarily ensure that each and every consumer will be made better off.

A second approach would be to permit mergers whose net effect on consumers across all the (possibly multiple) markets served by the merging parties is positive. Using this standard, a merger would be permitted even if consumers are harmed in market A, so long as the benefits received by consumers in other markets (B, C, . . . , Z) served by the merging firms are in aggregate greater. One might refer to this as a potential Pareto consumer welfare standard.

A third approach, one that has not, to my knowledge, been adopted explicitly by any major competition authority, is to permit mergers whose predicted effect on the total welfare of members of society as a whole is positive.[5] Application of this standard requires that

[5] The welfare standard employed in Canada lies somewhere between a consumer and a total welfare approach. Section 96 (1) of the 1986 Competition Act of Canada explicitly provides for an "efficiencies defense" for mergers that might result in higher prices for consumers. As interpreted by Canadian courts in the recent *Superior Propane* litigation, an efficiencies defense for mergers where consumers are likely to be harmed must employ a so-called "balancing weights" approach—i.e., an approach in which harm to low-income consumers is afforded disproportionately greater weight. Elaborating on the logic employed in this decision, Ross and Winter (2005) show that use of a balancing weights approach, where the weights are those revealed in government tax or redistribution policy generally, would only in the most extraordinary circumstances produce a ruling different from that generated by the total surplus rule. For an excellent discussion of the *Superior Propane* case, other recent Canadian court decisions, and an economic analysis of Canada's efficiency defense, see Thomas W. Ross & Ralph A. Winter, *The Efficiency Defense in Merger Law: Economic Foundations and Recent Canadian Developments,* 72 Antitrust L.J. 471, 471-505 (2005). *See also* Discussion *in* Report of the Advisory Panel on Efficiencies to Scott Sheridan, Commissioner of Competition (Aug. 2005).

weight be given not only to the welfare of those who consume the merging firm's products, but also to those doing the producing.[6]

In one very real sense, an economy's producers are consumers as well, albeit consumers of many items other than the ones they happen to produce. There is, of course, a difference between the act of consuming and the act of producing, and most individuals in our highly specialized economy do not restrict themselves to consuming only what they themselves produce; they enhance one another's welfare through trade. This distinction, however, hardly suggests a meaningful basis for weighting the welfare of individuals occupying these two roles unequally; much less, weighting the welfare of a market's producers at zero when determining whether a merger is, on balance, beneficial to society. In any event, it seems reasonable to place the burden of proof on those who would defend the use of a narrower, consumer welfare standard, rather than a total welfare standard that accounts for the wellbeing of all the members of an economy. As discussed later in this paper, it is far from clear that this burden has been carried.

This paper makes a case for employing the total welfare standard. In the course of doing so, it responds to a number of possible defenses for antitrust's current exclusive focus on the welfare of consumers in the relevant markets impacted directly by proposed mergers.

The issue is not a new one. In 1968, Oliver Williamson famously described, using what he termed the "naive tradeoff model," the tradeoff that arises when a merger simultaneously produces cost savings—from realization of efficiencies and higher prices—from greater market power.[7]

Williamson went on to present what he termed "illustrative" results, showing that it may take very small percentage cost savings to completely offset the negative welfare effects of even a significant increase in market power. Indeed, much of the subsequent commentary on Williamson's influential article dealt more with the implicit assumptions that generated this

---

[6] Although those most directly affected by a merger, and those for whom the merger's likely effects may be easiest to identify and calculate, are the merging firms and their customers, total welfare technically includes also the welfare of any and all who may be affected by the merger. This includes, in principle, the welfare of those who compete against the merging firms and, to the extent higher profits are shared with them, the workers at firms whose profits are affected. I do not, in this article, consider the effect of mergers on consumers, producers, or workers in countries outside of the competition authority's jurisdiction.

[7] Merging firms may be made better off in yet another way that can leave consumers worse off. Consider a situation where two duopolists had been colluding—tacitly, perhaps. If a merger makes it easier for them to price discriminate and increase output, this may leave consumers worse off (though it may also leave them better off).

FIGURE 1

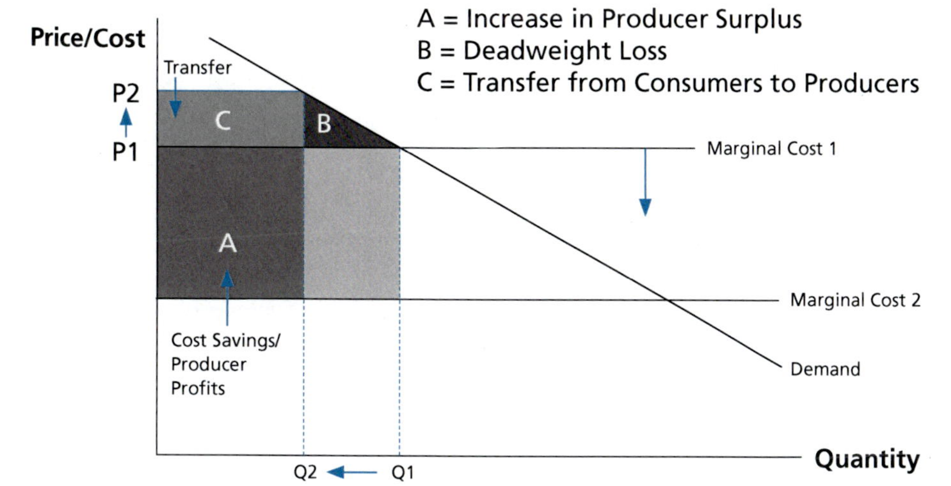

contentious result, than with the proposal that merger policy employ a total, rather than a consumer, welfare standard.[8]

II. WELFARE AND EFFICIENCY

The concepts of economic welfare and economic efficiency are closely related to one another. Economists say that an economy is operating at maximum efficiency when society is squeezing

[8] *See* Oliver E. Williamson, *Economies as an Antitrust Defense: The Welfare Tradeoffs*, 58 AM. ECON. REV. 18 (1968), reprinted in 1 COMPETITION POL'Y INT'L 217 (2005). In responding to critics and qualifying his admittedly naive model, Williamson recognized that accurately measuring a merger's net effect on total welfare properly incorporates any losses in producer surplus—that occur when, as is commonly the case, the merging firms were setting price above marginal cost even before exercising greater market power post-merger. Williamson concluded that adjusting for this did not materially affect his conclusions. For criticisms of Williamson's original article, see Michael E. DePrano & Jeffrey B. Nugent, *Economies as an Antitrust Defense: Comment*, 59 AM. ECON. REV. 947 (1969); *see also* Alan A. Fisher & Robert H. Lande, *Efficiency Considerations in Merger Enforcement*, 71 CAL. L. REV. 1580 (1983). For responses by Williamson to his critics, see Oliver Williamson, *Economies as an Antitrust Defense: Reply*, 59 AM. ECON. REV. 954, 954-959 (1969) and Oliver Williamson, *Economies as an Antitrust Defense Revisited*, 125 U. PA. L. REV. 669 (1977). For a more recent treatment of similar issues, see L.-H. RÖLLER, J. STENNEK, & F. VERBOVEN, EFFICIENCY GAINS FROM MERGERS (The Research Institute of Industrial Economics, IUI Working Paper Series, No. 543, 2000), *available at* http://swopec.hhs.se/iuiwop/papers/iuiwop0543.pdf.

the greatest value—the highest level of welfare—out of its scarce resources. The independent actions of profit and utility-maximizing economic agents work towards producing this desirable outcome in ways that are familiar to students of elementary microeconomics. Competition among firms to obtain the patronage of consumers spurs them to produce those goods and services that are most highly valued by consumers, to do so at the lowest possible cost (for example, by finding ways of producing the same quantity of output with fewer inputs), and to drive prices down towards the marginal cost of production (thereby resulting in output up to the point at which additional value to consumers no longer exceeds the additional cost to society). In this way, competition works—"as if by an invisible hand" as Adam Smith famously observed—to squeeze the greatest possible value out of society's scarce resources.

One of the ways in which production costs are minimized is by efficiently combining the inputs that produce the goods and services we ultimately consume. The entities that typically accumulate and process inputs into final products are called firms, though at times inputs may be combined by independent agents through arms-length contracts with one another. Firms will at times seek to grow through merger, though an alternative may be to grow internally, or perhaps to expand via arms-length contracts with other, still independent, firms.

III. MERGERS AND EFFICIENCY

Getting a product to market involves a number of discrete, yet critical, steps. These steps may include some or all of the following: basic research, applied research, product design, product manufacture, marketing, distribution, or service. Not uncommonly, firms that produce final products in close competition with one another have different strengths and weaknesses in these various steps. Auto firm A, for example, may be better than auto firm B when it comes to coming up with innovative ideas and quality control, while auto firm B may be better when it comes to marketing and post-sale servicing. Combining the best of both can produce synergies that in principle permit lower-cost production of an even better product.[9]

It is useful to discuss briefly why contracts that maintain the independence—especially the pricing independence—of two competitors with relatively different strengths will not always be a feasible or equally efficient method of obtaining the economic benefits expected from the merger. Industrial organization economists have been, at least since publication of Ronald Coase's landmark article on the theory of the firm, intrigued with the question of when and why the costs of organizing transactions within firms will tend to be lower than

[9] Many of these essentially complementary efficiencies may be available only by merging the operations of competitors.

the costs of organizing transactions across entities via contract.[10] Several decades after the appearance of Coase's article, work by others, particularly Oliver Williamson, put more theoretical flesh on the bare bones that Coase had first exposed.[11] Over time, a number of industry studies provided a degree of empirical support for today's commonly accepted notion that transactions organized within a firm can, in many cases, economize greatly on the transactions costs associated with writing, monitoring, and enforcing contracts.[12] While important theoretical questions about the efficiency of operations even within a firm continue to be studied, there is little disagreement that it will frequently be less costly to conduct transactions within a firm than to do so across firms. And unless it is equally costly for a firm to grow internally rather than through acquisition, this implies that cost savings may be merger specific. In other words, merger will at times be the most efficient means through which firms satisfy the demands of consumers.

A merger can be thought of as a special sort of contract, an all-encompassing one, if you will, whereby the decisions of two formerly independent firms will be subject to the authority of a single entity. Or, put differently, it can be thought of as when two formerly independent firms contract to become a single firm. Firms may merge to obtain greater market power. They may also merge to achieve efficiencies—i.e., to reduce costs.[13] The efficiencies potentially realizable through merger are numerous, as are the means through which these benefits can be achieved.[14]

Broadly speaking, efficiencies will tend often to take either of two forms: ones that lower marginal production costs, and ones that generate savings in fixed costs. Efficiencies can lower the cost of producing existing products. They can also promote the development

---

[10] *See* R.H. Coase, The Nature of the Firm, 4 Economica 386 (1937).

[11] *See* Oliver E. Williamson, Markets and Hierarchies: Analysis and Antitrust Implications (1975).

[12] *See* Benjamin Klein, Robert G. Crawford, & Armen Alchian, *Vertical Integration, Appropriable Rents, and the Competitive Contracting Process*, 21 J.L. & Econ. 297 (1978). *See also* Russell Pittman, *Specific Investments, Contracts, and Opportunism: The Evolution of Railroad Sidetrack Agreements*, 34 J.L. & Econ. 565 (1992); and Paul L. Joskow, *Contract Duration and Relationship-Specific Investments: Empirical Evidence from Coal Markets*, 77 Am. Econ Rev. 168 (1987).

[13] I am referring here to a lowering of the cost function, not to a reduction of costs that occurs purely as a consequence of reducing quality or output.

[14] This raises a question of how to treat reductions in marginal cost that arise because of procurement cost savings. The answer is that procurement cost savings arising from resource cost savings—e.g., fewer resources required when there are longer production runs—are welfare-enhancing. Indeed, they are efficiencies that likely result in greater output as well. Procurement cost savings that arise from merger-generated monoposony power, however, are less likely to generate increases in welfare. Unless the exercise in monopsony power is offsetting preexisting market power on the selling side, these benefits to the merged firm will likely result in lower output, and will in any event result in inefficient production of pre-merger levels of output.

of entirely new or better products. One way in which this latter type of benefit—dynamic efficiencies—can in theory be enhanced is for merging firms to eliminate redundant R&D activities and instead allocate the firms' limited assets towards multiple, alternative projects. Dynamic efficiencies may themselves be realized in a variety of ways, and one may ask whether efficiencies that make innovative activity more likely to occur, or likely to occur at lower cost, are more properly viewed as fixed cost savings or marginal cost savings. The important point is that whatever label one applies, and regardless of how the benefits from dynamic efficiencies are split between lowering prices and developing entirely new products or processes, dynamic efficiency generates an increase in total welfare.[15]

Distinctions between fixed and marginal cost tend to be particularly important when competition authorities employ a consumer, rather than a total, welfare standard

Distinctions between fixed and marginal cost tend to be particularly important when competition authorities employ a consumer, rather than a total, welfare standard. The reason is as follows: unlike changes in marginal cost, changes in fixed cost generally do not alter the firm's profit-maximizing price, or the level of output at which the firm maximizes its profits, unless they affect the firm's very viability.[16] As a result, pure fixed cost changes, no matter how large, may have no effect at all on the welfare of consumers in the relevant market.[17] In terms of their effect on a firm's profit-maximizing price, higher fixed costs can be compared

[15] Another oft-cited category of possible efficiencies from merger is realization of scale economies. For reasons given in Farrell and Shapiro, however, achieving through merger pure scale economies will often not be merger specific. Or if it is, the fact that the merging firms had not been achieving these efficiencies without merging may suggest strongly that the market is not performing competitively. Joseph Farrell & Carl Shapiro, *Scale Economies and Synergies in Horizontal Merger Analysis*, 68 Antitrust L.J. 685 (2001). Röller et al. categorize potential efficiencies from merger as either rationalization, economies of scale, technological progress, purchasing economies, and reduction of slack (managerial and X-efficiency) (*See* Roller et al., *supra* note 8). *See also,* William J. Kolasky & Andrew R. Dick, *The Merger Guidelines and the Integration of Efficiencies into Antitrust Review of Horizontal Mergers,* 71 Antitrust L.J. 207 (2003).

[16] Although it sometimes surprises attorneys to hear it, reducing the marginal cost of a firm with market power makes it profitable for the firm to reduce price and increase output. Because firms maximize profit by setting marginal revenue equal to marginal cost, fixed cost savings do not have this effect.

[17] Under a consumer welfare standard, even fixed cost savings would properly be given some weight if they were ultimately passed along to consumers in the form of lower prices. Arguing that all costs must be recovered in the long run, some would contend that fixed cost savings would, eventually, be reflected in lower prices. This intuition no doubt provides part of the rationale for the willingness of the U.S. antitrust agencies, as reflected in the Horizontal Merger Guidelines, to "consider the effects of cognizable efficiencies with no short-term, direct effect on prices in the relevant market." The extent to which fixed cost savings actually will be passed through, and how quickly that might occur, will depend at least in part on the strength of competition post merger.

with someone breaking into the company's headquarters and stealing a large sum of money from the firm's safe. Conversely, lower fixed costs are akin to some anonymous benefactor depositing a large sum of money into the firm's bank account. In the first case the firm is worse off, and in the second it is better off, yet in neither case is there reason to expect a change in the price the firm finds it most profitable to set, or the level of output the firm finds it most profitable to produce.

Importantly, however, unlike in the case of pure money transfers, fixed cost savings have significant efficiency implications for the economy as a whole. As discussed below, by freeing up resources for use elsewhere in the economy, fixed cost savings enhance an economy's total welfare. These potential benefits from merger are given zero weight when applying a narrow consumer welfare standard.[18]

IV. THE ACTUAL PARETO CONSUMER WELFARE STANDARD

As an initial matter, when a merger has no effect other than to lower the (quality-adjusted) price for final goods sold in a market, some consumers in that market will benefit and no consumers will be harmed. Those who had been consuming the product before the merger will be able to purchase their original quantities at a lower price, and additional surplus will be obtained by consumers who, at the now-lower price, consume even greater quantities than before. In addition, individuals who had in the past maximized their utility by consuming zero quantities of the product may be better off by making some purchases at the now-lower price. Thus, all consumers of the product appear to be better off.

[18] The Horizontal Merger Guidelines issued by the U.S. Department of Justice and the U.S. Federal Trade Commission outline the approach to efficiencies taken by the U.S. federal competition authorities. They state, "The Agency will not challenge a merger if cognizable efficiencies [i.e., efficiencies that are merger-specific, that have been verified and do not arise from anticompetitive reductions in output or service] are of a character and magnitude such that the merger is not likely to be anticompetitive in any relevant market." In a footnote, the Guidelines qualify this statement, noting that although the Agency generally focuses on whether cognizable efficiencies likely would be sufficient to prevent even short-term price increases in the relevant market, "The Agency also will consider the effects of cognizable efficiencies with no short-term, direct effect on prices in the relevant market," though the Guidelines state that benefits from such efficiencies "will be given less weight because they are less proximate and more difficult to predict." This qualification permits U.S. competition authorities, in some circumstances, to depart from what I am referring to as the consumer welfare standard. Nevertheless, neither the U.S. competition authorities, nor competition authorities in most other economies, appear willing to adopt explicitly and unambiguously a total welfare standard for merger enforcement. U.S. Dep't of Justice & Federal Trade Commission, Horizontal Merger Guidelines §4 n.36 (1992) (revised Apr. 8, 1997) [*hereinafter Merger Guidelines*].

Even in the case of price-lowering mergers, however, it will not necessarily be true that all consumers everywhere will be better off. An efficient merger may drive one or more rivals out of business, and consumers who preferred the version offered by exiting rivals may now find themselves worse off. Related to this point, efficiencies sometimes arise from combining complementary assets and standardizing on a single platform or a single standard. Where the two merging firms had previously been offering competing and incompatible methods of satisfying consumers, efficient standardization will typically strand the investments of consumers who had invested in the to-be-jettisoned standard. They will be left worse off, even though consumers in the market as a whole are better off from having a better, cheaper, more ubiquitous standard as a result of the merger.

Producers in the relevant markets may be either better off, or worse off. Certainly the merging firms believe that they will be better off, as evidenced by the fact that they have chosen to merge, presumably, voluntarily. Rivals of the merging firms are likely to be harmed, since a price-lowering merger may well force them to compete harder, perhaps by lowering their own prices, and they may well lose business to the more efficient merged firm. In addition, firms not even in the relevant markets may be worse off to the extent that demand for their product falls when consumer patronage shifts to products whose price has fallen as a result of the merger. While these latter categories of producers are worse off—indeed, producers may collectively be worse off—an actual Pareto consumer welfare standard would bless the merger.

As emphasized recently in work by Steve Salop, merger-generated efficiencies can in theory actually lower total welfare—as a consequence of shifting sales towards the merging parties and away from their rivals.[19] Salop presents an example where two relatively high-cost firms with relatively small shares achieve marginal cost savings through merger. As a consequence of lowering their marginal cost, they reduce price somewhat. This, in turn, results in greater sales for them and lower sales for what may be a (still) more efficient rival.[20] Although the reduction in the merged firm's marginal cost will likely lead to at least somewhat greater sales in the relevant product market, the pre-merger level of output will be produced at higher total cost.

[19] Steven C. Salop, *Question: What is the Real and Proper Antitrust Welfare Standard? Answer: The True Consumer Welfare Standard,* Presentation to Antitrust Modernization Commission (Nov. 4, 2005).

[20] In answer to the question "How do higher-cost firms manage to survive in the market?" Salop suggests that it may be because they provide a differentiated product. To the extent that consumers value the particular variety produced by the "high cost" firms, Salop may not be making the point as strongly as he might. Given that many oligopoly models—Cournot among them—generate equilibria where the lowest cost firm finds it profitable to price high enough to keep its rivals viable, the general point can be made even more strongly by simply assuming that all firms in the market produce and sell a homogenous product.

In such a circumstance, the net effect would be gains for consumers, but quite possibly lower total welfare—after one adjusts for the net negative effect on producers as a whole.[21]

Scenarios such as this may or may not be rare, yet they represent another category of cases—ones where prices are actually lowered by a merger—in which application of a pure consumer welfare standard would be costly to the economy as a whole. Taking fully into account such possibilities—akin in certain respects to what are termed "second best" considerations[22]—may be very difficult in practice. However, the example alerts us to the possibility that looking only at a merger's effect on the welfare of consumers and the merging firms can be too narrow a focus if it ignores inefficient shifts in production across firms and leads one falsely to conclude that a merger has raised total welfare, when in fact it has not. The original Williamson diagram, therefore, suggests incorrectly that when a merger results in lower prices total welfare inevitably rises. This is not a general result.

Though concern for the welfare of parties affected only indirectly by the effects of a merger ought not be completely irrelevant to enforcement decisions, difficulties associated with estimating such effects (ones that may well be second order), and requiring that a general equilibrium analysis be conducted of every merger, would seem to argue for imposing a fairly high burden of proof on those asking that competition authorities base enforcement decisions on such arguments.

V. FIXED COST SAVINGS AND TOTAL WELFARE

There are a number of situations in which merging parties anticipate capturing efficiencies that, under traditional consumer welfare criteria, would not help them avoid an adverse enforcement decision (or court ruling). Thus, the choice of standard may be of more than simply theoretical interest. Mergers contemplated because they will likely produce significant fixed cost savings tend to be of this form. Consider, for example, the situation where firm A and firm B compete with differentiated products, and where firm A happens to have a good deal of unutilized capacity in its factory. The reasons for this disequilibrium may be several, but let's

---

[21] Yet another somewhat counterintuitive result can occur in circumstances where a merger produces no cost savings at all, but where higher prices set by the merging firms induce customers to shift some of their patronage toward substitutes. If the products to which customers turn have relatively high price-cost margins and demand for the good whose price has risen is sufficiently inelastic, total welfare can increase precisely because price has gone up. I thank Ralph Winter for this observation.

[22] R. G. Lipsey & Kelvin Lancaster, *The General Theory of Second Best*, 24 Rev. Econ. Stud. 11 (1957).

assume that the available capacity is temporarily excessive because there has been a significant and unanticipated drop in demand for firm A's product.[23]

The excess capacity in the hands of firm A can, let us assume, be used to produce the entire projected output of competing firm B. In such circumstances—that I suspect are hardly unique—consolidating all the production of both firms in the partially vacant plant of firm A would clearly lower the total cost of producing this output. This is because part of the cost to society of producing firm B's output in firm B's plant is that resources are being used for this purpose that could be reallocated elsewhere in the economy, producing a net gain in total welfare. In particular, assuming the fixed cost savings are merger-specific, a cost of prohibiting a merger between firms A and B would be the opportunity cost of continuing to run the plant of firm B.[24] If firm B's plant would be closed by a merged firm, and particularly if the merged firm would continue supplying the market with all or nearly all of both firm A and firm B's pre-merger output, economic benefits could be substantial.

Benefits might consist of the value—net of their production costs—of alternative products produced out of the now empty plant. Or, if the highest alternative use of the plant is to tear it down and sell it as scrap, then the value of that scrap (net of demolition costs)—plus the value in its highest alternative use of the land on which the plant currently sits—would represent economic benefits from the merger. These would all be net benefits to the economy—an increase in total welfare. The fact that they do not involve a reduction in the merged firm's marginal cost—and thus do not result in any pass-through to the merged firm's consumers—does not change the fact that the merger is welfare enhancing.[25] Under a consumer welfare standard, the merger would be blocked if there is a small increase in market power.

---

[23] Unused capacity need not, of course, be excess in an economic sense. It may instead be serving a valuable function in the event that demand for the firm's product increases in the next period. By assumption, I am ruling out this explanation. In addition, the fact that factory capacity is durable implies that the firm cannot readily and immediately adjust its capacity to fit the now-smaller projected demand for the output of its product. Over time, of course, firms will adjust their investment decisions to reach a new, long-run equilibrium. Nevertheless, this will not necessarily happen quickly.

[24] As discussed in Farrell & Shapiro (2001), such efficiencies are more likely to be merger-specific when firm A can't simply produce and sell the total output of the two merging firms at constant cost through its own plant. This may be because the products of the merging firms are branded and contracting costs are substantial. See Farrell & Shapiro, *supra* note 15, at 12.

[25] Of course, if the marginal cost of production at firm A's plant is lower than the marginal cost of production at firm B's plant, efficiencies would be even greater—though in this case we would expect the lower marginal cost of production to translate into some pass-through to final consumers and a concomitant increase in consumer surplus (i.e., welfare).

VI. MARGINAL COST SAVINGS NOT FULLY PASSED THROUGH

As discussed above, fixed cost savings tend not to be passed on to consumers in the relevant product markets at all, while marginal cost savings in markets potentially raising competitive concerns generally result in lower prices. That having been said, the degree of pass-through from mergers that lower marginal costs will differ from case to case, as it is a function of many factors—including both demand conditions and the particular oligopolistic game being played by firms in the market.[26]

Much like fixed cost savings, those marginal cost savings that do not result in lower prices are both benefits to society as a whole and, under a consumer welfare standard, not an acceptable defense to a transaction that is likely to raise price.

VII. THE BENCHMARK: TOTAL WELFARE

Let us begin with the standard definition of total welfare. In any single market, total welfare is conventionally defined as total surplus—the difference between the value consumers place on output, minus what it costs society to produce that output. Across all markets, total welfare is simply the sum of all surplus, irrespective of how it happens to be divided between consumers and producers. In a hypothetical world populated by only a single individual, that individual would do best by organizing his or her affairs so as to maximize the total value obtained from the scarce resources he or she has to work with.[27]

Adding to the population does not obviously negate this core principle; however, it does introduce issues of distributional equity, which I discuss in some detail below. In any event, the difference between the value to consumers and the cost of production is exactly what economists mean by total welfare. From the standpoint of society as a whole, maximizing it would seem, at least at a first approximation, to be a desirable objective. Anything short of this is akin to asking society to make do with less, rather than with more.[28]

---

[26] A pure price taker—an infra marginal producer—will not find it profitable to pass on in the form of lower prices even marginal cost savings. Rather, it will keep those savings as rents.

[27] Of course, in such a world it is hard to imagine any need for a merger policy. Still, the point holds.

[28] It is worth noting that literal application of a pure consumer welfare standard, as that term is being defined here, would appear to immunize consumer buyer groups that exert efficiency-reducing monopsony power over sellers. I suspect that many supporters of a consumer welfare standard for sellers would be uncomfortable applying its logic equally to the buyer side of the market. Moreover, economic cost-benefit analyses of proposed government activities and regulations tend to employ a distribution-neutral framework, though these studies may attempt to estimate, or even propose ways of ameliorating, associated distributional consequences.

What reasons might there be for departing from this standard when developing merger policy? We can consider at least three categories of objections. One is that use of a total welfare standard conflicts with antitrust law, or at least with legal precedent. A second is that employing a total welfare standard would be more costly for antitrust agencies than employing one or another flavor of a consumer welfare standard. A third possible objection, one neatly abstracted away from in our example of a single individual populating the economy, is that the total welfare standard ignores important distributional considerations—ones that are better treated under some form of consumer welfare standard. Each of these objections is evaluated, and ultimately rejected, in the analysis below.[29]

VIII. LEGAL IMPEDIMENTS TO USE OF A TOTAL WELFARE STANDARD?

Section 7 of the Clayton Act prohibits mergers, the effect of which "may substantially reduce competition *in any line of commerce*." (emphasis added) It does not say anything about consumers.[30] An argument could certainly be made that the "in any line of commerce" language implies that mergers are illegal whenever the result is net harm in any relevant market (irrespective of whether the net benefits outside of that relevant market would be even greater). While under this argument one might condemn welfare-enhancing mergers whose primary benefit is to consumers in some other markets, it does not, by itself, support condemning mergers whose benefits to some in the relevant market (namely, those producing the goods being consumed), exceed the harms to others in the same relevant market (those doing the consuming).

---

[29] A somewhat different line of argument for employing a consumer welfare standard has been presented by Lyons. Lyons observes that because firms, rather than enforcement officials, get to select which mergers are proposed, they will select those mergers that are most profitable, not necessarily those that maximize welfare, from among the set that competition authorities permit. Lyons then shows that because of this self-selection effect, enforcement by competition authorities of a total welfare standard instead of a consumer welfare standard can, under some circumstances, actually lower total welfare. While Lyons' theoretical results are intriguing, his analysis fails to show that use of a total welfare standard is actually likely to produce such perverse outcomes, much less that use of a total, rather than a consumer welfare standard will systematically bias outcomes and lead to lower total welfare. *See* Bruce R. Lyons, Could Politicians Be More Right Than Economists? A Theory of Merger Standards (University of East Anglia Centre for Competition & Regulation Working Paper CCR 02-01, revised, May 2002).

[30] I recognize that there is a literature debating just what objective function those who legislated the Sherman Act were really seeking to maximize, and that there are those who feel strongly that the act was passed to protect the merging firms' consumers. This article takes no position on the original intent of U.S. merger policy's founding fathers. To the extent that legislative history truly presents a bar to use of a total welfare standard, an implication of this article is that new legislation to correct this error would be desirable. In any event, for those countries where there is less clearly a legal bar to use of a total welfare standard, such use would be in their economies' best interest.

Only a seemingly arbitrary decision to weigh more heavily the welfare of some individuals in society than others would do that. If, in particular, a merger causes harm to consumers of product A and yet the fixed cost savings from no longer producing and selling product A would exceed this harm, then treating the welfare of consumers and producers of product A equally would seem to imply that the merger enhances (total) welfare "in any line of commerce."

The literal language of Section 7 would seem, if anything, more likely to rule out use of a potential Pareto consumer welfare standard than to trump a total welfare standard. In the former case, at least the beneficiaries whose gains outweigh the harm to be suffered by individuals within a specific line of commerce (or relevant market) are by definition outside that line of commerce. Conceivably, therefore, consideration of these benefits might run afoul of the law's prohibition against mergers likely to reduce competition substantially "in any line of commerce."

Nevertheless, the federal antitrust agencies, if not yet the courts, have stated explicitly that under certain circumstances they will employ their prosecutorial discretion to not challenge such mergers. In particular, the most recent edition of the U.S. Department of Justice and U.S. Federal Trade Commission's Horizontal Merger Guidelines observes that:

> "In some cases . . . the Agency in its prosecutorial discretion will consider efficiencies not strictly in the relevant market, but so inextricably linked with it that a partial divestiture or other remedy could not feasibly eliminate the anticompetitive effect in the relevant market without sacrificing the efficiencies in the other market(s)."[31]

Incorporating into one's decision-making out-of-market consumer benefits that are inextricably linked to in-market consumer harms makes eminent economic sense. Less clear is why these benefits should, from either a legal or an economic perspective, receive greater weight than the benefits to producers—whether the latter are achieved in-market or out-of-market.

All of this having been said, the language of the Clayton Act explicitly concerns itself with maintaining competition, not welfare. Doesn't the concern with competition imply that the Clayton Act aims to protect the beneficiaries of competition—consumers?[32] Perhaps.

---

[31] Merger Guidelines, *supra* note 18, at 13.

[32] One might fairly observe that because the law talks about competition, not about benefits, mergers that reduce competition—for example, merger to monopoly—are at the heart of the statute's concerns. In this respect, use of a consumer welfare standard could perhaps be deemed a sensible way of making operational the statute's notion of reduced competition. On the other hand, to get from competition to consumer welfare requires the introduction of a benefit standard. Otherwise, the law is only protecting the act of rivalry itself, which as discussed earlier, the law has (appropriately, in the view of many) moved beyond.

And yet, even here the case for a consumer welfare standard is less than clear cut. Merger to monopoly, for example, reduces competition by definition.[33] Nevertheless, if the merger-specific marginal cost reductions are large enough, even in these cases the affected consumers are better off, and welfare (however defined) rises. Does the Clayton Act condemn such mergers? Should it do so? If we agree that the ultimate determinant of whether a merger under the law (a law that is conspicuously silent as to the welfare measure it endorses) depends (or should depend) on its effect on welfare rather than on competition per se, then it seems fair to consider whether the appropriate measure of welfare should be consumer welfare or total welfare.

Shifting towards a total welfare standard for review of future mergers would seem to provide guidance that is no less clear to potential merger parties

IX. COSTS OF CHANGE?

Once a precedent, or a policy, has been around for a sufficiently long period of time, individuals are likely to have come to rely on it. More specifically and more significantly from an economics perspective, the reliance that individuals place on a longstanding policy may have led them to sink investments in anticipation of the precedent not being overturned. Both from the standpoint of equity and efficiency, change—even change to a better policy (or standard)—can impose significant costs. Is this consideration likely to present a serious objection to shifting from a consumer to a total welfare standard in merger analysis? It is not likely that it would, and the application to merger policy of the *stare decisis* doctrine seems weak.

In particular, there seems little reason to believe that a change in standard would cause either inefficiency or an inequitable effect on those who have taken past actions in reliance on the current standard. A change in standard would not be applied retroactively to mergers that have already been consummated, and on a going forward basis it is hard to imagine significant costs of shifting to a total welfare standard for mergers that have not yet even been proposed. We hardly have a situation where market participants, relying on the consumer welfare precedent, have made significant sunk investments based on the assumption that a consumer welfare standard would continue to be used on into the future. Shifting towards a total welfare standard for review of future mergers would seem to provide guidance that is no less clear to potential merger parties. It would also have the added benefit of encouraging an even larger number of efficient mergers than have taken place in the past.

---

[33] And, it certainly satisfies the statute's concern with mergers that "tend to create a monopoly."

One cost of changing standards would be a need for the antitrust bar, consultants, and courts who have become educated in just what does or doesn't satisfy a consumer welfare test to become retrained in what constitutes an increase in total welfare. My sense is that these costs are likely to be relatively small. Certainly, they will be far smaller than the costs that were incurred in the course of moving over the past three decades towards a more economics-based approach to merger analysis generally.

X. RELATIVE COSTS OF ADMINISTERING THE ALTERNATIVE STANDARDS

If the costs—to competition agencies, firms, consultants, courts—of employing a total welfare standard were likely to be significantly higher than the costs of employing a consumer welfare standard, this would be an argument for sticking with what we have—warts and all. It is not obvious, however, that this is true. And even if it were, in determining how much weight to be given administrative ease when deciding on a welfare standard, one should be mindful of the old saying about looking under a street lamp for one's lost keys simply because the light there is better. Indeed, it is plausible that in many investigations it would be easier, rather than more difficult, to employ a total welfare standard.

Supporters of a consumer welfare standard might contend that applying it is fairly simple; all one needs to do is determine whether price will rise or fall. Unfortunately, even this is far more difficult to determine in practice than it is to state in principle—even if one were to assume away the potential for merger-specific improvements in product quality.

In order to gauge the actual effect on a product's consumers, economists require reasonably accurate information about the shape of the demand curve for that product within the relevant range. The costs of obtaining reliable information of this sort may be considerable. Absent this information, it is difficult to estimate confidently the extent to which marginal cost savings of any given amount will be passed on to consumers in the form of lower prices.[34]

In addition, estimating the price effect from a merger-generated reduction in marginal cost of any given amount requires information about the competitive game being played by market

[34] Werden, however, shows that in the case of differentiated products where merger leads to neither enhancements in quality nor changes in differentiation (such as, through repositioning), the marginal cost reduction necessary to offset the anticompetitive effect is independent of the shape of demand; it depends only on margins and diversion ratios. And, accurate information about these variables may be easier to obtain than information about demand. Werden further argues that, in these circumstances, a very large reduction in marginal cost is generally required to offset the price-increasing effects of an otherwise anticompetitive merger. *See* Gregory J.Werden, *A Robust Test for Consumer Welfare Enhancing Mergers Among Sellers of Differentiated Products*, 44 J. INDUS. ECON. 409 (1996).

participants. Cournot, Bertrand, and other specific types of oligopolistic competition have different implications for the extent of pass-through from a given cost reduction, just as they have different implications for the extent to which a merger will enhance market power. And, all of this is complicated even more by the fact that the type of competitive game being played may itself change as a result of the merger, implying either greater or lesser pass-through than if the game remained unchanged.[35]

Beyond these difficulties, and importantly, in order to apply the consumer welfare standard the analyst needs not simply an estimate of merger-specific efficiencies, but also an estimate of the anticipated merger-induced reduction in marginal cost. The practical difficulties of distinguishing between those cost savings that impact incremental sales, and thus will to some extent factor into future pricing, and those that are fixed, and hence are unlikely directly to affect the profit-maximizing price, can be substantial.[36] In my experience, considerable resources tend to be spent (and wasted) by merging parties, by their consultants, by the competition authorities themselves, and by the courts in attempting to draw what would, under a total welfare standard, be a far less important distinction.

It might be argued that even if the costs of implementing a consumer welfare test are non-trivial, they are necessarily less than the cost of calculating the total welfare effect of a merger. Why? Because calculating total welfare requires the analyst to do all of the above plus estimate and add in any fixed or marginal cost savings that will not be passed on to consumers.

While this is correct if one's goal is to calculate precisely a merger's total effect on welfare, it is not correct if one's purpose is instead to determine whether total welfare is likely to increase. There will surely be many situations where the analyst would be able to conclude from the likely magnitude of merger-specific cost savings—whether marginal or fixed—that these benefits to society would exceed any plausible deadweight welfare loss.[37] In such cases, a total welfare

[35] To be sure, this may complicate considerably the analysis of a merger's likely effects under any welfare standard.

[36] In addition, marginal cost savings will generally not be achieved immediately, implying a need properly to discount for the more distant effects on price. While even fixed cost savings may take time to materialize, these at least tend to be one-time cost savings, implying less need to discount a stream of future benefits.

[37] Treating as welfare neutral the pure transfer of surplus from consumers to producers from even a modest post-merger price increase—which is what a total welfare standard would do—the deadweight loss from many mergers would often be quite small relative to any significant cost savings. This, even after controlling for the factors that may have biased upwards the estimates contained in Williamson's naïve model. Moreover, as discussed in Roberts and Salop, firm-specific efficiencies generated by merger may, over time, spill over to the market as a whole as other firms in the economy gradually appropriate these benefits for themselves. Gary L. Roberts & Steven C. Salop, *Efficiencies in Dynamic Merger Analysis*, 19 World Competition L. & Econ. Rev. 5 (1996).

standard would likely be far easier than a consumer welfare standard to apply.[38] Moreover, if one is unable to estimate with a reasonably high degree of confidence claimed efficiencies that benefit producers rather than consumers (such as, merger-specific fixed cost savings), it would not be inconsistent with the use of a total welfare standard to evaluate the merger largely on the basis of what one believes likely to be the effect on final consumers alone. A total welfare standard may, therefore, not only be more desirable conceptually, but also less costly to implement.

XI. WELFARE STANDARDS AND THE FIRST THEOREM OF ANTITRUST

Finally, one might argue that employing a consumer welfare standard is less costly because it lends itself to ready application of what some might consider the "first theorem of antitrust"—i.e., if consumers like it, the merger is pro-competitive and should be permitted. If they dislike it, the merger is anticompetitive and should be blocked. Because pure fixed cost savings do not translate into lower prices for consumers in the relevant markets impacted by a merger, and because a total welfare standard explicitly permits a tradeoff between harms to consumers and (potentially larger) gains to producers, determining from the views of customers whether to challenge a merger provides at most only limited guidance under the total welfare standard.

The case for relying on the views of customers as a simple, shorthand way of determining whether a merger is likely to enhance consumer welfare is not, however, anywhere as strong as some suggest.[39] Indeed, difficulties in applying this proxy are an important reason why competition authorities do not simply poll customers for their bottom-line views on a merger, but dig more deeply into the rationale behind customer views, where possible; examine natural experiments; and rely increasingly on sophisticated empirical techniques—particularly econometric analysis. These efforts tend to belie the claim of some that the first theorem is a surefire and low-cost method of answering our ultimate questions.

Why can one not readily determine from the views of customers whether a merger is likely to satisfy the consumer welfare standard? The reasons are several.

---

[38] For a fuller discussion of the issues presented in this section, see Ken Heyer, *Predicting the Competitive Effects of Mergers by Listening to Customers*, 74 ANTITRUST L.J. (forthcoming 2006).

[39] It is worth recalling also from the discussion in Section III, *supra*, that even mergers likely to satisfy the consumer welfare standard, as currently applied, may result in harm to at least some consumers. Such may be the case, for example, where a merger efficiently leads the combined firm to focus on a single standard or platform (thereby stranding some groups of customers), or where merger-specific efficiencies in some markets are inextricably linked to competitive harm in others.

For one thing, typically there are many consumers with different demands and tastes. Polling a segment of them, particularly if price discrimination is not feasible, will not necessarily determine whether a merger is likely to produce a reduction in consumer welfare. Second, where the merger threatens potentially to raise price to each consumer by only a relatively small dollar amount, consumers are unlikely to have given serious thought to the question; they will rationally have found it unprofitable to invest in obtaining the information relevant to developing a strong and informed opinion.

Also very important is the fact that many, perhaps even most, mergers that come before competition authorities involve inputs, not final products. The immediate consumers of these inputs, and the ones most frequently quizzed about the merger's likely impact, are not themselves final consumers. Unfortunately, the effects on some, or even all, of these customers can be quite different from the effects on the ultimate, final, consumers to whom they sell. Purchasers of intermediate goods frequently employ different production techniques in turning out competing final goods. To the extent that some of these producers rely less heavily on a particular input than do others, the impact on the former group may be positive even if a merger threatens to raise the incremental costs for that firm and its rivals. In effect, firms that face relatively small cost increases may benefit on net from the fact that consumers shift towards them, and away from competitors whose costs have increased even more.[40]

In addition, where final demand is inelastic and pass-through is likely to be nearly complete, intermediate goods customers may (correctly) believe that they will not be very much harmed by even a substantial post-merger increase in the price of what they buy. Final consumers, of course, are unambiguously harmed. Moreover, purchasers of intermediate goods who themselves already have substantial stocks of the input—either warehoused, or incorporated into final products not yet sold—may benefit from the higher incremental costs now faced by all from expanding and/or entering their markets. Again, final consumers would be left worse off, even as some (or even all) intermediate good producers benefit.

Finally, in some circumstances pass-through of a cost increase will be greater than one hundred percent,[41] and economists have shown that, depending on final demand conditions,

---

[40] *See* Joseph Farrell, *Listening to Interested Parties in Antitrust Investigations: Competitors, Customers, Complementors, and Relativity*, 18 ANTITRUST 64 (Spring 2004). For one famous instance of a strategic effort by some firms to raise their rivals' costs as well as their own, see Oliver Williamson, *WAGE RATES AS A BARRIER TO ENTRY: THE PENNINGTON CASE IN PERSPECTIVE*, 82 Q.J. ECON 85 (1968).

[41] For example, this is an implication of Cournot competition.

higher marginal costs may actually increase the profits of intermediate goods customers.[42] The takeaway from all of this is not that the views of customers are irrelevant in determining the likely effects of a merger. Rather, it is that the translation from consumer views to implementation of even a consumer welfare standard is often far from a simple task.[43]

All of this having been said, employing a total welfare standard would not be an easy matter either. Moreover, for reasons I now discuss, strict adherence to a total welfare standard would potentially lead to approval of a number of mergers whose likely effect on consumers is significantly negative.

XII. DISTRIBUTIONAL CONSIDERATIONS

Distributional considerations raise at least two separate and distinct issues. The first is whether pure transfers among groups in society should be considered in merger policy. Again, the statute is silent on this issue.

A second is whether, even if we were to grant that wealth distribution considerations are an appropriate focus of antitrust policy, this provides clear support for use of a consumer welfare standard. Here we need to ask how confident we are of the presumption that consumers impacted adversely by a merger are less wealthy than owners of the firms that may be achieving cost savings in addition to the consumer surplus they are diverting. Surely not all mergers are likely to have this effect, and we should therefore consider the potentially enormous costs of calculating in each case the net distributional effect from employing a consumer welfare standard.

To see that anticompetitive mergers need not have an adverse distributional impact, consider a proposed merger of all Mercedes-Benz repair shops in a relevant geographic market. Assume that entry into the market is strictly prohibited; perhaps because of zoning restrictions enacted to prevent noise or congestion, or perhaps explicitly to protect these

[42] *See* Sheldon Kimmel, *Effects of Cost Changes on Oligopolists' Profits,* 40 J. Indus. Econ. 441 (1992). For an analysis of circumstances under which intermediate goods customers may be harmed even as consumers benefit, see Daniel P. O'Brien & Greg Shaffer, *Bargaining, Bundling, and Clout: The Portfolio Effects of Horizontal Mergers*, 36 RAND J Econ. 573 (2005).

[43] It is worth mentioning also, that while final consumers are an excellent source of information about their own demands they cannot generally be expected to opine intelligently on other factors relevant to whether a merger will prove anti-competitive. For example, it is not at all obvious that individual consumers will have reliable knowledge as to a proposed merger's prospects for generating merger-specific efficiencies, or whether in the face of a possible SSNIP (small but significant and non-transitory increase in price) entry can be expected to be timely, likely, and sufficient.

firms from additional competition. Under this fact pattern, should the antitrust authorities challenge the merger if our best economic analysis concluded that, post-merger the profit-maximizing price for repairing Mercedes-Benz automobiles would rise by 25 percent? Typically, one would think, a challenge would be appropriate, and that authorities should not be required first to determine whether the deadweight loss from a merger-induced price increase would be offset by a socially beneficial wealth transfer from rich automobile owners towards service station owners.[44]

Beyond the question of whether it is desirable in theory to take into account distributional effects,[45] it is not clear that one can at low cost confidently predict even the direction, much less the magnitude, of a merger's distributional consequences. The owners of publicly traded corporations proposing to merge in an effort to capture savings not fully passed on to consumers are quite often an ordinary cross section of Americans, and doubtless include the life savings of retirees, as well as the proverbial widows and orphans.[46] Moreover, many consumers who happen to be poor today will be wealthier tomorrow (and vice versa). Although in extreme cases the distributional consequences of a proposed merger may be relatively clear,[47] in most cases it will be far from obvious (and costly to determine) whether consumers of the merging firms' substitute products are disproportionately in the lower wealth brackets. Determining with any degree of confidence the impact on particular consumer groups of proposed mergers in intermediate goods markets is likely to be especially difficult.

While a policy requiring calculations of not only the likely price effects, but also the likely distributional consequences of mergers, would doubtless contribute significantly to the wealth of economic consultants and experts, the benefits to society from incurring these costs seem highly questionable. And if we are not even sure what a standard's distributional consequences are, it seems hard to justify use of that standard on the basis of its (unknown) distributional consequences.

---

44 If station owners are generally poorer than their customers, should station owner cartels be permitted? Should they be encouraged to form?

45 Arnold Harberger, in a paper, offers a plea for economists to accept as part of their "conventional framework for applied welfare economics," the postulate that "when evaluating the net benefits or costs of a given action (project, program, or policy), the costs and benefits accruing to each member of the relevant group (e.g., a nation) should normally be added without regard to the individual(s) to whom they accrue." Arnold Harberger, Three Basic Postulates for Applied Welfare Economics: An Interpretive Essay, 9 J. Econ. Lit. 785 (1971).

46 In addition, producer surplus, when not passed through to consumers in the form of lower prices, may be shared to some extent with suppliers of the firm's inputs—including labor.

47 Ralph Winter offers, as one possible example, a proposed merger of duopoly slumlords.

It is hardly obvious that a decision on whether to block a merger ought to depend in any way on whether, for example, service station owners are, on average, wealthier than their customers (or vice versa). And even if it were costless to determine whether the consumers or the producers affected by a merger are wealthier, surely questions of wealth distribution are better handled through targeted tax and subsidy programs, rather than via antitrust policy. Arguing that government tax and spend policies are a more appropriate means of dealing with issues of income (and wealth) distribution is not equivalent to proposing that government take on the job of neutralizing, in all cases, the consequences of the occasional price-increasing merger that may come to be permitted under a total welfare standard. The wealth of poorer citizens is regularly affected by any number of broad economic factors—including, for example, adverse changes in the supply and demand for their labor. And yet, economists generally deem it more efficient to deal with broad issues of wealth and income distribution at a macroeconomic level, rather than by interfering regularly with the normal, wealth-maximizing functioning of private markets.[48]

Finally, and importantly, a merger policy that contributes to the overall size and growth of the economy generates larger total wealth; and at least part of the proceeds can, if society wishes, be used by fiscal authorities to aid, through targeted taxation and spending programs, those deemed to be most needy, or otherwise most deserving.

XIII. SOME ADDITIONAL CONSIDERATIONS

A. The Costs of Rent-Seeking Behavior

Economists have long known that competition can be wasteful at times. That is to say, one really can have too much of a good thing. What does it mean to say, as a matter of economics, that something is "excessive"? Conduct can sensibly be defined as excessive when it is being engaged in past the point at which, from the standpoint of society as a whole, the value it adds is greater than its cost.[49] Pollution is one commonly used example of where negative externalities may be imposed by manufacturers on residents who are not compensated for harms they suffer. In such cases, it is easy to show that an activity—in this case, production by the manufacturers—may well proceed past the point at which its net value to the economy is positive.

[48] Indeed, the absolute adverse impact on an individual poor person of a merger permitted under the total welfare standard, but not permitted under the consumer welfare standard, seems likely to be quite modest in comparison with other factors impacting on a poor person's wealth. Even a 20 percent increase in the price paid for a $200 item amounts to a total of only $40.

[49] The maintained assumption is that rational actors engage only in conduct whose benefits to them are expected to exceed the costs to them.

Competition itself can in some cases create a negative externality—an uncompensated harm—that results in excessive entry or excessive product differentiation. The negative externality in these cases is felt not by consumers, but by incumbent producers. Nevertheless, it can result in entry and competition that, while beneficial to consumers in the market, is wasteful to the economy as a whole.[50]

Consider, for example, a market in which incumbent firms are earning significant margins and positive margins will remain even following competitive entry. In such cases, potential entrants will find that the costs of entering will be partly covered by revenues on business that the entrant steals" from incumbents. To the extent that business can be stolen without a substantial cut in price (or improvement in quality), the benefits to consumers may fall far short of the associated costs, in particular, the fixed costs of entry.[51]

Part of what makes entry into a market profitable can be the margins that are shifted from incumbents to the entrant. From the standpoint of society as a whole, however, these are merely transfers from one firm to another. Nevertheless, the prospect of capturing these margins can in some instances make entry profitable, despite the fact that, from the standpoint of the economy as a whole, entry does not pass a cost-benefit test.[52] In addition

---

[50] Antitrust scholars, most notably Richard Posner, have argued that the drive to obtain market power can transform rents into costs. Richard Posner, *The Social Costs of Monopoly and Regulation*, 83 J. Pol. Econ. 807 (1975). Whatever the power of this logic in general, the argument appears to have questionable applicability to mergers in particular. As Williamson summarizes after responding to this argument in some detail:

> Plausibility standards plainly vary. Those who are easily persuaded that managers enjoy extensive insularity [from stockholder control], that managers fully credentialize on the basis of low probability events, and that the marginal utility of money is fairly constant will conclude that exhaustive ex ante rent transformation occurs in the merger context, as required by Posner's theory. On the other hand, those who are skeptical of any of these assumptions will conclude that rent transformation will be incomplete. As for myself, I believe that the insularity assumption is the most doubtful. Absent this assumption, the entire argument collapses.

See Williamson, *supra* note 8, at 8.

[51] It is hard to imagine there being a serious competitive problem with a merger of two or more of the many high-price coffee shops located within walking distance of my office in downtown Washington, DC, and I admit to wondering whether some of the fixed costs incurred from all of this entry might not be wasteful from the standpoint of society as a whole.

[52] *See* Gregory N. Mankiw & Michael D. Whinston, *Free Entry and Social Inefficiency*, 17 RAND J. Econ. 48, 55-57 (1986), which discusses various entry biases and examines the tendency toward excessive entry in homogeneous product markets. *See also* Michael Spence, *Product Selection, Fixed Costs, and Monopolistic Competition*, 43 Rev. Econ. Stud. 217 (1976) and A.K. Dixit & J.E. Stiglitz, *Monopolistic Competition and Optimal Product Diversity*, 67 Am. Econ. Rev. 297 (1977), which discuss the possibility of free entry resulting in too little entry relative to the social optimum in a monopolistically competitive market. Finally, see Chiang-Tai Hsieh & Enrico Moretti, *Can Free Entry Be Inefficient? Fixed Commissions and Social Waste in the Real Estate Industry*, 111 J. Pol. Econ. 1076 (2003), which attempts empirically to estimate the cost of excess entry into the Real Estate Industry.

to investments in entry, investments in product differentiation can, for similar business-stealing reasons, be wasteful as well.[53]

These considerations suggest a theoretical case for actually prohibiting entry at times, though it is worth mentioning also that, in theory, markets can suffer equally from insufficient entry.[54] The antitrust laws are not employed to keep out competitive entry, nor would many propose that they be used for that purpose.[55] Consumers in markets where even excess entry occurs clearly benefit. The benefits include not only lower prices, but also the prospect for highly valued variety and better products, not to mention the incentive that the entry threat provides for incumbents to minimize costs and identify and satisfy consumer demands. Determining ex ante whether the costs of entry are likely to exceed its many potential benefits seems clearly too daunting a task to take on.[56] As with antitrust's *per se* prohibition of naked price fixing, courts sensibly eschew case-by-case analysis in circumstances where the expected cost exceeds the expected benefit.

Given how costly—and potentially harmful—it may be to implement a total welfare standard that takes these theoretical possibilities into account, one could argue that it would be best, all things considered, simply to stick with a consumer welfare standard. And yet, the difficulties of administering a total welfare standard do not seem so large, or so welfare-standard specific, that they offset the strong case for using what is otherwise a far more desirable welfare criterion. Determining whether a merger is likely to raise total

---

[53] *See* Michael Spence, *Product Differentiation and Welfare*, 66 AM. ECON. REV. 407 (1976). *See also* Steven C. Salop & Jeffrey M. Perloff, *Firm-Specific Information, Product Differentiation, and Industry Equilibrium*, 38 OXFORD ECON. PAPERS 184 (1986) and Dixit & Stiglitz, *id.*

[54] *See, e.g.*, Chaim Fershtman & Ariel Pakes, A Dynamic Oligopoly with Collusion and Price Wars, 31 RAND J. ECON. 207 (2000). There, the authors show that where fixed costs are significant, marginal costs are low, and post-entry pricing is Bertrand, total welfare can be enhanced by permitting postentry collusion. In certain circumstances total welfare can be enhanced also by having the government subsidize entry or limit the freedom of an incumbent to respond to an entrant's lower prices. *See, e.g.*, AARON S. EDLIN & JOSEPH FARRELL, THE AMERICAN AIRLINES CASE: A CHANCE TO CLARIFY PREDATION POLICY (Berkeley Competition Policy Center, Working Paper No. CPC02-33, Nov. 2002).

[55] The argument that entry should be prohibited on grounds that its costs exceed its benefits has, however, been employed in regulatory proceedings—typically by incumbents claiming to be natural monopolies. *See, e.g.*, Paul W. MacAvoy, Daniel F. Spulber & Bruce E. Stangle, *Is Competitive Entry Free? Bypass and Partial Deregulation in Natural Gas Markets*, 6 YALE J. ON REG. 209 (1989).

[56] Inefficiencies associated with requirements that potential entrants first obtain regulatory approval have been widely documented. For one discussion of the harmful effects of entry regulation in the trucking industry, see Thomas Gale Moore, *Trucking Deregulation*, The Concise Encyclopedia of Economics, *available at* http://www.econlib.org/library/Enc/TruckingDeregulation.html.

welfare requires an estimate of the merger's effect on allocative efficiency via the ability of firms profitably to raise price (or otherwise harm consumers of their products) and the cost savings, if any, that are specific to the merger. In principle, the analyst needs to evaluate these two effects and calculate their net welfare effect under either a consumer, or a total, welfare standard.[57]

B. Transparency

One might agree with the policy proposal put forward in this paper—that competition authorities should be employing a total welfare standard—yet also feel that if a change is to be made, it would be best that it not be made very publicly or transparently. A formal policy change of this type could well generate considerable flak and controversy. Might it be best, all things considered, to implement it through the use of prosecutorial discretion not to bring wrong or difficult cases?

Apart from objections in principle to the idea that open debate should be discouraged because the public would simply not support such a change, there are a number of practical adverse consequences from being less than candid about the standard that the competition agencies will apply. For one thing, if parties do not know that certain types of efficiencies are going to be credited by the authorities, they are far less likely to present the types of evidence and analysis required for those efficiencies to be credited. For another, in some circumstances the government may elect to file a case and the defendants will present to the court an efficiency justification that would in theory be credited under a total welfare standard, but that would not be credited under a consumer welfare standard. If total welfare is not the standard officially employed by antitrust officials, one can expect government prosecutors and their experts to argue strenuously that benefits unlikely to be fully passed through to consumers in the relevant markets of concern do not count. This would be, in my view, unfortunate, and may help lead a court to wrongly rule in favor of the plaintiff, or at least to rule in favor of the plaintiff for the wrong reasons. It may also complicate the ability of authorities to implicitly credit savings in producer surplus and appropriately to exercise prosecutorial discretion in the future.

---

[57] An optimal policy under conditions of uncertainty would take into account the costs of both type I and type II errors. Decisions would be made based on the expected value of a merger's effect on welfare, not simply a point estimate. *See* Ken Heyer, *A World of Uncertainty: Economics and the Globalization of Antitrust*, 72 Antitrust L.J. 375 (2005).

XIV. CONCLUSIONS

More and more antitrust practitioners, both in the United States and abroad, have expressed an interest in incorporating the effects of merger-generated efficiencies into merger analysis. The analysis in this article argues that if we are going to do it,[58] we might as well do it right, and that use of a total welfare standard appears to be not only the theoretically best standard to employ, but also one that can be employed with no significant increase in administrative costs.

And there is a somewhat broader point worth making. Use of a consumer welfare standard in antitrust inherently casts consumers as those who count, and producers as those who do not. This is unfortunate, in my view, for reasons that go well beyond those laid out in this article. For one thing, producers, it bears remembering, happen also to be consumers. Indeed, they have been seen shopping after work, and on their days off. Moreover, there seems good reason to value the welfare of those who produce what we consume as highly as those who do the consuming.

Defense of a welfare standard that ignores the welfare of producers contributes to a perception that producers exist only to benefit those to whom they sell, and that the welfare of those actually doing the producing—often at significant cost and risk—is itself of no value. It thus contributes to a mindset that favors all manner of efficiency-reducing policies to benefit select groups of consumers at the expense of producers, despite the negative effect such policies have on overall economic welfare, certainly in the long run, and often in the short run as well.

Quite apart from whatever economic benefits would result from putting antitrust policy on a more economically sensible footing, these considerations argue in favor of doing so as well.

---

58 Some serious antitrust scholars, including Richard Posner and Robert Bork, have concluded that explicit case-by-case consideration of merger-specific efficiencies, and by implication the use of an efficiencies defense, is simply too difficult to conduct in practice and should therefore not be a formal part of merger analysis and litigation. *See* Richard A. Posner, Antitrust Law (2nd ed. 2001) and Robert H. Bork, The Antitrust Paradox (1978).

INTERVIEW:
UPDATE ON "SCREENS FOR CONSPIRACIES AND THEIR MULTIPLE APPLICATIONS"

Scan our QR code with your mobile device to listen to the recorded interview. Note: you must have a scanner app or installed software to read the QR code.

As part of our Spring 2012 issue, CPI is presenting a retrospective of our best articles in the past and providing updates. One of our selections is "Screens for Conspiracies and their Multiple Applications," originally appearing in the Fall 2010 issue of the Journal. Providing some of her insights into this article, as well as reasons why the ideas explored in it are still relevant today, is co-author Rosa Abrantes-Metz. Rosa is currently a principal at Global Economics Group and adjunct associate professor at NYU's Stern School of Business, where she teaches industrial economics, monetary policy, and financial institutions. In the past, she has served as staff economist at the Federal Trade Commission and taught econometrics at the University of Chicago. Rosa is one of the leading developers of screens to detect conspiracies, manipulations, and fraud, and also uses these techniques on the other side to assist in defending against allegations of such behavior.

What were the most significant developments in screening since your article with co-author Patrick Bajari was published?

Lauren, thank you so much for this opportunity to talk to you about screens. Over the last couple of years since we published our article, there have been some pretty significant developments in the area of screening. The most important—to me personally, but also in terms of dimension and potential implications—is the alleged LIBOR conspiracy and manipulation with current investigations worldwide. The LIBOR is a benchmark rate to which, it is estimated, about $350 trillion in contracts are benchmarked against, so it is a very important number. Four years ago, following a couple of articles in the *Wall Street Journal* that first put into possibility a manipulation in these rates, I and co-authors Albert Metz, Mike Kraten, and Gim Seow, decided to take a look into this topic. We looked at the period flagged by the Wall Street Journal initially, and a variety of other periods as well, and put together a set of results in which we flagged situations that were unexpected—behavior that was unexpected by banks in a competitive setting, and that could potentially suggest the possibility not only of manipulation, but actually coordinated behavior by the banks implying the possibility of a conspiracy. Last year, we learned, that a few years after our paper came out, there were investigations by the SEC, CFTC, the DOJ, the European Commission, the OFT, and a variety of other regulatory and competition authorities into this matter. So I would say this is the most important development, in my view.

But over the last few years as well, competition authorities have started to increase their adoption of these methods. For example, the Mexican authority has flagged a bid-rigging cartel in pharmaceuticals. The Brazilians (CADE) have flagged gasoline cartels in a particular region. So these have also been significant developments in the area of detection.

And following this, in particular in the case of LIBOR, we are starting to see screens being applied in other areas as well, and for other purposes such as in complaints by plaintiffs. There are a variety of uses of screens in the LIBOR matters [by plaintiffs], and I expect they will also be used by defendants.[1]

Aside from detections, how have screens increased their use for other purposes?

The first purpose of a screen is detection. If a screen, which is an econometric model based on the theory of cheating, cannot detect alleged behavior, then it is really not useful for other purposes. But given that we have already established the power of several screens [in cases], then they can be used in a variety of other settings, and the exact same results that can be used to flag a conspiracy and to assist in proving it (though it is never the final proof, but it assists in proving) the existence of conspiracy, manipulation, or any other type of fraud, can just as well be used to assist in defending against allegations of that type of behavior. If one does screen the market and does not find any strange patterns, then there are only two possible

1 I have successfully developed new screening methodologies on behalf of defendants making use of only publicly available data. Their use should expand in the future.

reasons: that nothing illegal happened, or even if anything illegal happened, it had no material impact in the market. Then, through the use of other tools, one can try and separate between these two possibilities.

If one does screen the market and does not find any strange patterns, then there are only two possible reasons: that nothing illegal happened, or even if anything illegal happened, it had no material impact in the market.

But, screens can be used by defendants. I have certainly used them in this setting in the initial stages of investigations into manipulation and conspiracy cases, and even in other fraud cases, to assist in showing that there did not appear to be anything abnormal going on in the market. As for other places that have also successfully started to use screens–as I mentioned earlier, the LIBOR– it is possible that after *Twombly*, screens can be of additional help in the higher standards that are now required after it, to pass the initial stages of litigation.

Regulators and competition authorities worldwide have also started to use screens for detection. Another development that is starting to occur now and that is expected to become bigger over the next few years is the use of screens in antitrust compliance programs, given that regulators are using these methods and new regulations, for example in financial markets, that do require tighter compliance programs.[2] Several financial institutions and energy companies have started implementing some of these tools to try and flag potential illegal behavior internally.

What role should screens play when compared to leniency programs?

I see screens as a complement to leniency. Leniency programs have, of course, been very successful, but they do tend to flag cartels primarily in a particular set of industries. That does not necessarily mean that there aren't cartels in other industries, but leniency programs do not tend to flag these. At the same time, leniency is based on the idea of a whistleblower: there is somebody within the organization of the cartel who is not so happy with the way things are going and decides to complain. When cartels are very successful from their point of view, very profitable and raising prices significantly, it is less likely that a whistleblower will come through. So it is less likely that in those situations a leniency program will be able to detect a cartel, in which case a screen can come into play. See, for example, the case of the LIBOR. This is a case which, for me, is a standard example of how screens should complement leniency. We

[2] In fact, just a few days ago new guidelines for compliance were released in Chile in which the internal use of screens is recommended.

I'm not quite sure had screens not been applied to LIBOR that the alleged wrongdoings would have been detected through leniency.

[I and co-authors] applied screens to the market, some abnormal patterns came through, years later investigations did get started, and they got started before there were any leniency applications. Later on, several months after these investigations became public, one of the banks filed for leniency with the Department of Justice. This is exactly how screens and leniency can and should interact. I'm not quite sure had screens not been applied to LIBOR that the alleged wrongdoings would have been detected through leniency.

Additionally, I believe that screens can have an important role in deterring this type of behavior from even getting started. If market players know that competition authorities and regulators are using these methods, and if they're not even quite sure how exactly these methods are being used, and what exactly is being flagged, but they do know their data is being analyzed, they might have second thoughts about engaging in this type of behavior. So, complementarity and deterrence are the two ways in which screens can contribute to detection.

Lastly, what do you see in the future for screens?

I see, even just in the last two, three, or even five years, that this is an area that has grown very significantly, not just in terms of research, but also in terms of adoption by competition authorities. And through the adoption of competition authorities, market players will believe that these screens are credible and will want to use them as well. I think that this is a trend that is going to continue.

Obviously, screens are based on data availability, and if there are no data, one cannot apply these types of screens. Maybe other screens can be done, but not empirical screens. But over time there will be better and more frequent data, and there are more economists capable of appropriately analyzing these data and developing new techniques fitted for the market at hand. So, I think that the use of screens can only increase over time.

Thank you very much, Romy. This has been a terrific discussion of how screens can be used to promote goals in antitrust and competition policy.

Thank you so much, Lauren. This was a good opportunity to talk a little bit about this area of research and its applications to litigation, which I feel is a really fascinating area.

SCREENS FOR CONSPIRACIES AND THEIR MULTIPLE APPLICATIONS

*Rosa M. Abrantes-Metz & Patrick Bajari**

ABSTRACT

A screen is a statistical test designed to detect conspiracies aimed at illegally manipulating a market. Competition authorities, academics, and consultants have designed a variety of screens to detect competition problems, and the use of such screens has been increasing. In this paper, we first describe screens designed to detect bid- rigging, price-fixing, market- allocation schemes, and commodity-market manipulation. Next, we discuss the ways in which screens can be used by plaintiffs and defendants in antitrust cases. These include: (i) class certification, (ii) motions to dismiss after Twombly; (iii) estimating the effects and damages of collusion; (iv) assisting companies in deciding when and whether to file a leniency application; (v) assisting in disproving the existence of a conspiracy and manipulation or establishing its immateriality; and (vi) assisting managers in large companies to monitor for data manipulation (e.g. falsified reimbursement or accounting statements) and price-fixing in purchasing.

I. INTRODUCTION

Competition authorities pursue price-fixing conspiracies in three stages: detection, prosecution, and penalization. In the United States and Europe, antitrust authorities historically have relied on leniency applications for the detection stage. Leniency programs have identified cartels in numerous industries including vitamins, dynamic random access memory ("DRAM") chips, graphite electrodes, and fine art auctions. As a result, over $2.5 billion dollars in fines have been assessed in the United States alone from 1997 to 2004.[1]

* Rosa M. Abrantes-Metz is Principal at Global Economics Group and Adjunct Associate Professor at Leonard N. Stern School of Business, New York University. Patrick Bajari is Professor of Economics, University of Minnesota and Research Associate, National Bureau of Economic Research. We thank David Evans for comments and suggestions. The views expressed are the authors' and should not be attributed to any affiliated organizations or their clients.

[1] See Scott D. Hammond, *Cornerstones of an Effective Leniency Program*, ICN Workshop on Leniency Programs (2004), *available at* http://www.justice.gov/atr/public/speeches/206611.htm.

Recognizing the limitations of leniency programs, many antitrust agencies have started to search for alternative approaches to detecting conspiracies. One such approach is screening

While leniency programs have been a success for antitrust agencies, some collusion remains undetected. Indeed, the very fact that leniency applications continue to be filed at high rates is evidence that collusion still occurs. Moreover, leniency programs likely reflect a bias towards uncovering conspiracies close to the breaking point, meaning that the most successful and durable cartels likely remain undetected. Recognizing the limitations of leniency programs, many antitrust agencies have started to search for alternative approaches to detecting conspiracies. One such approach is screening.

A screen is a statistical test designed to identify industries where competition problems exist and, in such industries, which firms are involved in a conspiracy. Screens use commonly available data such as prices, costs, estimated market shares, or bids, and then use statistical tools to identify patterns in the data that are anomalous or highly improbable. Broadly speaking, collusion screens used in the literature employ two strategies.

The first is to search for improbable events. This type of screen is similar to looking for a cheat in a casino. For example, the probability that a gambler at a Las Vegas casino will place a winning bet in roulette is roughly 0.5 percent. During her shift, a roulette dealer may see a handful of players win five, six, or even seven times in a row. However, the probability of winning twenty times in a row is around one in one million. If a pit boss sees this occur, he may not be able to prove that cheating has occurred, but he would be well advised to watch closely or risk losing a lot of money. One set of collusive screens generalizes this idea by looking for events that are improbable unless firms in the industry have coordinated their actions.

The second type of screen uses the concept of a control group. In the 1980s, organized crime in New York City operated a concrete club that rigged bids on contracts over $2 million. During this period, the price of concrete was 70 percent higher in New York City than other U.S. cities. While it is true that the price of many goods and services is higher in New York City, few prices are 70 percent higher than in other large cities. Prices that are anomalous compared to other markets suggest a competition problem. In this simple example, a control group consisting of prices in other cities is used as a basis for comparing prices in New York.

Below, we describe how economists have implemented screens to search for competition problems. The examples we discuss are bid-rigging, price-fixing, market-allocation schemes, and manipulating commodities markets.

Screens are not only useful to antitrust agencies; they can also be powerful tools for plaintiffs and defendants in antitrust cases. We will describe the multiple uses screens have (i) during class certification, (ii) for motions to dismiss after *Twombly*; (iii) estimating the effects and damages of collusion; (iv) assisting companies in deciding when and whether to file a leniency application; (v) assisting in disproving the existence of a conspiracy and manipulation or establishing its immateriality; and (vi) assisting managers in large companies to monitor for data manipulation (e.g. falsified reimbursement or accounting statements) and price-fixing in purchasing.

Screens are not only useful to antitrust agencies; they can also be powerful tools for plaintiffs and defendants in antitrust cases

It is important to emphasize that screens do not *prove* collusion. Screens isolate outcomes that are improbable or anomalous. Screens will exhibit both false positives and false negatives. However, this does not mean that screens lack value. Doctors regularly screen their patients for diseases even though their methods exhibit both false positives and negatives. Even so, patients are screened because the expense of testing all patients for a rare disease is prohibitive. The process of screening identifies a subset of patients that are at a higher risk than others, which then allows the doctor to engage in the more extensive testing for just a selective few. Analogously, a good antitrust screen will narrow the set of possible conspiracies to a manageable few that merit further review.

A good screen should possess the following properties: (i) it should minimize the number of false positives and negatives; (ii) it should be easy to implement; (iii) it should be costly for firms to disguise collusive behavior; and (iv) it should have empirical support.

II. EXAMPLES OF SCREENS

In this section, we describe several screens and their empirical applications. We start with the example of competitive bidding because the strict rules of competitive bidding help to identify colluders. Next, we discuss screens when only price data are available. These include variance screens, which search for pockets of high or low variances in prices as a flag for competition problems. Finally, we discuss screens based on Benford's Law, which describes the rates at which certain digits occur in many data sets.

A. Bid-Rigging

Bid-rigging in competitive tenders is a productive setting to apply screens for three reasons. First, competitive tenders account for a large volume of economic output. Public sector procurement, which often uses some form of competitive bidding, accounts for about 15 percent of

There is a large body of empirical literature on collusion in auctions that implements various types of screens.

world output. In addition, competitive bidding is widely used in financial markets, privatization of public assets, real estate, and many other transactions. Second, bid-rigging is a common antitrust offense. For example, during the 1980s, bid-rigging accounted for more than half of the criminal cases filed by the Department of Justice's Antitrust Division ("DOJ"). Third, markets that use competitive bidding are frequently rich in data. In many countries, statutes require the public disclosure of bids.

There is a large body of empirical literature on collusion in auctions that implements various types of screens.[2] While these papers span a wide variety of industries, researchers have identified common patterns when collusion is known or suspected. We describe these patterns below.

B. Bid-Rigging Screens Based on Improbable Events

The first set of screens looks for improbable events in sealed bid auctions. In these settings, firms submit their bids simultaneously. These bids are then read at a fixed date. In the public sector, the contract is typically awarded to the lowest bidder. If firms do not collude, they cannot condition their bids on the bids of other firms. As a result, we should expect that the bids would be independent after we control for information that is observed by all bidders, such as variables that influence cost or market power.

On the other hand, if firms collude, they need to coordinate their actions. Frequently, this coordination destroys the independence of the bids and can be detected through the use of statistical hypothesis testing. Collusion is suspected when bids are "too correlated" with each other to be the result of independent actions by bidders. Searching for identical bids is a limiting case

---

[2] *See* Robert H. Porter & J. Douglas Zona, *Detection of Bid Rigging in Procurement Auctions*, 101 J. Pol. Econ. 518 (1993) (examining auctions for highway construction projects in Long Island); Laura H. Baldwin et al., *Bidder Collusion at Forest Service Timber Sales*, 105(4) J. Pol. Econ. 657 (1997) (examining timber auctions in the Pacific Northwest); Robert H. Porter & J. Douglas Zona, *Ohio School Milk Markets: An Analysis of Bidding*, 30 RAND J. Econ. 263 (1999) (examining the procurement of school milk in Ohio); Martin Pesendorfer, *A Study of Collusion in First-Price Auctions*, 67 Rev. Econ. Stud. 1 (2000); Peter Crampton & Jesse Schwartz, *Collusive Bidding: Lessons from the FCC Spectrum Auctions*, 17 J. Reg. Econ. 229 (2000); Patrick Bajari & Jungwon Yeo, *Auction Design and Tacit Collusion in FCC Spectrum Auctions*, forthcoming in Information Economics and Policy. Econ. & Pol'y; Patrick Bajari & Lixin Ye, *Deciding Between Competition and Collusion*, 85(4) Rev. Econ. Stat. 971 (2003); John List, Daniel Millimet, & Michael Price, *Inferring Treatment Status when Treating Assignment is Unknown: with an Application to Collusive Bidding Behavior in Canadian Softwood Timber Auctions*, mimeo University of Chicago (2004); John Asker, *A Study of the Internal Organisation of a Bidding Cartel*, 100(3) Am. Econ. Rev. 724 (2010); Robert Marshall & Leslie Marx, *The Vulnerability of Auctions to Bidder Collusion*, forthcoming in Q. J. Econ. (2007).

of this sort of screen. A famous example is bids received by the Tennessee Valley Authority to install conductor cables in the 1950s. Seven firms submitted identical bids of $198,438.24. This is analogous to a gambler making twenty winning bets in a row at the roulette wheel. The chances of seven bidders, acting independently, arriving at bids that agree to eight significant digits is almost zero and a very strong signal that firms have explicitly or implicitly arrived at a mechanism for coordinating bids.

We illustrate this screen with an example involving bids to supply school milk in Ohio between 1980 and 1990.[3] In Ohio, firms submitted sealed bids for contracts to supply schools with pint-size portions of milk. The bidders were typically processors or distributors of milk, and school milk typically represented less than 10 percent of their annual revenues. Based on court evidence, Robert Porter and Douglas Zona argued that a bidder's costs are easily explained by a small number of variables, which are readily observed and include the price of raw milk and transportation costs, which represent 7 percent of total costs. Competition in the school milk market is localized due to transportation costs. Firms that are close to a particular school have a cost advantage because of shorter delivery routes.

Porter and Zona constructed econometric models of submitting a bid and bid levels. Economic theory suggests that both decisions should depend on two factors. The first is costs, which the authors measured using data on the distance between a public school, the bidder's location, and the number of deliveries made by the bidder. The second is local market power, which the authors controlled for by variables measuring the locations of competing firms.

The first screen proposed by Porter and Zona examined the correlation in bidders' entry decisions. After controlling for information that was publicly observed at the time of bidding, the authors found that the bidding decisions of some firms in the sample was too high to be explained by pure randomness, which supported the hypothesis that many accused colluders coordinated their decisions to submit bids.

Next, Porter and Zona constructed econometric models that express bids as a function of costs (controlled for by the distance between a public school, the bidder's location, and the number of deliveries made by the bidder) and local market power (controlled for by variables measuring the locations of competing firms). Porter and Zona found that bids for the non-colluding firms were explained using these regression models while, in comparison, the bids of cartel members were too highly and persistently correlated to be explained by

[3] Robert H. Porter & J. Douglas Zona, *Ohio School Milk Markets: An Analysis of Bidding* (NBER Working Paper No. 6037 (1997)).

Therefore, a second screen proposed in the literature is to determine how well bids reflect costs

the data. Porter and Zona concluded that it was difficult to reconcile this high and persistent correlation in bids with the hypothesis that firms were bidding independently. This high degree of correlation is similar to a gambler in a casino who has "correctly guessed" which bet to place in roulette twenty times in a row. These events appear to be too improbable to have occurred at random.[4]

C. Bid-Rigging Screens Based on Control Groups

A second prediction of economic theory is that bids should reflect costs in reasonably competitive markets. The act of collusion, on the other hand, attenuates the relationship between bids and costs so that conspirators can earn profits above a normal competitive rate. Therefore, a second screen proposed in the literature is to determine how well bids reflect costs. In our motivating example, one of the pieces of evidence we used to help make our case about the concrete club in New York City was that the cost of concrete there was 70 percent higher than in other U.S. cities. In this example, costs in other cities are a control group for the costs in New York.

Patrick Bajari (a co-author of this article) and Lixin Ye[5] examined bids by highway contractors in the upper Midwest during the 1990s. Three of the firms in their sample had been convicted of collusion in the last decade. However, market observers believed that the industry was free of a market-wide conspiracy to rig bids. The authors used bids for a type of road repair known as seal coating. The standard job in their data was fairly small—the winning bids are approximately $175,000. State highway departments prepare cost estimates before bidding occurs. These cost estimates are largely based on bids made in other geographic markets. Companies like McGraw Hill sell "blue books," which are essentially price indexes for particular construction tasks with market-specific adjustments. Note that the ratio of the winning bid to the cost estimate is almost equal to one with a fairly small standard deviation. This suggests that bids

---

4 Other studies have performed similar tests with similar results in markets where collusion is strongly suspected. This includes Porter & Zona's (1993) analysis of paving contacts on Long Island in the 1980s, List et. al.'s (2004) examination of bids for Canadian timber, and Marshall & Marx's (2008) study of bidding decisions for Russian Oil and Gas leases. Taken together, these papers demonstrate the usefulness of a screen that tests for the independence of bid submissions and bid levels. In the introduction, we argued that a good screen should have few false positives. Bajari & Ye, *infra*, demonstrate that this screen appears to have this property in their study of bidding by contractors in Minnesota, North Dakota, and South Dakota during the late 1990s.

5 Patrick Bajari & Lixin Ye, *Deciding Between Competition and Collusion*, 85(4) Rev. Econ. Stat., 971-989 (2003).

TABLE 1 Summary Statistics from Bajari and Ye

Variable	# of Observations	Mean	Std Deviation
Total Bid	441	175,000	210,000
Winning Bid/Cost Estimate	139	1.0031	0.1573
Distance of Winning Firm	139	188.67	141.51
Distance of Second Lowest Bidder	139	213.75	152.01
Backlog of Winning Bidder	131	0.3376	0.3160
Backlog of Second Lowest Bidder	131	0.4326	0.3435

are comparable to properly deflated bids from other markets. The authors took this as positive evidence that most bids in the market are competitive.

Distance is an important determinant of costs in seal coating. Bajari and Ye used mapping software to measure the travel time in minutes from a bidder's location to the project site. The table above shows that the winning bidder is closer than the second lowest bidder, which is consistent with bids increasing in transportation costs, and supporting evidence of a competitive market.

Backlog is another important determinant of costs. Most firms in the data are small, with annual revenues under $20 million. As a result, they have limited capacity and could not win all of the projects awarded in a particular year. As firms near their capacity constraints, their bids should increase as a result. The authors measured an individual firm's capacity by tracking the number of projects it previously won and the completion dates for those projects. Capacities are normalized to always lie between zero and one. The table shows that bids increase with backlog, which is consistent with economic intuition.

Next, the authors model bids using regression analysis. They use control variables, such as the engineer's cost estimate, distance from the project, and backlog. The regression also controls for competitive factors, such as the distance of the closest rival to the project. They estimated the regression separately for the eleven largest firms in the market. This allows them to study how and if bids are determined differently across the firms.

The authors screen for collusion by comparing the regressions described above for pairs of firms. The intuition behind the screen is simple. If A and B are not colluding, their bids will only depend on cost and competitive factors. On the other hand, if A and B collude, these factors alone cannot explain their bids. As a result, we should expect A and B's bid regressions to differ, which can be detected using hypothesis testing. Bajari and Ye apply this test to the eleven largest firms in their data set. They find that they cannot reject the hypothesis of no collusion, with the exception of two firms recently sanctioned for bid rigging.

D. Screens Based on Price and Cost Information

Economists also can screen for collusion by searching for prices that appear to be the result of direct coordination or that fail to reflect costs. For example, the DOJ suggests that the following patterns might be indicative of collusive behavior. Identical prices may indicate a price-fixing conspiracy, especially when: (i) prices remain identical for long periods of time; (ii) prices previously were different among firms before they were identical; (iii) price increases do not appear to be explainable by increased costs; (iv) discounts are eliminated, particularly in a market where discounts historically were given, or (v) vendors are charging higher prices to local customers than to distant customers.[6]

In a recent paper by Rosa Abrantes-Metz (a co-author of this article), Luke Froeb, John Geweke, and Christopher Taylor, the authors build on the intuition suggested in the first pattern noted above.[7] The authors propose a screen based on a search for pockets of high and low price variances among gasoline stations within a single metropolitan area. The idea for the screen came from the observation of price and cost behavior during, and after, the fall of a bid-rigging conspiracy in the market for frozen perch fillets purchased by the Defense Personal Support Center between 1987 and 1989. This conspiracy showed that collusive prices are less volatile and less responsive to cost shocks than are competitive prices. This empirical finding is also a prediction of many theoretical models. A cartel can be thought of as a "filter" that attenuates cost shocks before passing them to price, thereby reducing price

---

[6] *See* Price Fixing, Bid Rigging, and Market Allocation Schemes: What They Are and What to Look For, *available at* http://www.usdoj.gov/atr/public/guidelines/primer-ncu.htm.

[7] Rosa Abrantes-Metz, Luke Froeb, John Geweke, & Christopher Taylor, *A Variance Screen for Collusion*, 24 Int'l J. of I.O. 467-486 (2006).

FIGURE 1 Frozen Perch Prices and Costs: 1/6/87 - 9/26/89

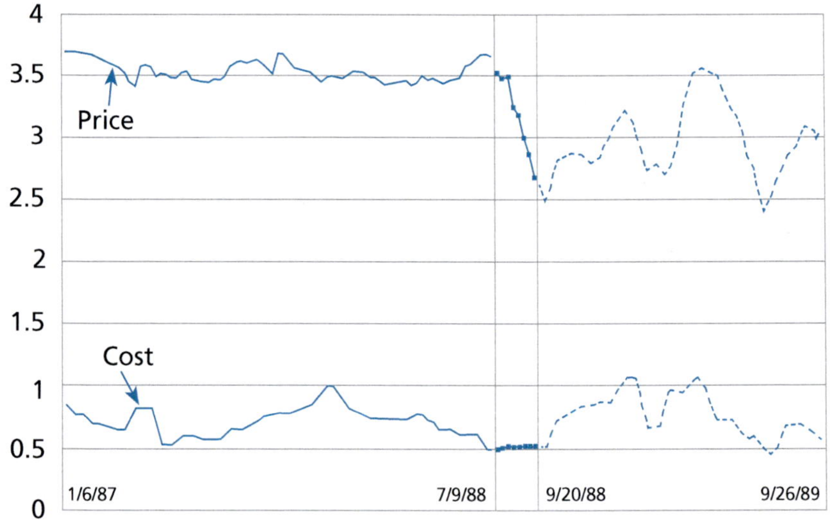

variance. The figure above, extracted from their paper, plots prices, in dollars per pound, for frozen perch filets paid by the Philadelphia Defense Personal Service Center from 1987 through September 1989. The cost data is the average monthly price of fresh perch, also in dollars per pound.

The authors compare prices and costs in the collusive regime (to the left of the vertical lines) to prices in the competitive regime (to the right of the vertical lines). The period between the two lines represents a transition from collusion to competition. This figure illustrates five features of the collusive and competitive regimes: (i) there was a structural break when the cartel collapsed, marked by a sudden drop in prices; (ii) the average price was higher during collusion than during competition; (iii) prices were more stable under collusion than under competition; (iv) prices followed costs movements more closely under competition than under collusion; and (v) gross margins were higher under collusion.

These five features are consistent with theoretical models of cartels. Also, the features of the data are consistent with the screens we discussed earlier and could be used by antitrust authorities to spot collusion. For example, the higher variance of prices in the competitive regime would be flagged by a well-designed variance screen.

As we will discuss in the next section, this variance screen has started to be used by a number of competition agencies in the United States and Europe.[8]

E. Screens Based on Quantities

Another potential screen uses data on quantity. The literature and evidence from prior cartels demonstrate that cartels may attempt to collude by fixing market shares.[9] Two screens are suggested by the literature: (i) markets shares that appear to be too stable over time and (ii) market shares for all firms in a particular market are negatively correlated over time. The first screen will detect an agreement by the cartel members to divide the market. Examples of cartels with stable market share agreements include cartels in copper plumbing tubes, organic peroxides, and several vitamins (A, E, and folic acid, in particular). In these industries, the cartel set shares at pre-cartel levels. Cartels in citric acid, sorbates, and zinc phosphate used the average of previous years. The second screen is suggested by dynamic models of collusion.[10] In these models, if a cartel member deviates from the collusive agreement, it will need to compensate other cartel members in subsequent time periods. As a result, abnormally high shares for a particular firm in one period should be followed by a reduction in shares the following period.

F. Screens Based on Mathematical Laws

In many data sets, the distribution of digits has a naturally, regularly occurring pattern. Benford's Law is a mathematical formula that describes this regularly occurring distribution of digits. Studies have shown that the law applies to a surprisingly large number of data sets, including populations of cities, street addresses of the first 348 persons named in *American Men of Science* (1934), electricity usage, word frequency, the daily returns to the Dow Jones, and even the

---

8 At the Italian Competition Authority, two economists "tested" the price variance screen on actual cartels in two different industries: the motor fuel market (gasoline and diesel); and the market for personal care and baby food products sold in pharmacies. The authors found that had the variance screen been applied to the data, it would successfully have detected these cartels. *See* Fabio Esposito & Massimo Ferrero, *Variance Screens for Detecting Collusions: An Application to Two Cartel Cases in Italy*, Italian Competition Authority, Working Paper (2006).

9 *See* Harrington, *Behavioral Screening and the Detection of Cartels*, Eur. Competition Law Annual 2006: Enforcement of Prohibition of Cartels (Claus-Dieter Ehlermann & Isabela Atanasiu, eds.) (2007).

10 *See* Susan Athey & Kyle Bagwell, *Optimal Collusion with Private Information*, 32(3) RAND J. Econ, 428-465 (2001) and Susan Athey, Kyle Bagwell & Chris Sanchirico, *Collusion and Price Rigidity*, 71 Rev. Econ. Studies, 317-349 (2004).

distribution of digits for the opening prices of 780 stocks on the Toronto Stock Exchange over a period of 300 days starting on June 30, 1998. Since Benford's Law is a naturally occurring pattern in many data sets, violations of the Law can be used to detect irregularities. In the past, violations of Benford's Law have been used to detect data tampering, manipulation of financial ratios, and tax evasion.[11]

Rosa Abrantes-Metz, Sofia Villas-Boas & George Judge use Benford's Law to test for conspiracies in several applied settings. The authors also use Benford's Law to test for manipulation of the Libor rate.[12] Similar to the findings in Abrantes-Metz, Kraten, Metz & Seow, their results indicate possible collusion for a specific period.[13,14]

III. THE USE OF SCREENS BY ANTITRUST AGENCIES

In this section we discuss efforts by antitrust agencies in the United States and Europe to detect conspiracies through the use of screens.[15] Screening efforts in the United States date back the 1970s when the DOJ formed an "identical bids" unit to investigate government procurement auctions in which identical bids were submitted. During the six years of its existence, no conspiracies were uncovered.

In October 2006, the DOJ created the National Procurement Fraud Task Force to promote prevention, early detection, and prosecution of fraud in federal procurement contracts.

---

11 Others who have used Benford's law to check the validity of purported scientific data in the social sciences include Hal Varian, *Benford's Law*, 26 Amer. Statistician, 65-66 (1972); Charles Carslaw, *Anomalies in Income Numbers: Evidence of Goal Oriented Behavior*, 63(2) Acct. Rev. 321-327 (1988); Mark Nigrini, *A Taxpayer Compliance Application of Benford's Law*, 18(1) J. Amer. Taxation Assn. 72- 91 (1996); Cindy Durtschi, William Hillson & Carl Pacini, *The Effective Use of Benford's Law to Assist in Detecting Fraud in Accounting Data*, 5 J. Forensic Acct., 17-34 (2004); C. Geyer & P. Williamson, *Detecting Fraud in Data Sets Using Benford's Law,* 33 Comm. In. Stat., 229-246 (2004); D. Giles, *Benford's Law and Naturally Occurring Prices in Certain Ebay Auctions*, 14(3) Applied Econ. Letters 157-161 (2007); John Nye & Charles Moul, *The Political Economy of Numbers: On the Application of Benford's Law to International Macroeconomic Statistics*, 7(1) The B.E. Journal of Macroeconomics (2007); George Judge & Laura Schechter, *Detecting problems in Survey Data using Benford's Law*, J. Human Resources, forthcoming (2009).

12 Rosa Abrantes-Metz, Sofia Villas-Boas, & George Judge, *Tracking the Libor Rate*, Applied Econ. Letters, forthcoming (2010).

13 Abrantes-Metz, Villas-Boas, and Judge are also testing the power of Benford's Law to detect manipulations in commodities markets and in price-fixing cartels.

14 Rosa Abrantes-Metz, Michael Kraten, Albert Metz & Gim Seow, *LIBOR Manipulation?* Working Paper (2008), *available at* http://papers.ssrn.com/sol3/cf_dev/AbsByAuth.cfm?per_id=339863.

15 A more detailed discussion can be found in Rosa Abrantes-Metz & Luke Froeb, *Competition Authorities are Screening for Conspiracies: What are they Likely to Find?* The American Bar Association Section of Antitrust Law Economics Committee Newsletter (2008).

This variance screen was referred to in the FTC's post-hurricane Katrina and Rita investigations to refute allegations of gasoline price manipulation

The Task Force focuses on defective pricing, false claims, grant fraud, labor mischarging, and bid-rigging.[16] And more recently, the DOJ announced proactive efforts in partnership with state and local agencies to protect stimulus funds provided for by the American Recovery and Reinvestment Act of 2009 from fraud, waste, and abuse. These efforts include spotting behavior consistent with red flags for collusion.[17]

In the late 1990s, Federal Trade Commission ("FTC") Chief Economist Jonathan Baker proposed a screen based on the behavior of prices over the business cycle. He hypothesized that the exercise of market power would cause prices to increase coming out of a business cycle trough. FTC economists searched for industries that experienced price increases during periods where output was not rising (to rule out demand increases). This screen flagged 600 industries for potential collusion, 25 of which were chosen for investigation. Of the 25, no benign reason for the price increases could be found for 3. One industry was already under extensive investigation by the DOJ. What happened as a result of these investigations is not a matter of public record.

More recently at the FTC, Abrantes-Metz, Froeb, Geweke and Taylor developed the price variance screen for collusion described in the previous section while Froeb was the Chief Economist at the Federal Trade Commission.[18] The authors used it to screen for conspiracies in gasoline retail stations in a localized area by searching for pockets of low variance and high means. Figure 2 below, which is extracted from their paper, represents the 279 gasoline stations studied in Louisville, Kentucky. Each gasoline station is represented by the average value of prices over the period studied and by the standard deviation of those prices. The authors look for a group of stations in the lower right-hand-side corner of the figure, characterized by high mean and low price variance, which is consistent with possible collusive behavior. No such group was found.

This variance screen was referred to in the FTC's post-hurricane Katrina and Rita investigations to refute allegations of gasoline price manipulation.[19]

---

[16] The National Procurement Fraud Task Force Web page is located at http://www.usdoj.gov/criminal/npftf/.

[17] Scott D. Hammond, Director of Criminal Enforcement, Antitrust Division, U.S. Dep't of Justice: *Follow the Money: An Update on Stimulus Spending, Transparency and Fraud Prevention*, Testimony Before the Committee on Homeland Security and Governmental Affairs of the United States Senate (Sept. 10, 2009), *available at* http://www.usdoj.gov/atr/public/testimony/250274.htm.

[18] *Supra* note 10.

[19] Federal Trade Commission, *Gasoline Price Changes: The Dynamic of Supply, Demand, and Competition* (2005), http://www.ftc.gov/reports/gasprices05/050705gaspricesrpt.pdf.

FIGURE 2 All Brands, 279 Stations

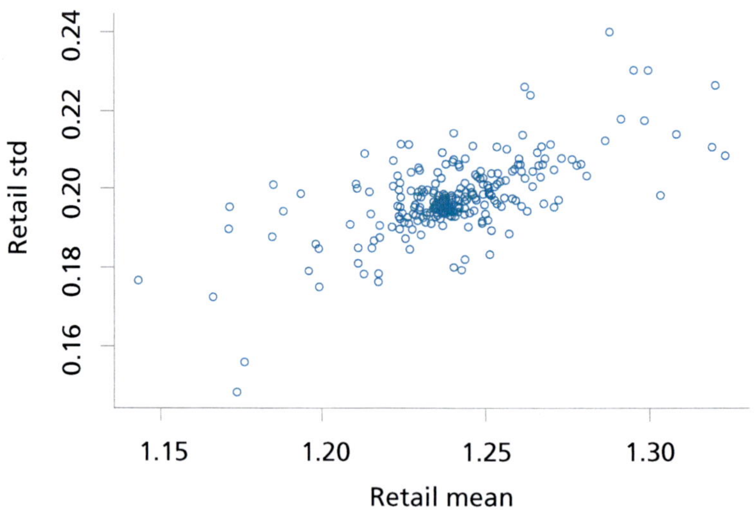

(Extracted from Abrantes-Metz, Froeb, Geweke and Taylor (2006))

The FTC uses screens in gasoline markets in its official monitoring program.[20] The FTC uses gasoline prices at major supply points like New Orleans as a competitive benchmark to screen retail prices in 360 cities and wholesale prices in 20 major urban areas. When the screen identifies persistent and significantly high prices, further investigation is conducted. To date, all of these anomalous prices have come down in a short period of time or have been found to be caused by non-collusive events like pipeline breaks or refinery outages.

In Great Britain, Grout and Sonderegger of the Office of Fair Trading identified industry-level variables that predict cartel activity.[21] The authors built an econometric model to predict collusion at the industry level using data from prior price-fixing cases obtained from the DOJ and the European Commission. The study concludes that industry turnover, cost measures, concentration measures, entry barriers, and employee costs, among other factors, help explain the prevalence of

[20] Federal Trade Commission, *Gasoline and Diesel Price Monitoring, available at* http://www.ftc.gov/ftc/oilgas/gas_price.htm.

[21] Paul A. Grout & Silvia Sonderegger, *Predicting Cartels, Office of Fair Trading*, Economic discussion paper (March 2005).

collusion in an industry. Competition authorities in the Netherlands use a similar approach to screen for cartels employing data on leniency applications and industry characteristics.

Other European antitrust agencies are actively using screens to detect conspiracies, namely in gasoline and diesel markets. For example, the European Commission's market monitoring program is a two-step, industry-level approach.[22] First, the program identifies industries at risk of collusion, using characteristics such as a small number of firms, more homogeneous products, and more stable demand. Having identified these at-risk industries, the second stage establishes a "reasonable theory of harm" and a "focused in-depth analysis" to test the theory of harm. Screens play roles in both stages of this EC approach.

IV. MULTIPLE USES OF SCREENS

Screens are more than just detection tools for antitrust agencies. They can also be used during litigation in the prosecution and penalization stages by plaintiffs, defendants, and antitrust agencies. Additionally, screens can be quite useful to companies in a pre-litigation setting.

During the prosecution and penalization stages, screens can be used in class action suits, to assist in establishing or rejecting certification, and during motions to dismiss, particularly after *Twombly*. At a later stage in litigation, plaintiffs and defendants can apply screens to determine if an alleged cartel caused harm. Finally, experts can apply screens when estimating but-for prices and in providing support in damages estimation.

A. Use of Screens in the Class Action Certification Stage

Screening methodologies might prove very useful in the class certification stage, in which factual claims are alleged to be common across class members. The use of screens could help illustrate different price patterns among the alleged participants in the alleged cartel, as well as in showing that the prices charged to each type of consumer were different enough after controlling for relevant market conditions.

B. Use of Screens During Motions to Dismiss After *Twombly*

Suppose plaintiffs file a complaint in which they infer the existence of a conspiracy, based on a screen, and for which there are no sufficient facts plausibly supporting the existence of explicitly

---

[22] Hans Friederiszuck & Frank Maier-Rigaud, *Triggering Inspections Ex Officio: Moving Beyond a Passive EU Cartel Policy*, 4 J. Comp. L. & Econ. 89 (2008).

coordinated behavior rather than independent strategic behavior. This is particularly important after the Supreme Court decision in *Bell Atlantic Corp. v. Twombly*[23] in which it is stated that "an allegation of parallel conduct and a bare assertion of conspiracy" does not by itself justify a claim for relief under Section 1 of the Sherman Act since the complaint does not provide sufficient facts to plausibly support the inference of a conspiracy as opposed to independent action.[24] This decision marks a clear turn in the standards required in these types of cases by requiring enough factual matter and plausibility that a collusive agreement existed. Previously, and for the last fifty years, the Court allowed cases to proceed unless it appeared likely beyond doubt that plaintiffs would not be able to prove the facts in support of their claims.[25]

With the higher standards imposed by Twombly, *screens can be of particular importance as it is now required that the economic expert opines on plausibility*

With the higher standards imposed by *Twombly*, screens can be of particular importance as it is now required that the economic expert opines on plausibility, i.e., on "how likely is it that such evidence was in fact produced under an agreement among alleged conspirators?"

Screens have been used on stock options backdating cases and survived some motions to dismiss. Plaintiffs have used screening methodologies based on abnormally high returns on particular days to assist in their argument for evidence of stock options backdating and spring-loading, and defendants have argued for the low power of some of these screens to correctly identify such situations for the current case and putting forward their own screens.

C. Use of Screens in Damages and Effects Calculations

Screens can also provide useful information for the estimation of overcharges and damages, for two reasons. First, screens can be used to uncover the time periods during which a cartel operated effectively. As discussed above, studies of previous cartels indicate that they may fail to change prices and quantities from a competitive level during many time periods. Second, many screens require the economist to study the relationship between prices and costs in normally functioning markets. This can assist the expert in estimating the but-for price in a damage estimate. Froeb and Shor use data from the cartel in Figure 1 to estimate but-for competitive prices during collusion, based on the observed relationship between prices and costs after the break of the cartel.[26]

---

23 Twombly, 127 S. Ct. 1955, 1965 (2007).

24 *Id.*, 1961, 1965-66.

25 Conley v. Gibson, 355 U.S. 41 (1957).

26 Luke Froeb & Mikahel Shor, *Auctions, Evidence and Antitrust*, in Econometrics: Legal, Practical and Technical Issues (John Harkrider ed.) (2005).

In addition, screens allow the economic expert to predict which effects and damages a competition authority may estimate when a cartel is alleged. Above, we surveyed the screens used by various competition authorities. The alleged effects of a cartel are likely to be closely related to the screen used to detect the cartel in the first place. Many alleged cartels are international. Even if an alleged colluder's business is primarily in the United States, collusion may be detected by screens used by European authorities. If collusion is suspected in Europe, the screen is likely to be used by U.S. antitrust authorities and may become an issue in U.S. courtrooms as a result.

D. Uses of Screens in Pre-Litigation

Screens can help firms decide whether it would be beneficial to apply for leniency. Applicants need to compare the benefits obtained from applying versus the risk of prosecution and penalties. Leniency programs differ substantially between the United States and Europe. The U.S. leniency program applies only to the first reporting firm and only applies before an investigation has begun. In Europe, however, there are also benefits to the second and third reporting parties.

E. Use of Screens by Defendants in Manipulation Cases

An additional use of screens is by defendants who are accused of market manipulation. Abrantes-Metz and Addanki developed a screen for manipulation in commodities markets.[27] The idea behind the test is to see whether short-run futures market prices are an unbiased predictor of spot market prices. This is a key prediction of economic models of competitive financial and commodities markets. If markets are manipulated, there may be a divergence between spot and futures prices.

This screen was applied on behalf of the defendants in a case and was used as supporting empirical evidence of the absence (or non-materiality) of anticompetitive behavior. As a benchmark to test the method, the authors applied it to the famous Hunt Brothers silver manipulation episode of 1979-1980. The authors demonstrated that this screen was able to detect this well-known instance of market manipulation but that the same manipulation features found in the silver episode were not verified in the case at hand, representing evidence inconsistent with the alleged manipulation for the case at hand.

---

[27] Rosa Abrantes-Metz & Sumanth Addanki, *Is the Market being Fooled? An Error-Based Test for Manipulation*, Working Paper (2007), *available at* http://papers.ssrn.com/sol3/cf_dev/ AbsByAuth.cfm?per_id= 339863.

F. Use of Screens for Internal Monitoring

Finally, screens described above could also be used by managers to monitor for fraud in accounting and reimbursement statements, collusion on employee compensation surveys, or other forms of data manipulation. Furthermore, screens could be used to detect for price-fixing in purchasing or procurement and enhance robustness of compliance programs as explained in Abrantes-Metz, Bajari, & Murphy.[28] However, note that the methods we have discussed are powerful and can be used to detect a much wider range of attempts by employees or suppliers to manipulate data.

V. CONCLUSION

A screen is a statistical test designed to detect conspiracies aimed at illegally manipulating a market. Competition authorities, academics, and consultants have designed a variety of screens to detect competition problems. In this paper, we first describe screens designed to detect bid-rigging, price-fixing, market allocation schemes, and commodity market manipulation. Next, we discuss the ways in which screens can be used by plaintiffs and defendants in antitrust cases. We also describe the use of screens for internal company use and in enhancing compliance programs. The use of empirical screens has been increasing over time. Given the increased data availability and computer power, we expect such a trend to continue into the future.

---

[28] Rosa Abrantes-Metz, Patrick Bajari & Joseph Murphy, *Enhancing Compliance Programs Through Antitrust Screening*, The Antitrust Counselor, forthcoming (2010).

JOSEPH SCHUMPETER ON COMPETITION

*Thomas K. McCraw**

ABSTRACT:
The following documents illustrate the relevance of Schumpeter's thought to competition policy. Part I is an introduction to Schumpeter's ideas; Part II a series of excerpts from his book, Capitalism, Socialism and Democracy;[1] *Part III a 1951 critique of his stance toward antitrust by the economist Edward S. Mason; and Part IV an evaluation of the current use of Schumpeter's theories in discussions of competition policy.*

I. INTRODUCTION

During the 1980s, there began a spirited revival of interest in the writings of Joseph Schumpeter (1883-1950), spurred by renewed attention to his seminal works on entrepreneurship and innovation. The movement gathered so much strength that citations to Schumpeter by scholars and journalists began to exceed those to Keynes, a phenomenon that would have seemed unthinkable only a few years earlier. In 2000, *Business Week* ran a two-page spread titled "America's Hottest Economist Died 50 Years Ago."[2]

This upsurge of interest has migrated to numerous areas of inquiry, including competition policy. Three pertinent articles among many that might be cited are Schmalensee's "Antitrust in Schumpeterian Industries",[3] Katz and Shelanski's " 'Schumpeterian' "

* The author is the Isidor Straus Professor of History Emeritus at Harvard Business School. A Pulitzer Prize-winning historian, he is the author of *Prophet of Innovation: Joseph Schumpeter and Creative Destruction* (Cambridge, Mass.: Belknap Press of Harvard University Press, 2007).

1 Joseph A. Schumpeter, Capitalism, Socialism and Democracy, (1st edition 1942) [hereinafter Capitalism].

2 Charles J. Whalen, *America's Hottest Economist Died 50 Years Ago*, Bus. Wk. (Dec. 11, 2000).

3 Richard Schmalensee, *Antitrust in Schumpeterian Industries*, 90 Am. Econ. Rev. 192-196 (2000).

Competition and Antitrust Policy in High-Tech Markets",[4] and Baker's "Beyond Schumpeter vs. Arrow: How Antitrust Fosters Innovation".[5]

Taken as a whole, Schumpeter's writings fall into the tradition of grand social theory exemplified by European thinkers such as August Comte, Karl Marx, John Stuart Mill, and Max Weber

This sudden attention to Schumpeter's work by antitrust scholars is a bit surprising, because very little of his vast body of writing even purports to address antitrust directly. In all, he published eleven books and scores of articles and reviews—a staggering total of about 3.5 million words. But the word "antitrust" appears almost nowhere.

A reading of Schumpeter's work in its entirety makes it clear that he disavowed advocacy of any kind. He opposed the development of "schools" of economic thought, even though he had tremendous respect for the achievements of great scholars across the ideological spectrum, from his fellow Austrians Mises and Hayek on the far Right to Marx on the far Left. Schumpeter believed economics to be a science, and he conceived the task of scientists as the quest for truth, not the service of policy. He was convinced that direct pursuit of the second goal would inevitably corrupt the first. So, if one searches his work for explicit guides to antitrust policy, one may find, as Gertrude Stein said of the city of Oakland, that "There is no there there."

This is probably why Schumpeter's writings were neglected for so long by antitrust scholars and policymakers. He makes no appearance, for example, in Bork's *The Antitrust Paradox*.[6] Nor is his name prominent in most other antitrust treaties and texts that appeared either before or after Bork's book. There is no explicit there there.

Taken as a whole, Schumpeter's writings fall into the tradition of grand social theory exemplified by European thinkers such as August Comte, Karl Marx, John Stuart Mill, and Max Weber. Although he spent his academic career as a professor of economics—teaching at two universities in Austria and one in Germany before moving permanently to Harvard in 1932, his work freely crosses disciplinary lines. In addition to economics, it encompasses sociology, psychology, law, business, and some mathematics.[7]

---

[4] Michael L. Katz & Howard A. Shelanski, *"Schumpeterian" Competition and Antitrust Policy in High-Tech Markets*, 14 Competition 47 (2005).

[5] Jonathan B. Baker, *Beyond Schumpeter vs. Arrow: How Antitrust Fosters Innovation*, 74 Antitrust L.J. 575-602 (2007).

[6] Robert Bork, The Antitrust Paradox: A Policy at War with Itself (1978).

[7] He had little talent for advanced math, but he thought it vitally important: along with Irving Fisher and Ragnar Frisch, he founded the Econometric Society, and he wrote the lead article for the first issue of *Econometrica*.

He was a leader not only in the study of entrepreneurship, but also in his emphasis on credit creation, business strategy, and—above all—innovation

Among all the sister disciplines of economics, Schumpeter most prized history. Concerning what he regarded as the three basic building blocks of economics—theory, statistics, and history—he wrote that the last "is by far the most important." In his final book, he issued this remarkable credo:

> "I wish to state right now that if, starting my work in economics afresh, I were told that I could study only one of the three but could have my choice, it would be economic history that I should choose. And this on three grounds. First, the subject matter of economics is essentially a unique process in historic time. Nobody can hope to understand the economic phenomena of any, including the present, epoch who has not an adequate command of historical facts and an adequate amount of historical sense or of what may be described as historical experience. Second, the historical report cannot be purely economic but must inevitably reflect also "institutional" facts that are not purely economic: therefore it affords the best method for understanding how economic and non-economic facts are related to one another and how the various social sciences should be related to one another. Third, it is, I believe, the fact that most of the fundamental errors currently committed in economic analysis are due to lack of historical experience more often than to any other shortcoming of the economist's equipment."[8]

Schumpeter came to this conclusion reluctantly. For almost his entire life he regarded himself primarily as a theorist, and he achieved some unique successes. His book *The Theory of Economic Development*[9] is one of the classic economic texts of the twentieth century. It remains to this day the best argument for the addition of entrepreneurship as a fourth factor of production along with land, labor, and capital. He was a leader not only in the study of entrepreneurship, but also in his emphasis on credit creation, business strategy, and—above all—innovation.

It was during the 1930s, some 25 years after his first important publications, that Schumpeter began fully to appreciate the importance of history. His 1,095-page *Business Cycles*[10] is as much a work of history as of theory; and his history (which highlights innovation and covers the entire capitalist epoch in Britain, Germany, and the United States), coheres far better than his theory. The latter is spoiled by a heroic but futile attempt to fit patterns of booms and busts

---

[8] Joseph Schumpeter, History of Economic Analysis, 12-13 (1954).

[9] Joseph Schumpeter, The Theory of Economic Development (1911, Eng. Translation 1934)

[10] Joseph Schumpeter, Business Cycles: A Theoretical, Historical, and Statistical Analysis of the Capitalist Process (1939) [hereinafter Cycles].

into determinate periods defined by other theorists: Joseph Kitchin (40 month cycles), Clément Juglar (8-10 year) and Nikolai Kondratieff (50-60 year).

Among its many virtues, Capitalism, Socialism and Democracy *contains one of the best explications of capitalism ever written*

But even in this book, written during the Great Depression, Schumpeter explicitly disavows advocacy and offers no solution to the economic crisis. "I recommend no policy and propose no plan," he writes in the preface; his book can "be used to derive practical conclusions of the most conservative or the most radical complexion." *Business Cycles* was an exercise in value-neutral science, and in this respect it typified nearly all of Schumpeter's writings. Some 33 years earlier, in the preface to his very first book, he had written something quite similar: "I hold aloof from practical politics and recognize no purpose other than knowledge."[11]

The subtitle of *Business Cycles*—"A Theoretical, Historical, and Statistical Analysis of the Capitalist Process"—well expresses the extraordinary reach of what Schumpeter was trying to do in 1939. Although the book failed as the magnum opus he was hoping for, the immense amount of empirical research on specific firms and industries that went into it prepared him, as nothing else could have done, to write his most famous work, *Capitalism, Socialism and Democracy*. The book appeared only three years after Business Cycles and is one of the seminal nonfiction works of the last hundred years, in any field. For competition policy, it is the most relevant of all his works, but, again, it offers no explicit formulas.

Although very much a book of its time—Schumpeter wrote it in 30 months during 1939-1942, against the uniquely atypical backdrop of the Great Depression and World War II—it is also a book for the ages. Among its many virtues, *Capitalism, Socialism and Democracy* contains one of the best explications of capitalism ever written. The book's most quoted phrase, "creative destruction," is perhaps second only to Adam Smith's "invisible hand" as the best-known metaphor in all of economics, a discipline rich in metaphors.

II. PASSAGES FROM CAPITALISM, SOCIALISM AND DEMOCRACY

The analysis in *Capitalism, Socialism and Democracy* is profound, and it provides at least some implicit guides to competition policy—though one must be extremely careful in applying anything Schumpeter says to a particular case or controversy. In parts of the book, he may appear to prefer large firms to small ones, but this is not what he believed, as his many

---

11 *Id.* at vi. *Also* JOSEPH SCHUMPETER, DAS WESEN UND DER HAUPTINHALT VON THEORETICHEN NATIONALÖKONOMIE (THE NATURE AND CONTENT OF THEORETICAL ECONOMICS) (1908) i-vi (Erich Schneider trans.).

other writings clearly show. His litmus test for competition policy, and almost any other policy, has little to do directly with firm size or industry structure, and everything to do with innovation. This is clear in *The Theory of Economic Development* and equally so in *Business Cycles*, where he writes repeatedly of "New Men" founding "New Firms" and thereby forcing "Innovation" (he capitalizes all three terms). The problem in specific cases involving public policy—as the mixed record of antitrust shows so clearly—is in making such a judgment *about the future* with much accuracy.

In *Capitalism, Socialism and Democracy*, Schumpeter felt it necessary to explain the workings of big business because when he began writing the book during the late 1930s, large firms were under very severe attack. They stood in lower popular repute than at any other time in American history. Hence the candid tone and very strong language in the following excerpts from the book, which contain the heart of Schumpeter's analysis of capitalism (footnotes are quoted as cited):

> "If we look more closely at the conditions (. . .) that must be fulfilled in order to produce perfect competition, we realize immediately that outside of agricultural mass production there cannot be many instances of it. (. . .) every grocer, every filling station, every manufacturer of gloves or shaving cream or handsaws has a small and precarious market of his own, which he tries—must try—to build up and to keep by price strategy, quality strategy—"product differentiation"—and advertising. Thus we get a completely different pattern which there seems to be no reason to expect to yield the results of perfect competition and which fits much better into the monopolistic schema. In these cases we speak of Monopolistic Competition. Their theory has been one of the major contributions to postwar economics.[12] (. . .)
>
> As soon as the prevalence of monopolistic competition or of oligopoly or of combinations of the two is recognized, many of the propositions which the Marshall-Wicksell generation of economists used to teach with the utmost confidence become either inapplicable or much more difficult to prove. This holds true, in the first place, of the propositions turning on the fundamental concept of equilibrium, i.e. a determinate state of the economic organism, toward which any given state of it is always gravitating and which displays certain simple properties. In the general case of oligopoly there is in fact no

[12] See, in particular, E.S. CHAMBERLIN, THEORY OF MONOPOLISTIC COMPETITION (1933), and JOAN ROBINSON, THE ECONOMICS OF IMPERFECT COMPETITION (1933).

determinate equilibrium at all and the possibility presents itself that there may be an endless sequence of moves and countermoves, an indefinite state of warfare between firms. (. . .)

The theories of monopolistic and oligopolistic competition and their popular variants may in two ways be made to serve the view that capitalist reality is unfavorable to maximum performance in production. One may hold that it always has been so and that all along output has been expanding in spite of the secular sabotage perpetrated by the managing bourgeoisie. Advocates of this proposition would have to produce evidence to the effect that the observed rate of increase can be accounted for by a sequence of favorable circumstances unconnected with the mechanism of private enterprise and strong enough to overcome the latter's resistance However, those who espouse this variant at least avoid the trouble about historical fact that the advocates of the alternative proposition have to face. This avers that capitalist reality once tended to favor maximum productive performance, or at all events productive performance so considerable as to constitute a major element in any serious appraisal of the system; but that the later spread of monopolist structures, killing competition, has by now reversed that tendency.

First, this involves the creation of an entirely imaginary golden age of perfect competition that at some time somehow metamorphosed itself into the monopolistic age, whereas it is quite clear that perfect competition has at no time been more of a reality than it is at present. Secondly, it is necessary to point out that the rate of increase in output did not decrease from the nineties from which, I suppose, the prevalence of the largest-size concerns, at least in manufacturing industry, would have to be dated; that there is nothing in the behavior of the time series of total output to suggest a "break in trend"; and, most important of all, that the modern standard of life of the masses evolved during the period of relatively unfettered "big business." If we list the items that enter the modern workman's budget and from 1899 on observe the course of their prices not in terms of money but in terms of the hours of labor that will buy them—i.e., each year's money prices divided by each year's hourly wage rates—we cannot fail to be struck by the rate of the advance which, considering the spectacular improvement in qualities, seems to have been greater and not smaller than it ever was before. If we economists were given less to wishful thinking and more

The essential point to grasp is that in dealing with capitalism we are dealing with an evolutionary process

to the observation of facts, doubts would immediately arise as to the realistic virtues of a theory that would have led us to expect a very different result. Nor is this all. As soon as we go into details and inquire into the individual items in which progress was most conspicuous, the trail leads not to the doors of those firms that work under conditions of comparatively free competition but precisely to the doors of the large concerns—which, as in the case of agricultural machinery, also account for much of the progress in the competitive sector—and a shocking suspicion dawns upon us that big business may have had more to do with creating that standard of life than with keeping it down.

The conclusions alluded to at the end of the preceding chapter are in fact almost completely false. Yet they follow from observations and theorems that are almost completely[13] true. Both economists and popular writers have once more run away with some fragments of reality they happened to grasp. These fragments themselves were mostly seen correctly. Their formal properties were mostly developed correctly. But no conclusions about capitalist reality as a whole follow from such fragmentary analyses. If we draw them nevertheless, we can be right only by accident. That has been done. And the lucky accident did not happen.

The essential point to grasp is that in dealing with capitalism we are dealing with an evolutionary process. It may seem strange that anyone can fail to see so obvious a fact which moreover was long ago emphasized by Karl Marx. Yet that fragmentary analysis which yields the bulk of our propositions about the functioning of modern capitalism persistently neglects it. Let us restate the point and see how it bears upon our problem.

---

[13] As a matter of fact, these observations and theorems are not completely satisfactory. The usual expositions of the doctrine of imperfect competition fail in particular to give due attention to the many and important cases in which, even as a matter of static theory, imperfect competition approximates the results of perfect competition. There are other cases in which it does not do this, but offers compensations which, while not entering any output index, yet contribute to what the output index is in the last resort intended to measure—the cases in which a firm defends its market by establishing a name for quality and service for instance. However, in order to simplify matters, we will not take issue with that doctrine on its own ground.

Capitalism, then, is by nature a form or method of economic change and not only never is but never can be stationary. And this evolutionary character of the capitalist process is not merely due to the fact that economic life goes on in a social and natural environment which changes and by its change alters the data of economic action; this fact is important and these changes (wars, revolutions and so on) often condition industrial change, but they are not its prime movers. Nor is this evolutionary character due to a quasi-automatic increase in population and capital or to the vagaries of monetary systems of which exactly the same thing holds true. The fundamental impulse that sets and keeps the capitalist engine in motion comes from the new consumers' goods, the new methods of production or transportation, the new markets, the new forms of industrial organization that capitalist enterprise creates.

This process of Creative Destruction is the essential fact about capitalism. It is what capitalism consists in and what every capitalist concern has got to live in

As we have seen in the preceding chapter, the contents of the laborer's budget, say from 1760 to 1940, did not simply grow on unchanging lines but they underwent a process of qualitative change. Similarly, the history of the productive apparatus of a typical farm, from the beginnings of the rationalization of crop rotation, plowing and fattening to the mechanized thing of today—linking up with elevators and railroads—is a history of revolutions. (. . .) of industrial mutation—if I may use that biological term—that incessantly revolutionizes[14] the economic structure *from within*, incessantly destroying the old one, incessantly creating a new one. This process of Creative Destruction is the essential fact about capitalism. It is what capitalism consists in and what every capitalist concern has got to live in. This fact bears upon our problem in two ways.

First, since we are dealing with a process whose every element takes considerable time in revealing its true features and ultimate effects, there is no point in appraising the performance of that process *ex visu* of a given point of time; we must judge

[14] Those revolutions are not strictly incessant; they occur in discrete rushes which are separated from each other by spans of comparative quiet. The process as a whole works incessantly however, in the sense that there always is either revolution or absorption of the results of revolution, both together forming what are known as business cycles.

its performance over time, as it unfolds through decades or centuries. A system—any system, economic or other—that at *every* given point of time fully utilizes its possibilities to the best advantage may yet in the long run be inferior to a system that does so at *no* given point of time, because the latter's failure to do so may be a condition for the level or speed of long-run performance.

Second, since we are dealing with an organic process, analysis of what happens in any particular part of it—say, in an individual concern or industry—may indeed clarify details of mechanism but is inconclusive beyond that. Every piece of business strategy acquires its true significance only against the background of that process and within the situation created by it. It must be seen in its role in the perennial gale of creative destruction; it cannot be understood irrespective of it or, in fact, on the hypothesis that there is a perennial lull.

But economists who, *ex visu* of a point of time, look for example at the behavior of an oligopolist industry—an industry which consists of a few big firms—and observe the well-known moves and countermoves within it that seem to aim at nothing but high prices and restrictions of output are making precisely that hypothesis. They accept the data of the momentary situation as if there were no past or future to it and think that they have understood what there is to understand if they interpret the behavior of those firms by means of the principle of maximizing profits with reference to those data. The usual theorist's paper and the usual government commission's report practically never try to see that behavior, on the one hand, as a result of a piece of past history and, on the other hand, as an attempt to deal with a situation that is sure to change presently—as an attempt by those firms to keep on their feet, on ground that is slipping away from under them. In other words, the problem that is usually being visualized is how capitalism administers existing structures, whereas the relevant problem is how it creates and destroys them. As long as this is not recognized, the investigator does a meaningless job. As soon as it is recognized, his outlook on capitalist practice and its social results changes considerably.[15] (. . .)

[15] It should be understood that it is only our appraisal of economic performance and not our moral judgment that can be so changed. Owing to its autonomy, moral approval or disapproval is entirely independent of our appraisal of social (or any other) results, unless we happen to adopt a moral system such as utilitarianism which makes moral approval and disapproval turn on them *ex definitione*.

It is hardly necessary to point out that competition of the kind we now have in mind acts not only when in being but also when it is merely an ever-present threat. It disciplines before it attacks. The businessman feels himself to be in a competitive situation even if he is alone in his field or if, though not alone, he holds a position such that investigating government experts fail to see any effective competition between him and any other firms in the same or a neighboring field and in consequence conclude that his talk, under examination, about his competitive sorrows is all make-believe. In many cases, though not in all, this will in the long run enforce behavior very similar to the perfectly competitive pattern. (. . .)

In the case of retail trade the competition that matters arises not from additional shops of the same type, but from the department store, the chain store, the mail-order house and the supermarket which are bound to destroy those pyramids sooner or later.[16] Now a theoretical construction which neglects this essential element of the case neglects all that is most typically capitalist about it; even if correct in logic as well as in fact, it is like Hamlet without the Danish prince. (. . .)

Practically any investment entails, as a necessary complement of entrepreneurial action, certain safeguarding activities such as insuring or hedging. Long-range investing under rapidly changing conditions, especially under conditions that change or may change at any moment under the impact of new commodities and technologies, is like shooting at a target that is not only indistinct but moving—and moving jerkily at that. Hence it becomes necessary to resort to such protecting devices as patents or temporary secrecy of processes or, in some cases, long-period contracts secured in advance. But these protecting devices which most economists accept as normal elements of rational management[17] are only special cases of a larger class comprising many others which most economists condemn although they do not differ fundamentally from the recognized ones.

---

[16] The mere threat of their attack cannot, in the particular conditions, environmental and personal, or small-scale retail trade, have its usual disciplining influence, for the small man is too much hampered by his cost structure and, however well he may manage within his inescapable limitations, he can never adapt himself to the methods of competitors who can afford to sell at the price at which he buys.

[17] Some economists, however, consider that even those devices are obstructions to progress which, though perhaps necessary in capitalist society, would be absent in a socialist one. There is some truth in this. But that does not affect the proposition that the protection afford by patents and so on is, in the conditions of a profit economy, on balance a propelling and not an inhibiting factor.

If for instance a war risk is insurable, nobody objects to a firm's collecting the cost of this insurance from the buyers of its products. But that risk is no less an element in long-run costs, if there are no facilities for insuring against it, in which case a price strategy aiming at the same end will seem to involve unnecessary restriction and to be productive of excess profits. Similarly, if a patent cannot be secured or would not, if secured, effectively protect, other means may have to be used in order to justify the investment. Among them are a price policy that will make it possible to write off more quickly than would otherwise be rational, or additional investment in order to provide excess capacity to be used only for aggression or defense. Again, if long-period contracts cannot be entered into in advance, other means may have to be devised in order to tie prospective customers to the investing firm.

In analyzing such business strategy ex visu of a given point of time, the investigating economist or government agent sees price policies that seem to him predatory and restrictions of output that seem to him synonymous with loss of opportunities to produce. He does not see that restrictions of this type are, in the conditions of the perennial gale, incidents, often unavoidable incidents, of a long-run process of expansion which they protect rather than impede. There is no more of paradox in this than there is in saying that motorcars are traveling faster they otherwise would *because* they are provided with brakes.

2. This stands out most clearly in the case of those sectors of the economy which at any time happen to embody the impact of new things and methods on the existing industrial structure. The best way of getting a vivid and realistic idea of industrial strategy is indeed to visualize the behavior of new concerns or industries that introduce new commodities or processes (such as the aluminum industry) or else reorganize a part or the whole of an industry (such as, for instance, the old Standard Oil Company).

As we have seen, such concerns are aggressors by nature and wield the really effective weapon of competition. Their intrusion can only in the rarest of cases fail to improve total output in quantity or quality, both through the new method itself—even if at no time used to full advantage—and through the pressure it exerts on the preexisting firms. But these aggressors are so circumstanced as to require, for purposes of attack and defense, also pieces of armor other than price and quality of their product which, moreover, must be strategically manipulated all along so that at any point of time they seem to be doing nothing but restricting their output and keeping prices high.

Old concerns and established industries, whether or not directly attacked, still live in the perennial gale

On the one hand, largest-scale plans could in many cases not materialize at all if it were not known from the outset that competition will be discouraged by heavy capital requirements or lack of experience, or that means are available to discourage or checkmate it so as to gain the time and space for further developments. (. . .)

Again this requires strategy that in the short run is often restrictive. In the majority of successful cases this strategy just manages to serve its purpose. In some cases, however, it is so successful as to yield profits far above what is necessary in order to induce the corresponding investment. These cases then provide the baits that lure capital on to untried trails. Their presence explains in part how it is possible for so large a section of the capitalist world to work for nothing: in the midst of the prosperous twenties just about half of the business corporations in the United States were run at a loss, at zero profits, or at profits which, if they had been foreseen, would have been inadequate to call forth the effort and expenditure involved.

Our argument however extends beyond the cases of new concerns, methods and industries. Old concerns and established industries, whether or not directly attacked, still live in the perennial gale. Situations emerge in the process of creative destruction in which many firms may have to perish that nevertheless would be able to live on vigorously and usefully if they could weather a particular storm. (. . .)

All this is of course nothing but the tritest common sense. But it is being overlooked with a persistence so stubborn as sometimes to raise the question of sincerity. And it follows that, within the process of creative destruction, all the realities of which theorists are in the habit of relegating to books and courses on business cycles, there is another side to industrial self-organization than that which these theorists are contemplating. (. . .)

It is certainly as conceivable that an all-pervading cartel system might sabotage all progress as it is that it might realize, with smaller social and private costs, all that perfect competition is supposed to realize. This is why our argument does not amount to a case against state regulation. It does show that there is no general case for indiscriminate "trust-busting" or for the prosecution of everything that qualifies as a restraint of trade. Rational as distinguished from vindictive regulation by public authority turns out to be an extremely delicate problem which not every government agency, particularly when in full cry against big business, can be trusted to solve.[18] (. . .)

Of course, plenty of cases of genuine price rigidity remain—of prices which are being kept constant as a matter of business policy or which remain unchanged because it is difficult to change, say, a price set by a cartel after laborious negotiations. In order to appraise the influence of this fact on the long-run development of output, it is first of all necessary to realize that this rigidity is essentially a short-run phenomenon. There are no major instances of long-run rigidity of prices. Whichever manufacturing industry or group of manufactured articles of any importance we choose to investigate over a period of time, we practically always find that in the long run prices do not fail to adapt themselves to technological progress—frequently they fall spectacularly in response to it[19]—unless prevented from doing so by monetary events and policies or, in some cases, by autonomous changes in wage rates which of course should be taken into account by appropriate corrections exactly as should changes in quality of products. And our previous analysis shows sufficiently why in the process of capitalist evolution this must be so.

What the business strategy in question really aims at—all, in any case, that it can achieve—is to avoid seasonal, random and cyclical fluctuations in prices and to move only in response to the more fundamental changes in the conditions

[18] Unfortunately, this statement is almost as effective a bar to agreement on policy as the most thoroughgoing denial of any case for government regulation could be. In fact it may embitter discussion. Politicians, public officers, and economists can stand what I may politely term the whole-hog opposition of "economic royalists." Doubts about their competence, such as crowd upon us particularly when we see the legal mind at work, are much more difficult for them to stand.

[19] They do not as a rule fall as they would under conditions of perfect competition. But this is true only *ceteris paribus*, and this proviso robs the proposition of all practical importance. I have adverted to this point before and shall return to it below.

that underlie those fluctuations. Since these more fundamental changes take time in declaring themselves, this involves moving slowly by discrete steps—keeping to a price until new relatively durable contours have emerged into view. In technical language, this strategy aims at moving along a step function that will approximate trends. (. . .)

Progress entails, as we have seen, destruction of capital values in the strata with which the new commodity or method of production competes

Perhaps the reader feels some surprise that so little remains of a doctrine of which so much has been made in the last few years. The rigidity of prices has become, with some people, the outstanding defect of the capitalist engine and—almost—the fundamental factor in the explanation of depressions. But there is nothing to wonder at in this. Individuals and groups snatch at anything that will qualify as a discovery lending support to the political tendencies of the hour. The doctrine of price rigidity, with a modicum of truth to its credit, is not the worst case of this kind by a long way.

Another doctrine has crystallized into a slogan, viz., that in the era of big business the maintenance of the value of existing investment—conservation of capital—becomes the chief aim of entrepreneurial activity and bids fair to put a stop to all cost-reducing improvement. Hence the capitalist order becomes incompatible with progress.

Progress entails, as we have seen, destruction of capital values in the strata with which the new commodity or method of production competes. In perfect competition the old investments must be adapted at a sacrifice or abandoned; but when there is no perfect competition and when each Industrial field is controlled by a few big concerns, these can in various ways fight the threatening attack on their capital structure and try to avoid losses on their capital accounts; that is to say, they can and will fight progress itself.

So far as this doctrine merely formulates a particular aspect of restrictive business strategy, there is no need to add anything to the argument already sketched in this chapter. Both as to the limits of that strategy and as to its functions in the process of creative destruction, we should only be repeating what has been said before. This becomes still more obvious if we observe that conserving capital values is the same thing as conserving profits. Modern theory tends in fact to use the concept Present Net Value of Assets (= capital values) in place of the concept of Profits. Both asset values and profits are of course not being simply conserved but maximized. (. . .)

I have entitled this chapter as I did [Monopolistic Practices] because most of it deals with the facts and problems that common parlance associates with monopoly or monopolistic practice. So far I have as much as possible refrained from using those terms in order to reserve for a separate section some comments on a few topics specifically connected with them. Nothing will be said however that we have not already met in one form or another.

(a) To begin with, there is the term itself. Monopolist means Single Seller. Literally therefore anyone is a monopolist who sells anything that is not in every respect, wrapping and location and service included, exactly like what other people sell: every grocer, or every haberdasher, or every seller of "Good Humors" on a road that is not simply lined with sellers of the same brand of ice cream. This however is not what we mean when talking about monopolists. We mean only those single sellers whose markets are not open to the intrusion of would-be producers of the same commodity and of actual producers of similar ones or, speaking slightly more technically, only those single sellers who face a given demand schedule that is severely independent of their own action as well as of any reactions to their action by other concerns. The traditional Cournot-Marshall theory of monopoly as extended and amended by later authors holds only if we define it in this way and there is, so it seems, no point in calling anything a monopoly to which that theory does not apply.

But if accordingly we do define it like this, then it becomes evident immediately that pure cases of long-run monopoly must be of the rarest occurrence and that even tolerable approximations to the requirements of the concept must be still rarer than are cases of perfect competition. The power to exploit at pleasure a given pattern of demand—or one that changes independently of the monopolist's action and of the reactions it provokes—can under the conditions of intact capitalism hardly persist for a period long enough to matter for the analysis of total output, unless buttressed by public authority, for instance, in the case of fiscal monopolies. A modern business concern not so protected—i.e., even if protected by import duties or import prohibitions—and yet wielding that power (except temporarily) is not easy to find or even to imagine. Even railroads and power and light concerns had first to create the demand for their services and, when they had done so, to defend their market against competition. Outside the field of public utilities, the position of a single seller can in general be conquered—and retained for decades— only on the condition that he does not behave like a monopolist. Short-run monopoly will be touched upon presently.

Why then all this talk about monopoly? The answer is not without interest for the student of the psychology of political discussion. Of course, the concept of monopoly is being loosely used just like any other. (. . .) But this is not all. Economists, government agents, journalists and politicians in this country obviously love the word because it has come to be a term of opprobrium which is sure to rouse the public's hostility against any interest so labeled. In the Anglo-American world monopoly has been cursed and associated with functionless exploitation ever since, in the sixteenth and seventeenth centuries, it was English administrative practice to create monopoly positions in large numbers which, on the one hand, answered fairly well to the theoretical pattern of monopolist behavior and, on the other hand, fully justified the wave of indignation that impressed even the great Elizabeth.

Nothing is so retentive as a nation's memory. Our time offers other and more important instances of a nation's reaction to what happened centuries ago. That practice made the English-speaking public so monopoly-conscious that it acquired a habit of attributing to that sinister power practically everything it disliked about business. To the typical liberal bourgeois in particular, monopoly became the father of almost all abuses—in fact, it became his pet bogey. Adam Smith,[20] thinking primarily of monopolies of the Tudor and Stuart type, frowned on them in awful dignity. (. . .) And in this country monopoly is being made practically synonymous with any large-scale business.

---

[20] There was more excuse for that uncritical attitude in the case of Adam Smith and the classics in general than there is in the case of their successors because big business in our sense had not then emerged. But even so they went too far. In part this was due to the fact that they had no satisfactory theory of monopoly which induced them not only to apply the term rather promiscuously (Adam Smith and even Senior interpreted for instance the rent of land as a monopoly gain) but also to look upon the monopolists' power of exploitation as practically unlimited which is of course wrong even for the most extreme cases.

The theory of simple and discriminating monopoly teaches that, excepting a limiting case, monopoly price is higher and monopoly output smaller than competitive price and competitive output. This is true provided that the method and organization of production—and everything else—are exactly the same in both cases. Actually however there are superior methods available to the monopolist which either are not available at all to a crowd of competitors or are not available to them so readily: for there are advantages which, though not strictly unattainable on the competitive level of enterprise, are as a matter of fact secured only on the monopoly level, for instance, because monopolization may increase the sphere of influence of the better, and decrease the sphere of influence of the inferior, brains,[21] or because the monopoly enjoys a disproportionately higher financial standing. Whenever this is so, then that proposition is no longer true. In other words, this element of the case for competition may fail completely because monopoly prices are not necessarily higher or monopoly outputs smaller than competitive prices and outputs would be at the levels of productive and organization efficiency that are within the reach of the type of firm compatible with the competitive hypothesis.

There cannot be any reasonable doubt that under the conditions of our epoch such superiority is as a matter of fact the outstanding feature of the typical large-scale unit of control, though mere size is neither necessary nor sufficient for it. These units not only arise in the process of creative destruction and function in a way entirely different from the static schema, but in many cases of decisive importance they provide the necessary form for the achievement. They largely create what they exploit. Hence the usual conclusion about their influence on long-run output would be invalid even if they were genuine monopolies in the technical sense of the term. (. . .)

In the short run, genuine monopoly positions or positions approximating monopoly are much more frequent. The grocer in a village on the Ohio may be a true monopolist for hours or even days during an inundation. Every successful corner may spell monopoly for the moment. A firm specializing in

21 The reader should observe that while, as a broad rule, that particular type of superiority is simply indisputable, the inferior brains, especially if their owners are entirely eliminated, are not likely to admit it and that the public's and the recording economist's hearts go out to them and not to the others. This may have something to do with a tendency to discount the cost or quality advantages of quasi-monopolist combination that is at present as pronounced as was the exaggeration of them in the typical prospectus or announcement of sponsors of such combinations.

paper labels for beer bottles may be so circumstanced—potential competitors realizing that what seem to be good profits would be immediately destroyed by their entering the field—that it can move at pleasure on a moderate but still finite stretch of the demand curve, at least until the metal label smashes that demand curve to pieces.

New methods of production or new commodities, especially the latter, do not *per se* confer monopoly, even if used or produced by a single firm. The product of the new method has to compete with the products of the old ones and the new commodity has to be introduced, i.e. its demand schedule has to be built up. As a rule neither patents nor monopolistic practices avail against that. But they may in cases of spectacular superiority of the new device, particularly if it can be leased like shoe machinery; or in cases of new commodities, the permanent demand schedule for which has been established before the patent has expired.

Thus it is true that there is or may be an element of genuine monopoly gain in those entrepreneurial profits which are the prizes offered by capitalist society to the successful innovator. But the quantitative importance of that element, its volatile nature and its function in the process in which it emerges put it in a class by itself. The main value to a concern of a single seller position that is secured by patent or monopolistic strategy does not consist so much in the opportunity to behave temporarily according to the monopolist schema, as in the protection it affords against temporary disorganization of the market and the space it secures for long-range planning. Here however the argument merges into the analysis submitted before.

Glancing back we realize that most of the facts and arguments touched upon in this chapter tend to dim the halo that once surrounded perfect competition as much as they suggest a more favorable view of its alternative. (. . .)

If we try to visualize how perfect competition works or would work in the process of creative destruction, we arrive at a still more discouraging result. This will not surprise us, considering that all the essential facts of that process are absent from the general schema of economic life that yields the traditional propositions about perfect competition. At the risk of repetition I will illustrate the point once more.

In this respect, perfect competition is not only impossible but inferior, and has no title to being set up as a model of ideal efficiency

Perfect competition implies free entry into every industry. It is quite true, within that general theory, that free entry into all industries is a condition for optimal allocation of resources and hence for maximizing output. If our economic world consisted of a number of established industries producing familiar commodities by established and substantially invariant methods and if nothing happened except that additional men and additional savings combine in order to set up new firms of the existing type, then impediments to their entry into any industry they wish to enter would spell loss to the community. But perfectly free entry into a new field may make it impossible to enter it at all. The introduction of new methods of production and new commodities is hardly conceivable with perfect—and perfectly prompt—competition from the start. And this means that the bulk of what we call economic progress is incompatible with it. As a matter of fact, perfect competition is and always has been temporarily suspended whenever anything new is being introduced. (. . .)

The firm of the type that is compatible with perfect competition is in many cases inferior in internal, especially technological, efficiency. If it is, then it wastes opportunities. It may also in its endeavors to improve its methods of production waste capital because it is in a less favorable position to evolve and to judge new possibilities. And, as we have seen before, a perfectly competitive industry is much more apt to be routed—and to scatter the bacilli of depression—under the impact of progress or of external disturbance than is big business. In the last resort, American agriculture, English coal mining, the English textile industry are costing consumers much more and are affecting total output much more injuriously than they would if controlled, each of them, by a dozen good brains. (. . .)

In this respect, perfect competition is not only impossible but inferior, and has no title to being set up as a model of ideal efficiency. It is hence a mistake to base the theory of government regulation of industry on the principle that big business should be made to work as the respective industry would work in perfect competition."[22]

---

[22] Capitalism, *supra* note 1, at 78-106.

III. PASSAGES FROM EDWARD S. MASON'S CRITIQUE OF 1951

Mason (1899-1992) was a good friend and a member of what Schumpeter called his "inner circle" of younger colleagues. Along with two other Harvard economists (E.H. Chamberlin and Joe S. Bain), Mason was one of the pioneers of industrial organization theory. He and Bain led the development of the structure-conduct-performance paradigm that dominated the sub-field of industrial organization from about the late 1940s to the 1980s, when it began to yield to game theory and other approaches.

The following excerpts comprise about 20 percent of Mason's article in *The Review of Economics and Statistics*.[23] This issue was dedicated to Schumpeter and its contents were devoted entirely to his work (he had died in 1950). In addition to Mason, the 14 contributors comprised something of an all-star lineup of the profession at that time: Paul Samuelson, Alvin Hansen, Jan Tinbergen, Gottfried Haberler, Fritz Machlup, Seymour Harris, E.H. Chamberlin, Erich Schneider, Arthur Marget, David McCord Wright, Wolfgang Stolper, Arthur Smithies, and A.P. Usher. Six of these economists had been Ph.D. students of Schumpeter's.

Overall, the authors were appropriately generous, but most pulled no punches in their evaluations. Tinbergen, for example, argued (correctly) that Schumpeter was not really a mathematical economist. Chamberlin argued (incorrectly) that Schumpeter had misunderstood his work on monopolistic competition. Mason, as is evident in the following passages, credits Schumpeter with real insight but contends that he provides no practical guide to antitrust policy. This is a fair assessment within the limits of the structure-conduct-performance framework in which Mason was writing, although part of the last sentence in his first paragraph (on the necessity of market power for innovation) is a gross distortion of Schumpeter's thinking. On the whole, Mason's comments go far in explaining why, for so long, Schumpeter's analysis had so little impact on competition theory (footnotes are quoted as cited):

> "These chapters [VII and VIII of *Capitalism, Socialism and Democracy*] which bring together and sharpen earlier views on the role of the large firm in the competitive process, represent one of the most effective as well as most drastic critiques extant concerning traditional patterns of anti-trust thought. The critique is drastic and effective because it plausibly undermines the two main pillars of the traditional ideology: first that market power is the proper object of

[23] Edward Mason, *Schumpeter on Monopoly and the Large Firm*, 33 Rev. Econ. & Stat. 139-144 (1951).

Schumpeter maintains that his argument is not a case against all anti-monopoly policy but only a particular variety of policy

attack since power means the ability to exploit; and, second, that the preservation of competition, meaning the exclusion of position of market power, will assure the efficient use of resources. The essence of Schumpeter's position is that market power is necessary to innovation and that innovation is the core of effective competition. (. . .)

Schumpeter maintains that his argument is not a case against all anti-monopoly policy but only a particular variety of policy. There may be "cases of restrictive or regulating strategy" that have "that injurious effect on the long-run development of output which is uncritically attributed to all of them."[24] He does not, however, give us much help in determining what business practices or strategies might be expected to produce expansive rather than restrictive results. What he has to say in criticism of existing policy constitutes a challenge that every serious student of the "monopoly problem" must take to heart. But whether his view of competition as the process of "creative destruction" could be made to yield principles applicable by government agencies and the courts in pursuit of a "rational" as opposed to a "vindictive" anti-monopoly policy is a different matter.

American anti-trust policy, as distinguished from the anti-monopoly policy of most other countries, purports to be—and to some extent is—an attack upon positions of market power. Whereas legislation and administrative practice elsewhere has emphasized *abuse* of power, including the charging of unreasonable prices, as the proper object of attack, and has recognized the possibility of "good" monopolies, American practice, within certain areas at least, has attacked market power as such. "The reasonable prices fixed today—may become the unreasonable prices of tomorrow" runs the language of a famous anti-trust decision.[25] And with respect to certain kinds of agreements in restraint of trade, i.e., certain attempts to secure a position of market power, the judicial position has been that they are unreasonable and illegal *per se*.

---

[24] Capitalism, *supra* note 1, at 91.

[25] U.S. vs. Trenton Potteries Co. et al. 273 U.S. 392.

Needless to say, however, U.S. anti-trust policy has not been entirely consistent. Large firms enjoying a position of market power have remained immune, while associations with much less power have been broken up. (. . .)

Schumpeter is on surer—and also more important—ground in his evaluation of the results of innovation, that is to say, the relation of innovation to effective competition. Here he denies completely the significance for public policy purposes of any standard of evaluation derived from pure competition, marginal cost-price relationships, or other formulations of static economic analysis. His general position is best stated in a proposition quoted with approval by Pigou.

> A system—any system, economic or other—that at every point of time fully utilizes its possibilities to the best advantage may yet in the long run be inferior to a system that does so at no given time, because the latter's failure to do so may be a condition for the level or speed of long-run performance.[26] (. . .)

During the nineteenth century innovation, according to Schumpeter, was typically the product of new firms. "The new processes do not, and generally cannot, evolve out of the old firms, but place themselves side by side with them and attack them."[27] In the twentieth century epoch of "trustified" capitalism, however, innovations issue from existing firms and, as indicated above, usually from large ones. Furthermore, although the creation of giant firms represents a high form of innovating ability that could not be expected to be brought to fruition except in a capitalism that gives full scope to exceptional talent, the process of concentration ends up by making innovations quasi-automatic.

> It meets with much less friction, as failure in any particular case loses its dangers, and tends to be carried out as a matter of course on the advice of specialists. Progress becomes "automized," increasingly impersonal and decreasingly a matter of leadership and individual initiative.[28] (. . .)

---

[26] The quotation is from CAPITALISM, *supra* note 1, at 83. It is cited in A.C. Pigou, LAPSES FROM FULL EMPLOYMENT 71 (1945).

[27] "The Instability of Capitalism," 28 ECON. J. 384 (1928).

[28] *Ibid., Cf.* also *Der Unternehmer in der Volkswirtschaft von heute, in* STRUKTUR WANDLUNGEN DER DEUTSCHEN VOLKSWIRTSCHAFT, I (1928), p. 303, where these ideas are worked out in greater detail.

Particularly serious difficulties are presented when the attempt is made to apply Schumpeter's analysis in the field of public policy

Particularly serious difficulties are presented when the attempt is made to apply Schumpeter's analysis in the field of public policy. Here the problems presented are what to do about a specific agreement in restraint of trade, a particular combination of hitherto independent firms, or a concrete set of business practices. If one took at face value his admonition that, since we are dealing with an organic process that takes time, a judgment on the consequences of any particular part of it—say a combination of hitherto independent firms—can only be an historical judgment, as these consequences "unfold over decades," and a partial judgment, since the repercussions reverberate throughout an economy which is in process of "organic development," informed public action would clearly be impossible. However, Schumpeter assures us that what he is opposed to is not every anti-monopoly policy but only certain kinds of monopoly policy.[29]

What a "sensible" as opposed to a "vindictive" anti-monopoly policy would presumably emphasize are mainly the possibility that various restrictive activities may be a necessary concomitant to innovation with its accompanying investment decisions, and that a firm producing new products and processes may be a more effective stimulant to efficient behavior on the part of others than a large number of routine competitors. What this appears to boil down to in terms of practical application is a useful admonition that the existence of a large firm or a few large firms in a market is not necessarily incompatible with effective competition. (. . .)

Schumpeter most certainly exaggerated the extent of the influence exerted on American business organization and business practices by anti-trust policy. Furthermore, he painted a picture of anti-trust objectives and of the ideological justification of these objectives that is in many respects distorted and out of focus. Nevertheless, his powerful attack on the limitations of static economic analysis as an intellectual foundation for a public anti-monopoly policy is highly salutary and profoundly correct. And his discussion of the political environ-

29 Capitalism, *supra* note 1, at 134.

ment in which public policy toward business organization and business practices actually gets shaped is a useful corrective to the thinking of those colleagues who conceive that policy can be divorced from politics. Finally, although it is difficult to the point of impossibility to derive from Schumpeter's "process of creative destruction" an analytical framework on which applicable and effective anti-trust standards might be built, his analysis suggests lines of research and invokes considerations that must play a role in formulating an acceptable public policy in this area."

IV. CURRENT USE OF SCHUMPETER'S THEORIES

For three decades after the appearance of Mason's article in 1951, relatively few economists read or cited Schumpeter. But then the Schumpeterian revival began in earnest. In a retrospective analysis of *Capitalism, Socialism and Democracy*, published in 1981, another all-star lineup once again paid tribute to his work. His great student Paul Samuelson wrote that "a century after Schumpeter's birth, we take his writings seriously and treat them as living contributions to contemporary debate."[30] In 1983, the centennial of the birth of both Keynes and Schumpeter, *Forbes*[31] ran a cover story, written by Peter Drucker, arguing that it was Schumpeter, not Keynes, who would provide the better guide to the economic changes that were beginning to engulf the world. In 1984, the German economist Herbert Giersh suggested in the *American Economic Review*[32] that the Age of Keynes was about to yield to the Age of Schumpeter. In the 1991 edition of his best-selling *The Worldly Philosophers*,[33] Robert Heilbroner devoted an entire chapter to Schumpeter, and concluded that more than any other great economist depicted in his book, "Schumpeter speaks to us with a voice that is unmistakably contemporary." Time has proved all of these judgments correct.

---

[30] Paul Samuelson, *Schumpeter's Capitalism, Socialism and Democracy* in SCHUMPETER'S VISION: CAPITALISM, SOCIALISM, AND DEMOCRACY AFTER 40 YEARS 21 (Arnold Heertje, ed., 1981).

[31] Peter Drucker, *Schumpeter and Keynes*, FORBES 124 (May 23, 1983).

[32] Herbert Giersh, *The Age of Schumpeter*, 74 AM. ECON. REV. 103-109 (1984).

[33] ROBERT HEILBRONER, THE WORLDLY PHILOSOPHER: THE LIVES, TIMES, AND IDEAS OF THE GREAT ECONOMIC THINKERS 291 (6th ed., 1991).

Before we get too enthusiastic about Schumpeter's work as a beacon of public policy, however, we should keep in mind three caveats:

1. Grand social theorists are not always reliable guides in specific cases. Their ideas can easily be distorted, either deliberately or inadvertently, in service to some immediate goal that the theorists themselves would not have supported. Karl Marx, for example, who urged that "workers of the world unite," would never have endorsed the "socialism in one country" doctrine set forth by Nikolai Bukharin and adopted by Joseph Stalin in 1925, let alone the Stalinist terrors that became institutionalized in 1927. The same point holds true of great economists who did not aspire to grand social theory. Many ostensibly "Keynesian" public policies—especially in the U.K. and the U.S. between about 1950 and 1980—would not likely have been approved by Keynes had he been alive to evaluate them.

2. In the case of Joseph Schumpeter, he addressed so many topics over so long a period (his first work appeared in 1905, his last posthumously, in 1954), that he frequently adjusted his thinking. He wrote so voluminously during this half-century that it is not hard to find apparently contradictory statements in his work, most of which reflect altered external conditions. This characteristic is so pronounced in Schumpeter's writings that it calls to mind the famous lines from the poet Walt Whitman's *Song of Myself* (1851):

   "Do I contradict myself?
   Very well, I contradict myself.
   (I am large, I contain multitudes)."

3. Beyond arguing against mindless trust busting and the conflation of big business with monopoly, Schumpeter very seldom addressed antitrust concerns directly. His central interests had much less to do with industrial organization per se than with entrepreneurship, innovation, business cycles, and the history of economic analysis. The courses he taught at Harvard were mostly on economic theory and on the history of economics as a discipline.

During the 1960s, before Schumpeter's work was taken up for purposes of antitrust analysis, a substantial related literature began to develop around what, unfortunately, became known as "the Schumpeter hypothesis." This alleged hypothesis held that large firms were better at innovation than small firms. Numerous articles appeared—many from prominent scholars—either supporting or attacking the hypothesis. But, as Anne Mayhew correctly pointed out in 1980, Schumpeter had never even formulated such a hypothesis.[34]

Throughout his career, Schumpeter admired entrepreneurial startups, and he almost surely would have been delighted by phenomena such as the evolution of Silicon Valley, a center of creative destruction if there ever was one

It is true, as is evident in the quoted excerpts from *Capitalism, Socialism and Democracy*, that Schumpeter thought that certain kinds of innovation required teams of researchers. But it is equally clear from his writings that he believed innovation could emerge from almost any source: the lone entrepreneur (the New Man founding a New Firm); the medium-sized company; or the giant corporation with its institutionalized R&D labs.

Throughout his career, Schumpeter admired entrepreneurial startups, and he almost surely would have been delighted by phenomena such as the evolution of Silicon Valley, a center of creative destruction if there ever was one. As for whether he would have taken the side of a company such as Microsoft in its major antitrust suits, it's impossible to say. From the totality of his writings, and allowing for certain self-contradictions, it seems likely that he'd have admired Microsoft greatly in its early years, but would then have turned his preferences to some (not all) of its many scrappy challengers.

[34] About 20 useful articles have appeared on the misnamed "Schumpeter hypothesis." Some of the most useful are Franklin Fisher and Peter Temin, *Returns to Scale in Research and Development: What Does the Schumpeterian Hypothesis Imply?*, 81 J. Pol. Econ.56-70 (1973); F.M Scherer, *Schumpeter and Plausible Capitalism*, 30 J. Econ. Literature 1416-1433 (1992); and Tom Nicholas, *Why Schumpeter was Right: Innovation, Market Power, and Creative Destruction in 1920s America*, 63 J. Econ. Hist. 1023-1058 (2003). Part of this debate is analyzed in David Reisman, Schumpeter's Market: Enterprise and Evolution, Ch. 5 (2004). A particularly good example of the frequent misreadings of the "Schumpeter hypothesis" is J.B. Rosenberg, *Research and Market Share: A Reappraisal of the Schumpeter Hypothesis*, 25 J. Ind. Econ. 101-112 (1976): "Schumpeter believed that technological innovations are more likely to be initiated by large rather than small firms" at 101. This statement, and many like it from other scholars, is incorrect, but plausible from a selective reading of Schumpeter's sometimes contradictory and ambiguous language. See the useful corrective by Anne Mayhew, *Schumpeterian Capitalism versus the "Schumpeterian Thesis"*, 14 J. Econ. Issues 583-592 (1980). Mayhew points out that most of the support for the existence of the "Schumpeterian thesis" derives from a single sentence on p. 106 of Capitalism, Socialism and Democracy—a sentence which is often taken out of context and which does not begin to express the complexity of Schumpeter's thinking. That sentence is: "What we have got to accept is that . . . [the large-scale establishment] has come to be the most powerful engine of . . . progress and in particular of the long run expansion of total output."

It is here that Schumpeter's enthusiasm for history becomes most relevant to his stance toward competition policy. One of the many lessons of history, as the Cambridge historian F.W. Maitland once said, is that "What is now in the past was once in the future." To put it another way, we simply cannot know with much certainty what the long-term consequences of particular antitrust decisions are going to be. Often the losers of the case turn out to be winners over the long haul, and vice-versa. In the landmark cases of Standard Oil and American Tobacco in 1911, for example, the companies lost and were forcibly split up; but both became more efficient over the long run. Conversely, U.S. Steel won its prolonged case in 1920 (in large part because it had stopped competing as fiercely as its constituent company Carnegie Steel had done). But by 1938 it had lost about two-thirds of the market share it had held at the time of its formation in 1901.[35]

In the case against IBM that began in 1969, antitrust pressures forced the company, over time, to alter its monopolistic practices. Had that not occurred, it seems unlikely that innovation in information technology would have grown at the blinding speed we now take for granted. The same is true of the 1984 breakup of AT&T under antitrust pressures. At the time of that breakup, many economists believed it to be a tragic mistake—some because it endangered (and ultimately killed) Bell Labs, one of the nation's finest centers of R&D. Yet we now know that for IBM, its competitors, and AT&T's successor firms, the long-term consequences of antitrust pressures unleashed immense entrepreneurial energy that otherwise might have remained dormant. That energy produced exactly the types of innovations that we most identify with Joseph Schumpeter.

A similar historical uncertainty emerges when we apply the "what is now in the past was once in the future" test to the related subject of deregulation. During the three decades since that movement began in the 1970s, the unanticipated consequences have been almost as numerous as the intended ones. In the case of airlines, the results have been painful but mostly positive; for railroads and trucking, clearly positive; for telecommunications, very positive; for electric utilities, mixed but on balance likely negative; for financial institutions, numerous innovations (complex derivatives, structured investment vehicles, credit default swaps), but some of them potentially catastrophic for the national economy.

[35] F. M. Scherer has often pointed out this pattern of unexpected consequences from wins and losses in big antitrust cases, including most of those mentioned here. On U.S. Steel, see also Thomas K. McCraw & Forest Reinhardt, *Losing to Win: U.S. Steel's Pricing, Investment Decisions, and Market Share*, 1901-1938, 49 J. ECON. HIST. 593-619 (1989).

These judgments themselves, of course, must be tentative and premature. Only in the long term can we be more certain. And Schumpeter almost always thought in the long term. This characteristic could hardly be more conspicuous than in the quoted passages from *Capitalism, Socialism and Democracy*, in which he writes of the "meaningless job" of drawing economic conclusions "*ex visu* of a point of time," about "a situation that is sure to change presently." Judges and juries must inevitably draw economic conclusions in antitrust cases, but it is not what Schumpeter chose to do. He almost never expressed an opinion of how pending legislation should be decided, and it is very hard to imagine his taking part in any case as a consultant or expert witness.

Schumpeter had been trained at the University of Vienna as a lawyer as well as an economist, but he had left the practice of law in 1908—a step that tells us a great deal about his preferred way of thinking. In the area of competition policy, his main fear during the 1930s and 1940s was of what he called "indiscriminate trust busting." No such eventuality came to pass, as we now know, despite some unwise Supreme Court decisions during the 1940s. From the vantage point of our own time, indiscriminate trust busting seems the precise opposite of what has occurred since the 1940s.[36]

In 1943, a year after the appearance of Capitalism, Socialism and Democracy, Schumpeter wrote in his diary, "Two kinds of people I distrust: architects who profess to build cheaply, and economists who profess to give simple answers." So it would be quite an irony if his name became attached to a particular approach to antitrust. Economists and others are free to invoke his name in specific cases, of course, but in doing so they should tread carefully—very carefully.[37]

---

[36] Schumpeter used this phrase not only in CAPITALISM but also in his presidential address to the American Economic Association in December 1948. See his discussion of the monopoly question in Joseph Schumpeter, *Science and Ideology*, 29 AM. ECON. REV. 347-349 (1949). Italics in original.

[37] One of the best articles on this question is Michael Katz & Howard Shelanski, *"Schumpeterian" Competition and Antitrust Policy in High-Tech Markets,* 14 COMPETITION 47 ff. (2005). Less impressive is Michael Carrier, *Two Puzzles Resolved: Of the Schumpeter-Arrow Stalemate and Pharmaceutical Innovation Markets*, 93 IOWA L. REV. 393 (Feb. 2008), which, like many of the articles cited in note 34 above, makes the mistake of identifying Schumpeter's position as favoring industry concentration as a means to innovation.

A NOTE ON DIRECTOR & LEVI (1956)

Keith Hylton[1]*

In their uninformatively titled article, "Law and the Future: Trade Regulation,"[1] Director and Levi set out a research agenda as well as some of the major propositions of what later came to be known as the Chicago School of antitrust. A better sense of its eventual importance to the antitrust literature would have been conveyed if the article had been titled "The Chicago School of Antitrust: A Manifesto." Of course, calling the article "The Chicago Manifesto" would have made the title more informative today, but less informative when it was written.

Therein lies the story of one of the most successful intellectual innovations of the legal academy. For when Director and Levi wrote "Law and the Future," the Chicago School of Antitrust was relatively unknown outside of the University of Chicago Law School, and even there, consisted of nothing more than critical discussion of antitrust cases in the classroom of one Aaron Director.

We are all familiar with the importance of those arguments today, primarily through the impression that they made on Director's students. The Chicago School of Antitrust has arguably become the core of serious antitrust analysis. "Law and the Future" is the only published article in which Director himself, rather than one of his students, sets forth the Chicago School arguments. The article discusses the economic analysis of market power, abuses of market power, and collusion.

Of the major Chicago School arguments, the one that receives the most attention is the "single monopoly power" thesis, which holds that various leveraging strategies such as tying cannot expand the monopoly power of a firm because any attempt to impose additional restrictions on consumers, beyond the monopoly price and output combination, will require concessions from the monopolist. Director and Levi briefly note that the single-power proposition does not necessarily apply when the monopolist adopts constraints that burden rivals more than itself, a view later explored in the post-Chicago literature.

---

* The author is a Professor of Law at Boston University School of Law and co-editor of *Competition Policy International*.

[1] Aaron Director & Edward Levi, *Law and the Future: Trade Regulation*, 51 NORTHWESTERN L. REV. 281 (1956), reprinted in 3(2) COMPETITION POL'Y INT'L 253 (2006).

LAW AND THE FUTURE: TRADE REGULATION

Aaron Director and Edward H. Levi***

Originally published in *Northwestern University Law Review*, Vol. 51, No. 281, 1956. Reprinted by special permission of Northwestern University School of Law, *Northwestern University Law Review*.

ABSTRACT:
In this note we do not attempt to predict the future of the anti-trust laws. Rather we wish to direct attention to certain problem areas for study. We assume for the purposes of this discussion that an over-riding belief in both free enterprise and in competition will prevail over future possible NRA attempts. We assume also that despite the extension of a government regulation of one form or another, there will still be a place for regulation by competition. The ability of the antitrust laws in weathering NRA and government regulation attempts in the past provides a basis for assuming the laws will continue. The durability of the antitrust laws is perhaps their main characteristic. In large measure, this is a common law durability, built on a case by case development, and exhibiting that flexibility is now limited by particularizing legislation enacted to accompany the Sherman Act. Throughout its history, indeed, the Sherman Act has exhibited the twin tendencies of flexibility and ambiguity, on the one hand, and a drive for certainty and automaticity, on the other. At the moment, the drive for certainty and automaticity seems paramount, but not without criticism and reaction. Much of this drive for certainty rests not so much on the concept of fair warning, which is inherent in any idea of the rule of law, but rather more on the belief that new and automatic applications of the laws will catch objectionable conduct and effects in their incipiency. The idea of incipiency seems to rest of economic doctrines, or, conclusions drawn from experience. Because of these doctrines or conclusions, certain types of conduct are deemed harmful in themselves, although the harm in the particular case may not be visible. Economic theory or experience thus substitutes for an observed effect.

* Professor of Economics, University of Chicago Law School. Ph.D., Yale Univ., 1924.
** Professor of Law and Dean, University of Chicago Law School. Ph.D. Univ. of Chicago, 1932, J.D., 1935; J.S.D., Yale Univ., 1938.

In no area, of course, is the law self-contained, that is, completely independent of the teachings of other disciplines or the assumptions, which may change, of underlying philosophy. The common law, itself, provides the mechanism for moving from doctrines outside the law into felt distinctions which make the law. As much as any field of law, however, and more than most, the antitrust laws in their evolution have exhibited an explicit interdependence with economic and political thought. Many of the cases, of course, reflect the law's skepticism for economists and economics.[1] But the antitrust laws have been greatly influenced by economic doctrine. At times the legal and economic theory have appeared to be the same. New problems for the antitrust laws are therefore created if it an be shown that, in term of present day situations, much of the reliance on economic doctrine if unjustified. Even if this can be shown, it is possible, perhaps probable, that the law will continue on its own, for the law is not economics. The main lines of the law, then, may remain the same, but the statement of reasons for the law may change, and this in itself should have an interstitial effect in the cases. Indeed, there is uncertainty whether the dominant theme of the antitrust laws is to be the evolution of laws of fair conduct, which may have nothing whatever to do with economics, or the evolution of minimal rules protecting competition or prohibiting monopoly or monopolizing in an economic sense. But this uncertainty only becomes meaningful as the issues concerning the underlying economic doctrines are sharpened.

We believe the conclusions of economics do not justify the application of the antitrust laws in many situations in which the laws are now being applied. We conclude, therefore, that there are new problems for the antitrust laws, and that the future perhaps will be occupied, at least in part, with their resolution. The new problems for the antitrust laws have to do with size, the concept of abuse, and with the application of the idea of collusion. They exist, therefore, in the central field of antitrust enforcement.

The problems are new. The earlier history of the Sherman Act involved its enforcement against units of great relative size which had acquired that position largely through mergers and acquisitions and which, in most cases, had engaged in conduct which was characterized as abusive. Under this analysis, there were three elements combined in the cases. First, there was great relative size. Since the relative size which was reached, although not always maintained, was sufficiently great, the firm could be characterized with some assurance as a monopoly, and its behavior in an important respect could be predicted. Second, this size was obtained through acquisitions. Great importance could be attached to this method of growth. A perennial fear

---

[1] *See* United States v. United States Steel Corp., 251 U.S. 417, 448 (1920). *Cf.* FTC vs. Cement Institute, 333 U.S. 683, 715 (1948).

in the application of the Sherman Act is that it will cut down units which have grown to great size only because of the economies of large scale, that is, in response to the demands for efficiency. But during this earlier period, the means of growth used by monopolies in many industries were mergers or acquisitions. It could be argued, although not without some doubt, that, presumptively, growth because of the economies of large scale would not take the form of merger or acquisition in so many industries. The underlying rationale behind this presumption is that it would strain credulity to believe that in so many industries the ideal arrangement for one firm would be merely the collection into one ownership unit of factories which were originally justified as parts of separate forms. In the reasoning of the law, the method of growth through mergers or combination thus could be used as some evidence of intention to monopolize, and as an answer to the efficiency argument. Third, there was present also conduct frequently described as abusive. There were instances of price cutting, exclusive arrangements or tying clauses, the receipt of rebates, and full line forcing. Perhaps this conduct was important because it colored the origin of the monopoly. Perhaps it was important because it characterized the way the monopoly was used. But since the abuses accompanied great relative size acquired through combination, no really separate decision had to be made as to whether it was these abuses which caused illegality. The abuses might have been merely incidental features of monopolies which were illegal because they had arrived at such size without the justification of efficiency.

But since the abuses accompanied great relative size acquired through combination, no really separate decision had to be made as to whether it was these abuses which caused illegality. The abuses might have been merely incidental features of monopolies which were illegal because they had arrived at such size without the justification of efficiency

The old *Standard Oil* case reflects this union of size, combination, and abuses. It was the "unification of power and control over petroleum and its products which was the inevitable result of the combining in the New Jersey corporation . . . aggregating so vast a capital" which gave rise "in the absence of countervailing circumstances, to say the least, to the *prima facie* presumption of intent and purpose to maintain the dominancy over the oil industry. . . ."[2] And this presumption was then made conclusive by considering conduct and results. This analysis left unanswered the question of the importance of the abuses in determining illegality. Specifically, it was not settled whether given sufficient size acquired through combination, an injury through abuses of that power would have to be shown to spell out a violation of the Sherman Act. As Judge Hand wrote in the *Corn Products* case, "perhaps it is yet an open

[2] Standard Oil of N.J. v. United States, 221 U.S. 1, 75 (1911).

question whether or not the test is to be found only in the combination of enough producing capacity to control supply and fix prices, or whether it must be shown that the combination had injured the public in the exercise of power."[3] But the combination of factors made it unnecessary to decide this question in *Corn Products*. There was also an open question as to the status of power less than monopoly but acquired through past abuses. This was the question which might have been reached in the *United States Steel Corporation* case[4] if past abuses had been found. But the *Steel Corporation* case, itself, marks a turning point. It is the beginning of the modern period for the Sherman Act when, with few exceptions, industrial combines are not monopolies. Some of the firms indeed might have been monopolies in the past, but there was little likelihood for most of them that such large relative size would be acquired again.

Today the industrial pattern is far different than it was at the beginning of the century. It is much less common than it was to have an industry in which one firm has seventy or more percent control over productive capacity or sales. There are likely to be at least three or four units of considerable relative size in an industry. The absolute size of these firms may be much greater than that once possessed by any single dominating firm. And large absolute size, of course, carries with it a power of its own. But it confuses concepts to call this monopoly power. And there is an additional change. The role of combination appears to be different. Whatever the ultimate conclusion may be, it has not yet been shown that such industrial concentration as exists is due in any widespread way to recent mergers and acquisitions. And this cannot be shown, of course, merely by counting the number of mergers and acquisitions which occur annually. The application of the antitrust laws to firms of less than monopoly size or to firms which acquired their size without combination presents new problems for the antitrust laws.

The *Aluminum Co.* case[5] hits one of these problems head on. The big step taken in *Alcoa* was to find illegality, perhaps without abuses, but in any event without recent combination. This finding of monopolizing without combination raises a serious question as to the application of the antitrust laws to monopolies born solely out of efficiency. The presence of combinations in the older cases was supposed to provide the necessary presumption that the growth in the form taken was not due to the drive towards efficiency and appropriate scale. Mergers thus appeared to minimize the point raised in *Alcoa* that monopoly may "have been thrust upon" the

---

3 United States v. Corn Products Refining Co., 234 Fed. 964, 1011 (S.D.N.Y. 1916). "If, however, it shall be eventually decided that it is the exercise of the power . . . and not the power alone, which is illegal, the case at bar is in the end no different. Under that theory the injuries to the public are shown by the means which the combination has employed in its efforts either to gain or to maintain its position." *Id.* at 1012.

4 United States v. United States Steel Corp., 251 U.S. 417 (1920).

5 United States v. Aluminum Co. of America, 148 F.2d 416 (2d Cir. 1945).

firm, and thus to satisfy, as Judge Hand indicates, the older cases on the question of "natural" or "normal" conduct, or on the question of intent.[6] Absent combination and abuses, it is possible to decide, as *Alcoa* appears to do, that monopoly as such is illegal as monopolizing. This means that the law has decided the monopoly behavior is not dependent on the circumstances which gave rise to the monopoly, and that perhaps even with access to an industry open, and without collusion, monopoly is not sufficiently self correcting. If stated without qualification, this would mean that a firm which grew to monopoly size because of the economies of large scale nevertheless would be illegal. The consequences of the law would be a less efficient system of production. This would not necessarily be a decisive criticism of the law, for, as Hand tells us, the Sherman Act has other objectives. The Congress which passed the statute, he reminds us, "was not necessarily actuated by economic motives alone. It is possible, because of its indirect social or moral effect, to prefer a system of small producers, each dependent for his success upon his own skill and character, to one in which the great mass of those engaged must accept the direction of a few.[7] And this maintenance of an organization of industry in small units was to be "in spite of possible cost."[8] Yet despite this language, the *Alcoa* opinion attempts to carve out a place for the argument of efficiency as a defense.

The *Alcoa* position on efficiency as a defense is somewhat complicated. The "successful competitor," we are told, "having been urged to compete, must not be turned upon when he wins."[9] The opinion draws a distinction between monopoly which has been "achieved" and monopoly which was been "thrust upon" the firm.[10] Persons "may unwittingly find themselves in possession of a monopoly, automatically, so to say; that is without having intended either to put an end to existing competition, or to prevent competition from arising when none had existed; they may become monopolists by force of accident."[11] Three illustrations are given:

> "A market may, for example, be so limited that it is impossible, to produce at all and meet the cost of production except by a plant large enough to supply the whole demand. Or there may be changes in taste or in cost which drive out all but one purveyor. A single producer, merely by virtue of his superior skill, foresight and industry."

---

[6] *Id.* at 429.
[7] *Id.* at 427.
[8] *Id.* at 429.
[9] *Id.* at 430.
[10] *Id.* at 429.
[11] *Id.* at 429-30.

The language appears to give full consideration to the requirements of efficiency. But there is balancing language on the other side. The issue for *Alcoa* is posed in this fashion: "The only question is whether it falls within the exception established in favor of those who do not seek, but cannot avoid, the control of a market."[12] On this issue, Judge Hand writes:

> "It was not inevitable that [Alcoa] should always anticipate increases in the demand for ingot and be prepared to supply them. Nothing compelled it to keep doubling and redoubling its capacity before others entered the field. It insists that it never excluded competitors; but we can think of no more effective exclusion than progressively to embrace each new opportunity as it opened, and to face every newcomer with new capacity already geared into a great organization, having the advantage of experience, trade connection, and the elite of personnel. Only in case we interpret 'exclusion' as limited to maneuvers not honestly industrial, but actuated solely by a desire to prevent competition, can such a course, indefatigably pursued be deemed not 'exclusionary.'"

Perhaps, then the successful competitor can be turned open when he wins, because he has been told not to compete.

Judge Wyzanski, in his opinion in the *United Shoe Machinery* case, describes the doctrine announced by Judge Hand in *Alcoa* as determining that "one who has acquired an overwhelming share of the market 'monopolizes' whenever he does business . . . apparently even if there is no showing that his business involves any exclusionary practice."[13] "But," Judge Wyzanski's opinion continues, "it will also be recalled that this doctrine is softened by Judge Hand's suggestion that the defendant may escape statutory liability if it bears the burden of proving that it owes its monopoly solely to superior skill, superior products, natural advantages (including accessibility to raw materials or markets), economic or technological efficiency (including scientific research), low margins of profit maintained permanently and without discrimination, or licenses conferred by, and used within, the limits of law (including patents on one's own inventions, or franchises granted directly to the enterprise by a public authority)." Perhaps, then, so far as efficiency is concerned, *Alcoa* only shifts the burden to the firm to justify its growth. It seems clear that *Alcoa*, in any event, has not settled the question of the weight to be given to the requirements of efficiency. In the enforcement of a regulatory statute, this issue might be

---

[12] *Id.* at 431.

[13] United States v. United Shoe Mach. Corp., 110 F. Supp. 295, 342 (D. Mass. 1953).

less troublesome, but it is different for a statute intended to remove restraints to enterprise as a means of fostering competition. For the artificial limitation on the growth of a firm is of as much concern as the artificial growth through combination in order to monopolize. This is a major unsolved problem in the field of antitrust.

The application of the monopoly concept to industries with three or four large units leads to curious anomalies. Thus what is deemed adequate relief for one industry, may be the starting point for bringing a case against another industry

Whatever difficulties the doctrine of *Alcoa* may have with the application of the law to growth because of efficiency, the case, since it deals with undoubted monopoly size, has a strong underlying basis for its assumption that this size carries with it the power to fix prices. In the case of the assured monopoly, one may predict a restriction on production because this restriction will be sensible from the standpoint of the firm. To be sure, even then the firm will wish to take into account problems of good will and the threat of governmental intervention. This restriction on production may provide adequate justification for a law which carries the burden of limiting economic expansion. But the application of the monopolizing concept of the law to units of lesser relative size raises special difficulties. For with units of lesser relative size, it cannot be said that there will be inevitably a restriction in production. If it is granted that there will be more competition if additional units are fashioned in the industry, this may not be an adequate basis to justify the application of the law. This is particularly true in terms of both the state of economics and of the history of the Sherman Act. For the Sherman Act, as has often been said, is directed against restraints and monopoly or monopolizing. It was not intended to compel all possible competition. The act arose out of an antipathy towards monopoly, and those restraints which were thought to have the consequences of monopoly. And it is in the identification and the prediction of the consequences of monopoly that economics has been the most to contribute. There is much greater uncertainty about the consequences of imperfect competition. The application of the monopoly concept to industries with three or four large units leads to curious anomalies. Thus what is deemed adequate relief for one industry, as, for example, the three firms in aluminum,[14] may be the starting point for bringing a case against another industry, such as tobacco.[15] It is in connection, with the application of the antitrust laws to firms of less than clear monopoly size, that the concepts of collusion and abuses have been expanded.

[14] United States v. Aluminum Co. of America, 91 F. Supp. 333 (S.D.N.Y. 1950).

[15] American Tobacco Co. v. United States, 328 U.S. 781 (1946).

Perhaps it can be said that what is emerging is a law limiting the uses of size. As Justice Holmes wrote in his dissent in *Northern Securities*, "it has occurred to me that it might be that when a combination reached a certain size it might have attributed to it more of the character of a monopoly merely by virtue of its size than would be attributed to a smaller one."[16] But since the units themselves do not have that position which would justify condemning them as monopolies, instead the law has developed to prohibit for them certain types of conduct deemed collusive or abusive. Thus without a finding of monopoly, collaborative efforts accompanied by the exclusion of others for competitive reasons are deemed unlawful in the *Associated Press* case;[17] vertical integration becomes unlawful in the motion picture industry,[18] although vertical integration per se is not illegal; tying arrangements are found illegal when based upon what is called a monopoly or dominant position, although the position in itself may be deemed lawful.[19] This places the concepts of collusion and abuses in a new light.

The concept of abuses is illustrated in Justice Douglas' opinion in *United States v. Griffith*.[20] The *Griffith* case is one of a sequence of antitrust cases dealing with the motion picture industry. In *Griffith*, affiliated exhibitors used a common agent or agents to negotiate with distributors. The exhibitors therefore "were concededly using their circuit buying power to obtain films." Moreover, "their closed towns were linked with their competitive towns." These practices apparently were decisive in finding a conspiracy in violation of both section one and section two of the Sherman Act. Justice Douglas explains that "anyone who owns and operates the single theatre in a town, or who acquires the exclusive right to exhibit a film, has a monopoly in the popular sense," although it is not necessarily illegal. Then, "if he uses that strategic position to acquire exclusive privileges in a city where he has competitors, he is employing his monopoly power as a trade weapon against his competitors. It may be a feeble, ineffective weapon where he has only one closed or monopoly town. But as those towns increase in number throughout a region, his monopoly power in them may be used with crushing effect on competitors in other places. . . . When the buying power of the entire circuit is used to negotiate films for his competitive as well as his closed towns, he is using monopoly power to expand his empire." This is "a misuse of monopoly power under the

[16] Northern Securities Co. v. United States, 193 U.S. 197, 407 (1904) (dissenting opinion).
[17] Associated Press v. United States, 326 U.S. 1 (1945).
[18] United States v. Paramount Pictures, Inc., 334 U.S. 131 (1948).
[19] *See* Times-Picayune Publishing Co. v. United States, 345 U.S. 594 (1953).
[20] 334 U.S. 100 (1948).

Sherman Act. If monopoly power can be used to beget monopoly, the Act becomes a feeble instrument indeed." There could be no doubt that the monopoly power of the circuit "had some effect on their competitors and on the growth" of the circuit.[21]

The doctrine of abuses sees them as exclusionary devices useful for getting a monopoly, or expanding it, or for moving from one monopoly to the creation of another. Thus when vertical integration is concerned, the inquiry is often as to the "leverage" of the device. When a tying clause is annexed to a patent, the courts regard this as an attempt to expand the scope of the patent, or as an attempt to create a new monopoly using the leverage of the patent monopoly. So in the *Griffith* case, buying power which joins the competitive with the closed towns, is a use of monopoly power to beget monopoly. It is natural that as the antitrust laws are applied to firms with less than assured monopoly size, new emphasis should be placed upon these exclusionary devices or abuses. Since the firms have not achieved positions which are regarded as illegal in themselves, it becomes important to see if their conduct threatens to bring to them greater monopoly power. The rule of *Griffith*, then, in contrast to *Alcoa* which dealt with assured monopoly size, emphasizes these exclusionary practices which are viewed as the means of achieving greater monopoly power and therefore as an illicit use of the power already possessed.[22] New importance therefore must be attached to the concept of abuses. In addition, the history of related legislation since the Sherman Act is to give independent status to these abuses. The abuses represent conduct which is thought to create monopoly and these are the practices to be caught under the Robinson-Patman Act, under section three and, to some extent, seven of the Clayton Act, and under section five of the Federal Trade Commission Act. The practices are to be caught in order to prevent monopoly in its incipiency.

We are not sure of the basis or the justification for the concept of abuses. Insofar as the practices involved are covered in special legislation, perhaps it may be suggested that all that is involved is a legislative determination that conduct should be banned. These enactments have introduced a certain automaticity into the law; to some extent they preclude or make unnecessary separate inquiry in each of the cases as to the effects, advantages, or disadvantages of the banned practices. But even so the enactments must be supposed to rest upon conclusions drawn from experience and supportable in general, even though they may not be true of an exceptional case. Moreover the interrelationship between the Sherman Act and the amenda-

21 *Id.* at 107-8, 109.

22 *See* Judge Wyzanski's discussion of the Griffith case in United States v. United Shoe Mach. Corp., 110 F. Supp. 295, 342 (D. Mass. 1953).

In point of fact even a firm with complete monopoly power over prices and output cannot both get the advantage of such power and impose additional coercive restrictions on suppliers and customers.

tory acts suggests that none of the special statutes is completely insulated from a pervasive concern with the doctrines of economics in the field of competition and monopoly. Indeed the attempt to apply the legislative standard with strictness has provoked criticism. The report of the Attorney General's Committee on section three of the Clayton Act, relating to exclusive dealing, for example, seems to prefer "full factual analysis of significant market data,"[23] and here as elsewhere it appears to favor incorporation of advances in economic teaching into the case law.[24] We may conclude that to an undefined extent it is of interest to the law to know whether the abuses in fact do create monopoly.

The economic teaching gives little support to the idea that the abuses create or extend monopoly. Firms that are competitive cannot impose coercive restrictions on their suppliers or their customers as a means of obtaining a monopoly. They lack the power to do this effectively. Firms which have some monopoly power over prices and output can impose coercive restrictions on suppliers and customers. In the normal case, however, they will lose revenue if they do impose such restrictions, and this casts some doubt on how prevalent or continued the practice would be. Such firms would lose revenue because they cannot both obtain the advantage of the original power and impose additional coercive restrictions so as to increase their monopoly power. The coercive restrictions on customers are possible only if the price which would be charged without the restriction is reduced. The restrictions therefore would not be sensible except as a means of price discrimination. If used as a means of price discrimination, the restrictions might be considered more an enjoyment of the original power than an extension of it. In point of fact even a firm with complete monopoly power over prices and output cannot both get the advantage of such power and impose additional coercive restrictions on suppliers and customers. At most such a firm, and of course one with only some monopoly power, can decide to impose additional costs upon itself for the sake of a restriction. Such a restriction might be valuable if the effect of it would be to impose greater costs on possible competitors. But except for this special case, there is no clearly apparent advantage to a firm with monopoly power as against one without such power.

---

[23] Report of the Attorney General's National Committee to Study the Antitrust Laws 143 (1955). The phrase is used in describing the Commission's handling of the Anchor Serum Co., F.T.C. Dkt. No. 5965 (Feb. 16, 1954), *aff'd*, 217 F.2d 867 (7th Cir. 1954), and Harley-Davidson Motor Co., F.T.C. Dkt. No. 5698 (July 7, 1954).

[24] *See* Report of the Attorney General's National Committee to Study the Antitrust Laws 132 (1955).

We realize that it is sometimes said that the restrictive practices support or extend monopolies because they can impose large capital requirements on existing or potential competitors. But this argument seems to require clarification and study. It is not evident whether the argument is based on an imperfection in the capital market, on the reluctance to assume the consequent risks, on the economies associated with raising large amounts of capital, or on the less efficient scale imposed on rival firms.

To a certain extent the economic analysis of the effect of the abuses may be relevant only to an interpretation of the meaning of the language of the law. We have suggested that in most instances the supposed abuses neither support nor enlarge monopoly power. Yet we realize that in the typical patent tying clause case, for example, the courts speak of the device as an attempt to expand the patent monopoly. In the *Carbice* case,[25] for example, where the patent was "for a particular kind of package employing solid carbon dioxide in a new combination," but not on the package nor on the dry-ice, the use of the patented combination was tied to the purchase of dry-ice. Justice Brandeis stated that "relief is denied because the Dry Ice Corporation is attempting, without sanction of law, to employ the patent to secure a limited monopoly of unpatented material used in applying the invention." This was beyond the "scope of the patentee's monopoly." In the *Mercoid* case, [26] the use of a combination patent on a heating system was tied to the purchase of stoker switches used in the combination. Justice Douglas stated that the case was "a graphic illustration of the evils of an expansion of the patent monopoly by private engagements." The practice in both of these cases could be described as an administrative device for collecting revenue from patents assumed to be valid.

The *Carbice* and *Mercoid* cases are perhaps exceptional in the tying clause field because they involve combination patents. The usual reference in this area would be to the practices as portrayed in the *Dick*,[27] *International Business Machines Corporation*,[28] and the block booking portions of the motion picture cases.[29] In the *Dick* case the use of the mimeograph machine was tied to the purchase of the supplies for it. The restriction was impliedly upheld, but Chief Justice White in dissenting wrote, "I have already indicated how, since the decision in the *Button Fastener* case, the attempt to increase the scope of the monopoly granted by a patent has become common by resorting to the devices of license restrictions

[25] Carbice Corp. v. American Patents Development Corp., 283 U.S. 27, 30, 33 (1931).

[26] Mercoid Corp. v. Mid-Continent Inv. Co. 320 U.S. 661, 666 (1944).

[27] Henry v. Dick Co., 224 U.S. 1 (1911).

[28] International Business Mach. Corp. v. United States, 298 U.S. 131 (1936).

[29] United States v. Paramount Pictures, Inc., 334 U.S. 131, 156 (1948).

the practices in each of the three cases can be explained best as methods of charging different prices to different customers and not as extensions of monopoly to other areas

manifested in various forms, all of which tend to increase monopoly and to burden the public in the exercise of their common rights. My mind cannot shake off the dread of the vast extension of such practices which must come from the decision of the court now rendered."[30] In the *International Business Machines* case, the use of the machines was tied to the cards utilized with it. Justice Stone characterized the effect of the condition as one "whose substantial benefit to the lessor is the elimination of business competition and the creation of monopoly. . . . "[31] Block booking is described in the *Paramount* case as the "practice of licensing, or offering for license, one feature or group of features on condition that the exhibitor will also license another feature or group of features released by the distributors during a given period."[32] The result was said "to add to the monopoly of the copyright in violation of the principle of the patent cases involving tying clauses." Nevertheless, we believe that the practices in each of the three cases can be explained best as methods of charging different prices to different customers and not as extensions of monopoly to other areas.

There are three remaining types of restrictive practices to which reference is frequently made. They are: (1) joint buying power linking open and closed situations as in the *Griffith* case; (2) exclusive arrangements as in the *Standard Fashion*[33] or *Standard Oil of California* cases;[34] and, (3) vertical integration. The joint buying power arrangement assumed to exist in *Griffith* includes within that power the strength of the monopoly of the theatres in the closed towns. This monopoly by itself is assumed to be lawful. If it is a monopoly, the owner will be enabled to obtain better prices from the suppliers than could be obtained by each of several independent exhibitors in that market. As we have suggested, it would seem that in order to impose additional coercive restrictions on the suppliers, as, for example, on the supplies for competitive markets, the monopoly owner would have to pay the suppliers for these additional restrictions. Nor would it seem to be in the interest of the suppliers to encourage the growth of monopoly among the exhibitors. Perhaps it could be argued and shown that

---

30 224 U.S. 1, 70 (1912).

31 298 U.S. 131, 140 (1936).

32 334 U.S. 131, 156, 158 (1948).

33 Standard Fashion Co. v. Magrabe-Houston Co., 258 U.S. 346 (1922).

34 Standard Oil of Calif. v. United States, 337 U.S. 293 (1949).

monopoly of the theatres confers larger resources upon the owner, but otherwise the monopolist has no obvious advantage for competitive areas over any other competitor who sets out to establish a monopoly. It would seem therefore that the method of buying supplies for a monopoly and a competitive market through a single course cannot be assumed to be effective as a means for extending a monopoly without additional evidence. There is no necessary effect on competitors. The case is not necessarily different from where the single source buys for many competitive theatres.

In the exclusive arrangement cases, the firm which is assumed to have some monopoly power imposes a cost upon itself in order to obtain the restriction forbidding its customer from handling the goods of others. There is an obvious monopoly problem if control over all the possible outlets were thus obtained, but most of the cases do not involve such control, nor would it be clear that firm with a monopoly over the supply would wish to obtain a monopoly over the outlets. Its monopoly over the supplies is not increased through its monopoly over the outlets, unless it can be said that the restrictions on the outlets impose greater costs on potential competitors than they do on the monopoly company itself. This may have been the situation in the *Standard Fashion* case. There a firm with widespread control over a variety of patterns for garments entered into exclusive arrangements with a multitude of outlets. A competitor with less control over the variety of patterns might, through this arrangement, have a greater cost imposes upon it to secure outlets. The reason for this is that there may well be economies for an outlet in handling a variety of patterns. But the *Standard Oil of California* case seems less justified on this basis. In that case no one firm had such a dominion over the products, and a single outlet handling the gasoline of a competitor would appear to have the same economies open to it as were open to Standard's stations. The vertical integration cases appear similar to the exclusive arrangement situations. Vertical integration, however, often appears explainable as a method of price discrimination. It will be said that vertical integration like exclusive arrangements and tying clauses increases a competitor's capital requirements, and so places him at a disadvantage. We have already indicated our belief in the need for further exploration and clarification of that line of argument.

If, then, there is doubt as to the economic support for the conclusions of law with respect to the effect of abuses, this does not mean the law will change. When the courts speak of expanding a monopoly, or of attempting to secure a monopoly through various exclusionary means, the language used may point to matters about which economics has little to say. For example, the scope of the monopoly conferred by a patent is a matter of law. Perhaps a combination patent cannot be enjoyed if the only means of collecting for its use is through the sale of one of the parts. Perhaps, also, the enjoyment of a patent is to be cut short to prevent price discrimination through the use of a tying device. Having conferred a monopoly in one area, the courts may feel that the incidents of that monopoly must be confined. Thus a restriction imposed on the use of products with a patented machine would have an effect upon the producers of the products. Moreover, even if the restriction does not bring a new monopoly into existence, it can be regarded as a restraint. The important point, however, is that the restrictions or abuses will not in most cases carry with them the normal incidents of monopoly. They will not in the normal case carry with them any decrease in production, nor, except for price discrimination, any increase in revenue, nor any increase in price. They may in fact, in some cases of price discrimination, result in an increase in production. In the language of the Robinson-Patman Act and of the Clayton Act, the abuses do not in most cases either tend to substantially lessen competition or tend to create a monopoly. If this were agreed upon, the law might not change, but its objectives would be clarified. The law would be seen as having less to do with competition and monopoly and more to do with merely a set of rules of fair conduct, perhaps emphasizing the protection of smaller firms. Clarification of the economic basis thus presents the opportunity of choice for the law.

The problem of collusion has always been central to the antitrust laws. Price-fixing agreements operate to affect the market price when they result in restriction in output which affect the market supply. It is difficult to provide an economic basis for a law against price-fixing agreements when the market price is unaffected. Moreover, price-fixing agreements, when adherence to them cannot be compelled through coercion or penalties, might be self-correcting either through the defection of members, which would be rewarding to the individual firm, or through the advent of new firms. But if a price-fixing agreement occurs between members of an industry controlling a substantial share of the market, then, when seen as in reality an agreement to control output, the consequences of this behavior may be predicted with some certainty. It becomes unnecessary to examine the consequences in the individual case in order to determine whether the resulting prices are different than competitive. Adopting the standard of competition, it becomes unnecessary to embark on what Judge Taft called a sea of doubt where reasonableness of the prices is in issue.[35] Accordingly, there is an economic foundation for the illegality of price fixing in itself when market price is affected. There is less foundation when it cannot be shown that the members of the arrangement control a substantial share of the market. And despite the repetition of the slogan that price fixing is illegal per se, the cases as yet do not hold, save possibly for

35 United States v. Addyston Pipe and Steel Co., 85 Fed. 271, 284 (6th Cir. 1898).

resale price control, that price-fixing agreements without power to affect the market price are illegal.[36] The clarification which economics can contribute at this point is to emphasize the importance of examining the effect of the agreement on production and the market supply. Yet surely the law may conclude on its own that if the participants believe the arrangement to be worthwhile for them, then there is sufficient likelihood market supply is affected so that a general prohibition is justified. The extension of the Sherman Act into the remoter nooks and crannies of commerce, because of the broadened view of commerce among the states, however, may be thought to raise some question as to the worthwhileness of a prohibition of all forms of price fixing regardless of market effect.

despite the repetition of the slogan that price fixing is illegal per se, the cases as yet do not hold, save possibly for resale price control, that price-fixing agreements without power to affect the market price are illegal

But the serious problem of collusion is to determine what conduct is to be characterized as the equivalent of an agreement to control output.[37] A facet of this problem concerns allowable trade association activities and the proper scope to be permitted to the uses of knowledge. The relative merits of knowledge and ignorance are not well defined in legal or economic doctrine. The counterpart of efficient scale in the size problem is the improvement of the market where collusion is concerned. Behavior designed to achieve these improvements cannot be readily isolated from behavior which can be interpreted as characterizing monopoly or effective agreements to control output. For example, dissemination of real or assumed knowledge as to pending market changes can bring about a restriction in output in the industry. The magnitude of the change for the individual firm, however, must be based on a prediction by that firm of the

---

[36] The opinion in United States v. Socony-Vacuum Oil Co., 310 U.S. 150 (1940), whittles away at the notion that a price-fixing agreement is illegal only if the group in it has the power to affect the market price. In the famous footnote 59 of that opinion Justice Douglas reminds us that "a person 'may be guilty of conspiring, although incapable of committing the objectionable offense.'" The thrust of footnote 59 is not entirely clear, for in part it reads as though control of the market price, which is not required, were being distinguished from an *influence* upon it of advantage to the members of the combination. In this respect the footnote echoes the language of the body of the opinion that it was immaterial "that other factors also may have contributed to that rise and stability of the markets." *Id.* at 219.We have Judge Hand's interpretation of the footnote to the effect that the plan would be unlawful "even if the parties did not have the power to fix prices, provided that they intended to do so." United States v. Aluminum Co. of America, 148 F.2d 416, 432 (1945). But footnote 59 is dictum, for in the actual case "proof that prices in the Mid-Western area were raised as a result of the activities of the combination was essential . . . in order to establish jurisdiction in the Western District of Wisconsin. 310 U.S. 150 at 224.

[37] As, for example, in American Tobacco Co. v. United States, 328 U.S. 781 (1946); FTC v. Cement Institute, 333 U.S. 683 (1948); Theatre Enterprises, Inc. v. Paramount Film Distributing Co., 346 U.S. 537 (1954).

behavior of other firms in the industry. It would appear to be extremely difficult and unwise for the law to assume that action taken on general knowledge implies a concert of action equivalent to collusion, conspiracy or agreement, and yet the result may be the same as that which follows from an agreement. It seems unworkable to suggest that illegality in such cases should be reserved for those instances where the restriction in individual output goes beyond the point justified by a common reaction and reaches that further restriction of output characteristic of a monopoly. This problem concerns also the application of the law to industries with several large firms when the attempt is made to deal with them as jointly monopolizing because of common patterns of behavior. Here it cannot be said that economic doctrine indicates with certainty that there will be collusion among the firms; it cannot be said that there will be inevitably a restriction in production.

The central problems in the field of antitrust as yet unsettled and pressing for solution concern size, abuses and collusion. We do not mean to suggest that there are simple economic or legal answers. The problems are difficult, and the law is not likely to meet them directly. Nor do we mean to suggest that the law must of necessity conform to the prescriptions of economic theory, let alone move within the confines of changing fashions in such theory. The law indeed can have a life of its own. But in this field of law more than any other, the general presumptions are of such a character that they cannot be readily isolated from the corresponding presumptions that in the future there may well be a recognition of the instability of the assumed foundation for some major antitrust doctrines. And this may lead to a re-evaluation of the scope and function of the antitrust laws.

Made in United States
Orlando, FL
04 November 2026

90206112R00148